UNITED NATIONS CONFERENCE ON TRADE AND DEVELOPMENT

TRADE AND DEVELOPMENT REPORT 2018

POWER, PLATFORMS AND THE FREE TRADE DELUSION

Report by the secretariat of the
United Nations Conference on Trade and Development

UNITED NATIONS
New York and Geneva, 2018

Note

Symbols of United Nations documents are composed of capital letters combined with figures. Mention of such a symbol indicates a reference to a United Nations document.

The designations employed and the presentation of the material in this publication do not imply the expression of any opinion whatsoever on the part of the Secretariat of the United Nations concerning the legal status of any country, territory, city or area, or of its authorities, or concerning the delimitation of its frontiers or boundaries.

Material in this publication may be freely quoted or reprinted, but acknowledgement is requested, together with a reference to the document number. A copy of the publication containing the quotation or reprint should be sent to the UNCTAD secretariat; e-mail: gdsinfo@unctad.org.

This publication has been edited externally.

UNCTAD/TDR/2018

UNITED NATIONS PUBLICATION
Sales No. E.18.II.D.7
ISBN 978-92-1-112931-1 eISBN 978-92-1-047322-4 ISSN 0255-4607 eISSN 2225-3262

Foreword

The world economy is again under stress. The immediate pressures are building around escalating tariffs and volatile financial flows but behind these threats to global stability is a wider failure, since 2008, to address the inequities and imbalances of our hyperglobalized world.

The growing mountain of debt, more than three times the size of global output, is symbolic of that failure. While the public sector in advanced economies has been obliged to borrow more since the crisis, it is the rapid growth of private indebtedness, particularly in the corporate sector, which needs to be monitored closely; this has, in the past, been a harbinger of crisis.

The growing indebtedness observed globally is closely linked to rising inequality. The two have been connected by the growing weight and influence of financial markets, a defining feature of hyperglobalization. Banks becoming too big to fail came to epitomize the reckless neglect of regulators prior to the crisis. But the ability of financial institutions to rig markets has survived the early rush of reform in the aftermath of the crisis and efforts are underway to push back even on the limited regulations that have been put in place.

Asymmetric power is not unique to financial markets; the global trade landscape is also dominated by big players. The ability of lead firms in global production networks to capture more of the value added has led to unequal trading relations even as developing countries have deepened their participation in global trade.

The digital world has bucked the gloomier post-crisis trend and is opening up new growth opportunities for developing countries. But the worrying spirit of monopoly risks distorting outcomes. Getting to grips with the policy and regulatory challenges this poses must be an integral part of rebalancing the global economy.

All these old and new pressures are weighing down on multilateralism. In our interdependent world, inward looking solutions do not offer a way forward; the challenge is to find ways to make multilateralism work for all and for the health of the planet. There is much to be done.

Mukhisa Kituyi
Secretary-General of UNCTAD

Contents

Chapter III

ECONOMIC DEVELOPMENT IN A DIGITAL WORLD:
PROSPECTS, PITFALLS AND POLICY OPTIONS

Chapter IV

BRIDGING GAPS OR WIDENING DIVIDES: INFRASTRUCTURE DEVELOPMENT
AND STRUCTURAL TRANSFORMATION

List of figures

Figure

List of tables and boxes

Table

Box

Explanatory notes

Classification by country or commodity group

The classification of countries in this *Report* has been adopted solely for the purposes of statistical or analytical convenience and does not necessarily imply any judgement concerning the stage of development of a particular country or area.

There is no established convention for the designation of "developing", "transition" and "developed" countries or areas in the United Nations system. This *Report* follows the classification as defined in the *UNCTAD Handbook of Statistics 2017* (United Nations publication, Sales No. E.17.II.D.7) for these three major country groupings (see http://unctad.org/en/PublicationsLibrary/tdstat42_en.pdf).

For statistical purposes, regional groupings and classifications by commodity group used in this *Report* follow generally those employed in the *UNCTAD Handbook of Statistics 2017* unless otherwise stated. The data for China do not include those for Hong Kong Special Administrative Region (Hong Kong SAR), Macao Special Administrative Region (Macao SAR) and Taiwan Province of China.

The terms "country" / "economy" refer, as appropriate, also to territories or areas.

References to "Latin America" in the text or tables include the Caribbean countries unless otherwise indicated.

References to "sub-Saharan Africa" in the text or tables include South Africa unless otherwise indicated.

Other notes

References in the text to *TDR* are to the *Trade and Development Report* (of a particular year). For example, *TDR 2017* refers to *Trade and Development Report 2017* (United Nations publication, Sales No. E.17.II.D.5).

References in the text to the United States are to the United States of America and those to the United Kingdom are to the United Kingdom of Great Britain and Northern Ireland.

The term "dollar" ($) refers to United States dollars, unless otherwise stated.

The term "billion" signifies 1,000 million.

The term "tons" refers to metric tons.

Annual rates of growth and change refer to compound rates.

Exports are valued FOB and imports CIF, unless otherwise specified.

Use of a dash (–) between dates representing years, e.g. 2015–2017, signifies the full period involved, including the initial and final years.

An oblique stroke (/) between two years, e.g. 2016/17, signifies a fiscal or crop year.

A dot (.) in a table indicates that the item is not applicable.

Two dots (..) in a table indicate that the data are not available, or are not separately reported.

A dash (–) or a zero (0) in a table indicates that the amount is nil or negligible.

Decimals and percentages do not necessarily add up to totals because of rounding.

Abbreviations

AI	artificial intelligence
BIT	bilateral investment treaty
CAD	computer-aided design
CIS	Commonwealth of Independent States
EPZ	export processing zone
EU-19	European Union (19 members of the eurozone)
EU-27	European Union 2007–2013 (27 countries)
FDI	foreign direct investment
FTA	free trade agreement
G20	Group of Twenty
GDP	gross domestic product
GFC	global financial crisis
GVC	global value chain
ICT	information and communication technology
IMF	International Monetary Fund
IoT	Internet of Things
IPR	intellectual property rights
LAC	Latin America and the Caribbean
LDCs	least developed countries
M&A	mergers and acquisitions
NAFTA	North American Free Trade Agreement
NCE	New Climate Economy
NIE	newly industrializing economy
OECD	Organisation for Economic Co-operation and Development
OPEC	Organization of the Petroleum Exporting Countries
R&D	research and development
SaaS	software as a service
TDR	Trade and Development Report
TiVA	OECD-WTO Trade in Value-Added initiative
TNC	transnational corporation
UNCTAD	United Nations Conference on Trade and Development
WIOD	World Input–Output Database
WTO	World Trade Organization

OVERVIEW

Technological changes are having a profound impact on the way we go about our daily lives. Digital innovations have already changed the way we earn, learn, shop and play. Collectively, as a fourth industrial revolution, they are changing the geography of production and the contours of work. But in the end, social and political actions – in the form of rules, norms and policies – will determine how the future unfolds.

In this respect, the digital revolution has the misfortune of unfolding in a neo-liberal era. Over the last four decades, a mixture of financial chicanery, unrestrained corporate power and economic austerity has shredded the social contract that emerged after the Second World War and replaced it with a different set of rules, norms and policies, at the national, regional and international levels. This has enabled capital – whether tangible or intangible, long-term or short-term, industrial or financial – to escape from regulatory oversight, expand into new areas of profit-making and restrict the influence of policymakers over how business is done.

This agenda has co-opted a vision of an interconnected digital world, free from artificial boundaries to the flow of information, lending a sense of technological euphoria to a belief in its own inevitability and immutability. Big business has responded by turning the mining and processing of data into a rent-seeking cornucopia.

Recent events – beginning with the financial crisis, through the sluggish recovery that has followed, to the fake news and data privacy scandals now grabbing headlines – have forced policymakers to face the inequities and imbalances produced by this agenda. Governments have begun to acknowledge the need to fill regulatory deficits that harm the public, to provide stronger safety nets for those adversely affected by technological progress and to invest in the skills needed for a twenty-first century workforce. But so far, actions have spoken more softly than words.

Despite the talk, this is neither a brave nor a new world. The globalization era before 1914 was also one of dramatic technological changes as telegraph cables, railroads and steamships speeded up and shrank the world; it was also a world of unchecked monopoly power, financial speculation, booms and busts, and rising inequality. Mark Twain castigated a "Gilded Age" of obscene private wealth, endemic political corruption and widespread social squalor; and, not unlike today's digital overlords, the railroad entrepreneurs of yesteryear were master manipulators of financial innovations, pricing techniques and political connections that boosted their profits even as they harmed business rivals and the public alike.

And much like today, the new communication technologies of the nineteenth century helped capital to reconfigure the global economy. Many commentators wistfully describe this as a "free trade" era, evoking David Ricardo's idea of comparative advantage to suggest that even technological laggards were better off specializing in what they did best and opening up to international trade. Here was a comforting win–win narrative for a winner-takes-most world, and an article of faith for the globalist cause, which led John Maynard Keynes, in his General Theory, to draw parallels with the Holy Inquisition.

In reality, international trade in the late nineteenth century was managed through an unholy mixture of colonial controls in the periphery and rising tariffs in the emerging core, often, as in the case of the United States, pushed to very high levels. But like today, talk of free trade provided a useful cover for the unhindered movement of capital and an accompanying set of rules – the gold standard, repressive labour laws, balanced budgets – that disciplined government spending and kept the costs of doing business in check.

As the growing imbalances and tensions of contemporary globalization play out in an increasingly financialized and digitalized world, the multilateral trading system is being stretched to its limit. Uncomfortable parallels with the 1930s have been quickly drawn. But if there is one lesson to take from the interwar years, it is that talking up free trade against a backdrop of austerity and widespread political mistrust will not hold the centre as things fall apart. And simply pledging to leave no one behind while appealing to the goodwill of corporations or the better angels of the super-rich are, at best, hopeful pleas for a more civic world and, at worst, wilful attempts to deflect from serious discussion of the real factors driving growing inequality, indebtedness and insecurity.

The response cannot be to retreat into some mythical vision of national exceptionalism, or to sit back and hope that a wave of digital exuberance will wash these problems away. There is, rather, an urgent need to rethink the multilateral system, if the digital age is to deliver on its promise.

In the absence of a progressive narrative and bold leadership, it is no surprise that the interregnum, as Antonio Gramsci would have predicted, is exhibiting disturbing signs of political morbidity. Finding the right narrative will be no easy task. For the moment, we might do best to recall the words of Mary Shelley – whose monstrous creation, Frankenstein, celebrating 200 years this year, has lost none of its power to evoke our fear of and fascination with technological progress – "the beginning is always today".

Pricking thumbs: Where is the global economy heading?

Ten years ago, in September 2008, Lehman Brothers declared bankruptcy. Suddenly, no one was quite sure who owed what to whom, who had risked too much and couldn't pay back, or who would go down next; interbank credit markets froze; Wall Street panicked; businesses went under, not just in the United States but across the world; politicians struggled for responses; and economic pundits were left wondering whether the Great Moderation was turning in to another Great Depression.

What is surprising, with hindsight, is the complacency in the run-up to the crisis. What is more surprising still is just how little has changed in its aftermath. The financial system, we are told, is simpler, safer and fairer. But banks have grown even bigger on the back of public money; opaque financial instruments are again *de rigueur*; shadow banking has grown into a $160 trillion business, twice the size of the global economy; over-the-counter derivatives have surpassed the $500 trillion figure; and (little surprise) bonus pools for bankers are overflowing once again.

On the back of trillions of dollars of publicly generated liquidity ("quantitative easing"), asset markets have rebounded, companies are merging on a mega scale and buying back shares has become the measure of managerial acumen. By contrast, the real economy has spluttered along through ephemeral bouts of optimism and intermittent talk of downside risk. While some countries have turned to asset markets to boost incomes, others have looked to export markets – but neither option has delivered growth on a sustained basis, and both have driven inequality even higher.

Arguably the greatest damage of all has been dwindling trust in the system. Here economists have no excuses, at least if they have bothered to read Adam Smith. In any system claiming to play by rules, perceptions of rigging are guaranteed eventually to undermine its legitimacy. The sense that those who caused the crisis not only got away with it but profited from it has been a lingering source of discontent since 2008; and that distrust has now infected the political institutions that tie citizens, communities and countries together, at the national, regional and international levels.

The paradox of twenty-first century globalization is that – despite an endless stream of talk about its flexibility, efficiency and competitiveness – advanced and developing economies are becoming increasingly brittle, sluggish and fractured. As inequality continues to rise and indebtedness mounts, with financial chicanery back in the economic driving seat and political systems drained of trust, what could possibly go wrong?

At some point in the past year, the mood music around the global economy changed. The perception of synchronized upswings across many different economies, developed and developing, suggested a positive prognosis for future growth. Upbeat forecasts of economic recovery have led central bankers and macroeconomic policymakers in advanced economies to accept that the time has come to reverse the easy money policies in place for the past decade.

The optimism hasn't lasted very long. Recent growth estimates have been lower than forecast and show some deceleration. Eurozone growth in the first quarter of 2018 is estimated to have decelerated relative to the previous quarter, and is now the slowest rate since the third quarter of 2016; in the United States, the annualized gross domestic product (GDP) growth rate for the first quarter has been revised downward, from 2.3 per cent to 2.0 per cent, significantly lower than the previous three quarters; and growth in the first quarter in Japan turned negative.

Developing economies are holding out better, with first quarter growth for 2018 beating expectations in China and India, but no improvement and even deceleration in Brazil and South Africa. The Russian Federation, like many other oil exporters, has seen the benefits of higher prices. Indeed, commodity exporting regions are generally enjoying the recovery in prices, albeit with some recent signs of a slowdown.

Overall, regional growth forecasts for this year are still on track. However, the number of countries appearing to be in some kind of financial stress has increased and forecasts for the medium term are being revised downwards. Already, as the talk of monetary policy normalization grows louder, a number of developing countries are struggling to cope with capital flow reversals, currency depreciation and associated instability.

The core concern is the continued strong dependence of tepid global growth on debt, in a context of shifting macroeconomic trends. By early 2018, global debt stocks had risen to nearly $250 trillion –three times global income – from $142 trillion a decade earlier. UNCTAD's most recent estimate is that the ratio of global debt to GDP is now nearly one third higher than in 2008.

Private debt has exploded, especially in emerging markets and developing countries, whose share of global debt stock increased from 7 per cent in 2007 to 26 per cent in 2017, while the ratio of credit to non-financial corporations to GDP in emerging market economies increased from 56 per cent in 2008 to 105 per cent in 2017.

Vulnerability is reflected in cross-border capital flows, which have not just become more volatile but turned negative for emerging and developing countries as a group since late 2014, with outflows especially large in the second quarter of 2018.

Clearly, markets turned unstable as soon as the central banks in advanced economies announced their intention to draw back on the monetary lever. This leaves the global economy on a policy tightrope: reversing the past loose monetary policy (in the absence of countervailing fiscal policy) could abort the halting global recovery; but not doing so simply kicks the policy risks down the road while fuelling further uncertainty and instability.

What is more, the implications of monetary policy tightening, whether now or later, could be severe because of the various asset bubbles that have emerged, even as the chances of global contagion from problems in any one region or segment now seem greater than ever. The synchronized movement of equity markets across the globe is one indicator of this. While property price movements in different countries have been less synchronized, they have also turned buoyant once again after some years of decline or stagnation after the Great Recession.

The cheap liquidity made available in developed country markets led to overheating in asset markets in both advanced and developing economies, as investors engaged in various forms of carry trade. The impact of the liquidity surge on equity markets has been marked, as valuations have touched levels not warranted by potential earnings. This has resulted in a fundamental disconnect between asset prices and real economic forces. With no support from fiscal policy, monetary measures failed to spur robust recovery of the real economy. While asset prices have exploded to unsustainable levels, nominal wages increased by much less, and stagnated in many countries. This has led to further increases in income inequality, which implied that sluggish household demand could only be boosted through renewed debt bubbles.

Meanwhile, debt expansion has not financed increased new investment. In advanced economies, the investment ratio dropped from 23 per cent on average in 2008 to 21 per cent in 2017. Even in emerging markets and developing countries, the ratio of investment to GDP was 32.3 per cent in 2017, only marginally higher than the 30.4 per cent achieved in the crisis year 2008, with some larger economies registering a drop over this period.

The policy dilemma is made more difficult by other "known unknowns": uncertainties about the movement of oil prices that also reflect geopolitical dynamics, and the possible trajectories and implications of trade wars that could result from the current muscle-flexing in the United States and its major trading partners. Trade picked up steam last year following several years of very sluggish growth and will likely continue to do so this year; but bets are off for what might happen beyond that.

In the absence of strong global demand, trade is unlikely to act as an independent engine of global growth. That said, a sharp escalation of tariffs and heightened talk of a trade war will only add to the underlying weakness in the global economy. Because tariffs operate in the first place by redistributing income among several actors, gauging their impact is not as straightforward as some of the more apocalyptic trade pundits are predicting. Still, they will almost certainly not have the desired effect of reducing the current account deficit in the United States; will raise uncertainty if tit-for-tat responses ensue; and will cause significant collateral damage for some developing countries, adding to the pressures already building from financial instability.

This is not, however, the start of the unravelling of the "post-war liberal order". That order has been eroded over the past 30 years by the rise of footloose capital, the abandonment of full employment policies, the steady decline of income going to labour, the erosion of social spending and the intertwining of corporate and political power. Trade wars are a symptom of an unbalanced hyperglobalized world.

Nor is the rise of emerging economies the source of problems. China's determination to assert its right to development has been greeted with a sense of anxiety, if not hostility, in many Western capitals, despite it adopting policies that have been part of the standard economic playbook used in these same countries as they climbed the development ladder. Indeed, China's success is exactly what those who gathered in Havana back in 1947 to design an International Trade Organization wanted and sought to encourage. The difference in discourse between then and now speaks to how far the current multilateral order has moved from its original intent.

The wretched spirit of monopoly

As discussed in last year's *Trade and Development Report*, increased market concentration and rising markups have become commonplace across many sectors and economies, with rent-seeking behaviour dominating at the top of the corporate food chain. These trends have inevitably extended across borders.

International trade has always been dominated by big firms. However, in the decades following the end of the Second World War, markets remained contested, as new entrants emerged and as countervailing bargaining power in the workplace, along with effective State regulations, constrained the power and reach of large corporations. Many of those constraints have been eroded in the era of hyperglobalization, even as more markets were opened up for business.

The resulting expansion of trade has been closely tied to the spread of global value chains (GVCs) governed by lead firms, principally headquartered in advanced economies. These have allowed more developing countries to participate in the international division of labour by providing specific links in these chains, drawing on their abundance of unskilled labour. The promise was that such fledgling manufacturing activities, through a mixture of upgrading and spillover effects, would quickly establish robust and inclusive growth paths aligned to their comparative advantage. Things have not turned out quite so simply.

The World Input–Output Database makes it possible to assess changes in the cross-country distribution of value added in manufactured output. The domestic share in this can be disaggregated into the shares received by management, marketing, research and development, and fabrication (or actual production), taking the capital share as a residual. From 2000 to 2014, both the domestic share of total value added and the domestic share of labour income in total value added declined in most countries, with the significant exception of China. The evidence for the domestic part of the capital share is more mixed; it increased sizeably in the United States and to a lesser extent in Mexico, while it declined in Brazil and China. However, the capital share is affected by transfer pricing and related practices, which cause returns on capital to show up in low-tax jurisdictions rather than the country where such returns originate.

The domestic share of fabrication declined in all countries other than Canada and China (in which country the share increased to 30 per cent in 2014). The picture for management and marketing activities is mixed, but the domestic share of research and development activities in total value added increased in most developed economies, particularly in Japan. There was also an increase in this share (from relatively low levels) in a range of developing economies, notably Brazil, China, Indonesia, Mexico, the Republic of Korea and Taiwan Province of China. Nevertheless, developed economies still recorded the highest levels of domestic shares of research and development activities in total value added.

One important factor behind these distributional trends has been the increased bargaining power of corporations, in part due to extremely concentrated export markets. Recent evidence from firm-level data on non-oil merchandise exports shows that, within the restricted circle of exporting firms, the top 1 per cent accounted for 57 per cent of country exports on average in 2014. The distribution of exports is thus highly skewed in favour of the largest firms. The concentration is even more extreme at the top of the distribution and increased further under hyperglobalization. After the global financial crisis, the 5 largest exporting firms, on average, accounted for 30 per cent of a country's total exports, and the 10 largest exporting firms for 42 per cent. This sheer size reinforced the gradual dilution of social and political accountability of large corporations to national constituencies and labour around the world.

In developing countries, the adverse impact of international trade on inequality has also resulted from the proliferation of special processing trade regimes and export-processing zones, which subsidize the organization of low-cost and low-productivity assembly work by the lead firms in control of GVCs, with limited benefits for the broader economy. The mixed outcomes of policies to promote processing trade often reflect the strategies of transnational corporations to capture value in GVCs that are designed on their own terms, with high value-added inputs and protected intellectual property content sold at high prices to processing exporters, and the actual production in developing countries accounting for only a tiny fraction of the value of exported final goods.

This raises questions about the strong bets made in many developing economies on the spillovers expected from processing trade, because unless developing countries manage to capture part of the surplus created by these GVCs and reinvest it in productive capacities and infrastructure, immediate gains in output and employment are unlikely to translate into a dynamic move up the development ladder.

China's particular success in using GVCs has crucially relied on its capacity to claim and use policy space to actively leverage trade through targeted industrial and other policies aiming at raising domestic value added in manufacturing exports. It has also relied on the ability of the Chinese authorities to develop independent financing mechanisms and acquire control over foreign assets, which are now being perceived by developed countries as a threat to their own business interests. Replicating these measures, however, is proving difficult elsewhere.

Along with the rise of export market concentration, large firms have increased their ability to extract rents from newer and more intangible barriers to competition, reflected in heightened protection for intellectual property rights and abilities to exploit national rules and regulations for profit shifting and tax avoidance purposes. The consequent increase in returns from monopolies generated by IPRs, as well as reduction in relative tax costs of larger companies, creates an uneven playing field. The empirical exercises carried out for this *Report* suggest that the surge in the profitability of top transnational corporations – a proxy for the very large firms dominating international trade and finance – together with their growing concentration, has acted as a major force pushing down the global labour income share, thus exacerbating personal income inequality.

The increase in profits of large "superstar" firms has been a major driver of global functional inequality, widening the gap between a small number of big winners and a large collection of smaller companies and workers that are being squeezed.

Given this winner-takes-most world, a key question is whether the spread of digital technologies risks further concentrating the benefits among a small number of first movers, both across and within countries, or whether it will operate to disrupt the status quo and promote greater inclusion.

All companies, if they are to enjoy efficiency gains and take innovative steps, should be able to collect and analyse the full range of data on the markets and cost conditions under which they operate. Lack of such information and the skills to manage it have long been seen as a constraint on the growth of most firms in developing countries, as well as on smaller firms in advanced economies.

The good news for developing countries is that data intelligence, created by the use of algorithms on big data, can help firms (both in the digital sector and beyond) to develop unique products and services, extend and coordinate complex supply chains, and underpin the world of algorithmic decision-making. Engaging in digital trade could be a promising first step, by encouraging the provision of hard and soft digital infrastructure, which is a basic requirement for people and enterprises to engage successfully in the digital economy. Anecdotal success stories point to firms from the South exploiting digital technologies to move in to pre- and post-production tasks in the value chain where value added is greatest. Significantly, China's ambitious new industrial strategy aims to make this an economy-wide goal by 2025.

The bad news comes from trends pointing in a different direction. The widening gaps across firms have been particularly marked in the digital world. Of the top 25 big tech firms (in terms of market capitalization) 14 are based in the United States, 3 in the European Union, 3 in China, 4 in other Asian countries and 1 in Africa. The top three big tech firms in the United States have an average market capitalization of more than $400 billion, compared with an average of $200 billion in the top big tech firms in China, $123 billion in Asia, $69 billion in Europe and $66 billion in Africa. What has been significant is the pace at which the benefits of market dominance have accrued in this sector: Amazon's profits-to-sales ratio increased from 10 per cent in 2005 to 23 per cent in 2015, while that for Alibaba increased from 10 per cent in 2011 to 32 per cent in 2015.

The size of these gaps and the speed with which they have opened up are, in large part, due to the extraction, processing and sale of data. Data, like ideas and knowledge more generally, and unlike most physical goods and services, if easily available, can be used simultaneously by multiple users. The challenge for business is twofold: to convert a seemingly abundant resource into a scarce asset and to realize the scale economies associated with network effects; if firms can achieve both, the returns appear to be limitless.

One way in which digitization is profoundly impacting distribution is through the emergence of platform monopolies. Using a combination of strengthened property rights, first-mover advantages, market power and other uncompetitive practices, these platforms control and use digitized data to organize and mediate transactions between the various actors, and have the capability of expanding the size of such ecosystems in a circular, feedback-driven process.

The trend towards greater concentration, in both the digital and analogue worlds of business, poses several macroeconomic risks and development challenges, which are starkly evident today. One concern is the negative impact that trade under hyperglobalization can have on aggregate demand, as it helps capital to progressively acquire a larger share of world income at the expense of labour. Many economists have noted that rising inequality, together with the higher propensity to save of the rich, creates a bias towards underconsumption or, alternatively, has encouraged debt-led consumption enabled by financial deregulation. Both of these processes tend to end badly.

Since the financial crisis, financial markets and major transnational financial institutions have, with some justification, become the principal villains in this story – but it is now evident that non-financial corporations cannot remain immune from criticism. Facing weaker prospective sales in a context of weak aggregate demand that has been compounded by the post-crisis turn to austerity, large corporations have cut back on investment, further depressing aggregate demand and contributing to slower trade in recent years. This breakdown of the profit investment nexus is one of the factors behind the reported slowdown in productivity growth, particularly in advanced economies.

In such an environment, incentives are strong for firms to seek to boost profitability through rent-seeking strategies, such as intensifying international competition between workers and between Governments to reduce labour and tax costs, crushing or buying up competitors to build up market dominance and increase markups, etc. The unfortunate truth is that the attempts of big firms to enhance their own market position through such strategies only make the broader economic system more fragile and vulnerable, since together they lead to more inequality, underconsumption, debt and, consequently, macroeconomic vulnerability.

One form of rent extraction attracting increasing attention is aggressive tax optimization by locating a firm's tax base in low-tax jurisdictions. The fact that United States companies generate more investment income from Luxembourg and Bermuda than from China and Germany is a reflection of corporate fiscal strategy, not economic fundamentals. The digital economy may exacerbate tax-base erosion because a multinational enterprise whose main assets are intellectual property or data can easily offshore such assets. While the Organization for Economic Cooperation and Development's Base Erosion and Profit Shifting initiative has taken some useful steps towards safeguarding fiscal revenues, taxing where activities are undertaken rather than where firms declare themselves as being headquartered redistributes rents and may be better suited to enlarging the tax bases of developing countries.

Bits and bots: Policy challenges in the digital era

Regulating digital super platforms and developing national marketing platforms is essential for developing countries to gain from e-commerce. Without this, linking into existing super platforms will only provide the companies that run them with more data, strengthening them further and facilitating their greater access to domestic markets.

Since Alexander Hamilton first set out his economic strategy for the fledgling United States, it has been understood that catching up requires active industrial policies to mobilize domestic resources and channel them in a productive direction. This is no less true when those resources are data in the form of binary digits. Indeed, given the economic power imbalances inherent in the data revolution, it will be even more crucial for countries to devise policies to ensure equitable distribution of gains arising from data which are generated within national boundaries.

To develop domestic digital capacities and digital infrastructure, some developing country Governments (such as those of Indonesia, the Philippines and Viet Nam) are using localization measures, just as many developed countries have done in both the earlier and current phases of digitalization. But most developing countries do not have such policies, implying that data are owned by those who gather and store it, mainly digital super platforms, which then have full exclusive and unlimited rights on it. National data policies should be designed to address four core issues: who can own data, how it can be collected, who can use it, and under what terms. It should also address the issue of data sovereignty, which relates to which data can leave the country and are thereby not governed under domestic law.

For developing countries, moving towards and benefiting from a digital future is obviously contingent upon the appropriate physical and digital infrastructure as well as digital capabilities. The challenges faced by these countries in ensuring such digital infrastructure are evident from the well-known and still-large gaps with developed countries: the active broadband subscription in the developed world (at 97 per cent) is more than double that in the developing world (48 per cent); in Africa, only 22 per cent of individuals use the Internet, as compared with 80 per cent in Europe. Even an economy such as India, with a more sophisticated digital sector, is lagging well behind in terms of Internet bandwidth, connection speed and network readiness.

To develop digital capabilities, efforts are needed at various levels: introducing digital education in schools and universities; upgrading the digital skills of the existing workforce; running special basic and advanced skill development programmes for the youth and older persons, including digital skills training programmes in existing professional development programmes; and providing financial support to develop digital entrepreneurship.

While skills development and infrastructure provision will be necessary, they are not sufficient to ensure developmental benefits; a more comprehensive strategy and a much fuller range of policy measures are needed. Industrial policies for digitalization should seek to exploit the strong synergies between supply-side and demand-side pressures in establishing a "digital virtuous circle" of emerging digital sectors and firms, rising investment and innovation, accelerating productivity growth and rising incomes and expanding markets. This may require moving towards a more mission-oriented industrial policy in a digital world to counter existing market asymmetries. For example, Governments could invest directly in infant digital platforms or acquire large equity stakes in them through sovereign digital wealth funds, in order to spread the fruits of high productivity growth from technological change more widely.

Mission-oriented industrial policy is also required because of the changed structure of finance for investment in the digital economy. Unlike tangible assets, intangible assets – such as data, software, market analysis, organizational design, patents, copyrights and the like – tend to be unique or most valuable within narrowly defined specific contexts, making them difficult to value as collateral. As a result, supporting investment in intangibles may well require an increased role for development banks as sources of finance, or of specialized financing vehicles, as well as policy measures designed to strengthen the profit–investment nexus, such as changing financial reporting requirements or imposing restrictions on share buybacks and dividend payments when investment is low, or preferential fiscal treatment of reinvested profits.

At the same time, the digital economy creates significant new regulatory policy challenges because the network effects and economies of scale associated with digitalization can cause rising inequality and generate barriers to market entry. The overwhelming control over digital platforms by a few firms points to the need for active consideration of policies to prevent anticompetitive behaviour by such firms, as well as potential misuse of data that are collected in the process.

One way of addressing rent-seeking strategies in a digital world would be to break up the large firms responsible for market concentration. An alternative would be to accept the tendency towards market concentration but regulate that tendency with a view to limiting a firm's ability to exploit its dominance. Given that a country's data may have public utility features, one option could be to regulate large firms as public utilities with direct public provision of the digitized services. This means that the digital economy would be considered similarly to traditional essential network industries, such as water and energy.

To keep up in the ongoing technological revolution, developing countries are in urgent need of international technology transfers from the developed countries and other developing countries that have been able to develop advanced digital technologies. International technology transfers have become much more complicated in the digital economy because technology and data analytics are being equated with trade secrets, and because some binding rules apply to source-code sharing. South–South digital cooperation can play an important role in helping developing countries grasp the rising opportunities in the digital world by providing mutual support for their digital infrastructure and capabilities.

Still, developing countries will need to preserve, and possibly expand, their available policy space to implement an industrialization strategy that should now include digital policies around data localization, management of data flows, technology transfers and custom duties on electronic transmissions. Some of the rules in existing trade agreements, as well as those under negotiation, restrict the flexibilities of the signatory Governments to adopt localization measures. Negotiations for the Trade in Services Agreement include a proposal that, for transferring data outside the national boundaries, the operator simply needs to establish a need to transfer data offshore "in connection with the conduct of its business". The Trans-Pacific Partnership document includes binding rules on Governments' ability to restrict the use or location of computing facilities inside national boundaries and prohibits Governments from designing policies requiring source-code sharing, except for national security reasons. Some of the proposals on e-commerce in the World Trade Organization include binding rules on cross-border data transfers and localization restrictions.

The international community is just beginning a dialogue on the required rules and regulations to manage all this, and agreement still needs to be reached on which issues relating to the digital economy are in the realm of the World Trade Organization and which fall under other international organizations. A premature commitment to rules with long-term impacts in this fast-moving area, where influential actors are driven by narrow business interests, should be avoided.

BRICS and mortar

There is no doubting that, as trade has accelerated under hyperglobalization, developing countries have captured a growing share of that trade, including by trading more with each other. However, turning these trends into a transformative development process has proved elusive across many parts of the South.

The significant metamorphosis of trade started in the mid-1980s and was particularly strong in East and South-East Asia, based on mutually reinforcing regional dynamics and State-targeted industrial policies that helped build strong links between profit, investment and exports. A rapid pace of domestic investment helped to tap both learning and scale economies, sustaining rapid productivity growth, driving the shift from resource-based to labour-intensive and subsequently to technology-intensive production and exports, and opening up Northern markets to those exports. In the absence of such linkages in other developing regions, the export of manufactures has been a poorer predictor of productivity growth during this period.

Over time, a gradual shift within Asia has seen China overtake Japan as the largest exporter from the region in 2004, and then become the world's largest exporter in 2007. This story has, somewhat casually, been rolled, under the BRICS (Brazil, Russian Federation, India, China and South Africa) acronym, into a wide narrative about the rise of large emerging economies. However, while their combined political weight has important geostrategic consequences, they are too varied a set of economic experiences to make for a collective economic force. Even within this group, China's experience is extraordinary. The share of BRICS in global output increased from 5.4 per cent in 1990 to 22.2 per cent in 2016. But excluding China, the share of "RIBS" in global output went up from 3.7 per cent to around 7.4 per cent – an increase, but not a spectacular one. This is mirrored in global export shares, where China significantly outpaces the others in the group. Indeed, in most of the rest of the developing world, outside East and South-East Asia, export shares remained roughly constant and in some cases even declined, other than during the rising phase of the commodity price supercycle, when major commodity exporters registered a temporary increase of their market shares.

The growth acceleration and structural transformation in East Asia have spilled over to the rest of the developing world, mainly in the form of boosted demand for raw materials. Nevertheless, again with the exception of some successful cases in Asia, there has been very little evidence of broad-based trade-induced structural change.

This is, in part, a reflection of asymmetric power relations between lead firms and suppliers in manufacturing value chains, and weak bargaining positions for developing countries. The experiences of Mexico and Central American countries as assembly manufacturers, for example, have been linked to the creation of enclave economies, with few domestic linkages and limited, if any, upgrading. The same can be said about the electronics and automotive industries in Eastern and Central Europe.

Trade in Value-Added (TiVA) data show that China has been more of an outlier, one of very few countries that managed to increase their shares of manufacturing domestic value added in gross exports (with a 12 percentage point increase between 1995 and 2014). Of 27 other developing countries recorded in TiVA, only 6 experienced increases, albeit of much smaller magnitudes. Instead, for many developing countries, trade under hyperglobalization strengthened the economic weight of extractive industries; 18 of the 27 developing countries experienced increases in shares of extractive industries in export value added. This may partly reflect price effects during the commodity boom, but the persistence of such effects over many years has strengthened incentives for investment in extractive industries, private and public, resulting in higher volumes, which in the long run is likely to have further entrenched dependence on extractive industries, with adverse implications for structural change.

Disaggregating developing countries' exports by the technological intensity of products points to significant differences in both structure and dynamics. On the one hand, the first-tier newly industrialized economies and China depict clear trends towards technological upgrading. By contrast, Africa and West Asia show limited progress as their exports remain extremely concentrated in commodities, with hardly any increase in shares of technology-intensive manufactures, regardless of their labour skill levels. Latin America and the rest of South, South-East and East Asia fell between these two extremes. In Latin America, the 1990s were a period of some structural change with technological upgrading, but this pattern was partly reversed during the commodity supercycle. As the commodity price boom receded, Latin America's trade structure returned to its position of the late 1990s, suggesting that technological upgrading has been limited at best. In the rest of South, South-East and East Asia, tendencies towards relative technological upgrading appeared in export data only in the 2000s, with a shift towards high-skill labour and technology-intensive goods. However, there is still some way to go to reach even the current structure of China, let alone the first-tier newly industrialized economies.

Overall, bilateral trade data suggest that intraregional trade seems to have the greatest potential in terms of providing support to move up the ladder, confirming the validity of previous UNCTAD calls for strengthening regional trade. By contrast, the expansion of East and South-East Asia has not triggered significant positive structural changes in the export structures of other developing regions; rather, it has intensified their role as providers of commodities. And with the slowdown of world trade since the global financial crisis, underlying structural weaknesses have been revealed in many countries. One of those weaknesses is the lack of a solid infrastructure base.

Whether measured as road density per square kilometre, access to energy, telephone connectivity (essential in the new digital era), piped water or basic sanitation facilities, infrastructure bottlenecks are obstacles to sustained growth in many developing regions, especially in South Asia and sub-Saharan Africa. This is, in part, a consequence of the neo-liberal turn in development policy that diluted the original goal of multilateral finance to fund infrastructure projects: for example, the ratio of infrastructure lending to total loans made by the World Bank in the 2000s was down 60 per cent from the figures for the 1960s. Combined with a wider policy assault on public investment, many developing countries have been left denuded of the infrastructure needed to compete effectively in more open markets.

However, infrastructure has made a comeback in recent years. The United Nations' ambitious 2030 Agenda for Sustainable Development requires big infrastructure projects if it is to stand any chance of success, with estimates of annual global investment needs in the range of several trillion dollars. China's Belt and Road Initiative, an estimated trillion-dollar infrastructure package, promises to extend its own investment–export model to a global stage.

But while headline-grabbing figures on the size of the financing gap have no doubt helped to raise awareness of the infrastructure challenge, there is a danger of missing the critical role it plays in structural transformation, and the importance of complementary policies and institutions in fostering that role. Moreover, if history is any guide, the later countries begin their development push, the bigger the resource mobilization challenge and the more necessary that infrastructure investments are properly planned and sequenced.

Regardless of a country's level of development, infrastructure represents a long-term investment in an uncertain future, and – given the significant scale economies, large sunk costs, strong complementarities and long gestation periods that tend to be involved – infrastructure planning is, as the American banker Felix Rohatyn has dubbed it, a "bold endeavour". At the same time, these same features make for both "natural monopolies" and significant coordination challenges that can generate big returns for private investors, but often require public sector involvement if they are to be delivered on the requisite scale and to full effect. An unfortunate consequence has been to turn the infrastructure challenge into a political football between the "market failure" and "government failure" camps.

What is needed instead is a paradigm shift that places infrastructure investment squarely in the context of structural transformation and provides an alternate perspective on how to plan, execute and coordinate those investments, particularly for developing countries that are building their industrial capacities. Doing so means revisiting, and refreshing, an older debate on development planning. In particular, Albert Hirschman's seminal study *The Strategy of Economic Development,* published 60 years ago, can provide a framework to link what was then commonly called "social overhead capital" (public infrastructure) and directly productive activities (private investment).

Hirschman associated planning with a model of "unbalanced growth", in which productive resources are best selectively targeted at sectors with the potential to build backward and forward linkages, thereby revealing gaps and generating price disruptions which stimulate further rounds of private investment, promoting organizational and other capabilities needed to keep the growth process going and sending the right signals to policymakers on where they should focus their infrastructure investments.

This approach, by tying financial viability to a wider set of developmental criteria, provides an alternative to the current fashion for reducing infrastructure planning to a portfolio choice, with a focus on the bankability of individual projects and risk-adjusted returns in line with the calculations of private investors.

Despite the current enthusiasm among policy makers for scaling up private sector involvement in infrastructure projects, financial markets in the era of hyperglobalization have avoided such projects in favour of more short-term lending and speculative positions in existing assets. Even when private sector participation in infrastructure has taken place, it has often pursued short-term financial gains over public service delivery, cherry picking projects accordingly and leading to substandard and fragmented infrastructure systems ill-suited to the promotion of accelerated growth and structural transformation.

The way forward requires instead a visionary but pragmatic experimentalism. Transformative development needs a more strategic approach, in which infrastructure development is planned to promote linkages that support industrial development and diversification. Such planning should pay due consideration to how infrastructure investments are structured, the key feedback loops between infrastructure and productivity growth, and the trade-offs involved in the choice of infrastructure. It matters which infrastructure investments are prioritized and how those priorities are reached. Some types of infrastructure (such as roads and telecommunications) have a greater impact on productivity than others (for example, air transport or sewage).

Planning forces policymakers to think about patient capital, since infrastructure investment typically begins to have an impact on private sector productivity only after some time and a threshold level of infrastructure investment has been reached. This also means that Governments need to be willing to take some risk; successful infrastructure programmes of the past have been as much the product of political ambition as of careful public accounting and cold statistical calculations. Finally, network effects of modern infrastructure as well as the complementarities between different types of infrastructure are important – energy promotion in rural areas will not necessarily lead to higher rates of returns among firms when roads or telecommunications are not concomitantly provided. These effects need to be factored into overall planning and coordination efforts.

As such, planning should be seen less as a top-down instruction manual and more as a coordinating umbrella embracing a wide range of differing interests and strategic choices, focusing on what sectors to prioritize and technologies to adopt, the macro coordination of investment decisions, the amount of resources required and how to mobilize them. From this perspective, the comeback of national development plans in many developing countries since the beginning of the new millennium is encouraging, even though an initial assessment of these initiatives suggests a continuing disconnect between infrastructure plans and a country's development strategy. More work is needed to connect a country's different stakeholders and the policy areas with which infrastructure overlaps, with attention to consistency, the development of capacities for planning, project preparation and execution, and a clear system of penalties to ensure that plans are followed through, as well as accountability to minimize unnecessary costs and ensure legitimacy. Ultimately, this requires bold political leadership.

Free trade troubadours

The growing backlash against hyperglobalization is not a surprise; that the international trading system is now on the frontline is more so, given that the roots of the heightened insecurity, indebtedness and inequality behind this backlash stem more from the financial system than the trade regime.

There should be little doubt that using tariffs to mitigate the problems of hyperglobalization will not only fail, but also runs the danger of adding to them, through a damaging cycle of retaliatory actions, heightened economic uncertainty, added pressure on wage earners and consumers, and eventually slower growth. Still, it would be foolish to dismiss those voicing concerns about damaging trade shocks as ignorant of the subtleties of Ricardian trade theory or simply the misguided victims of populist politicians. Indeed, while the gravity of discontent in the North is only now pulling towards trade issues, there are long-standing concerns among developing countries about the workings of the international trading system.

The dominant narrative of the current era has identified globalization with the growing reach of markets, an accelerating pace of technological change and the (welcome) erosion of political boundaries; the language of "free trade" has been used incessantly to promote the idea that even as global economic forces have broken free from local political oversight, a level playing field, governed through a mixture of formal rules, tacit norms and greater competition, will guarantee prosperity for all.

In reality, hyperglobalization has as much to do with profits and mobile capital as with prices and mobile phones, and is governed by large firms that have established increasingly dominant market positions and operate under "free trade" agreements that have been subject to intense corporate lobbying and all too frequently enacted with minimal public scrutiny. As described in previous *Reports*, this is a world where money and power have become inseparable and where capital – whether tangible or intangible, long-term or short-term, industrial or financial – has extricated itself from regulatory oversight and interference.

As a result, it is hardly surprising that the heightened anxiety among the growing number of casualties of hyperglobalization has led to much more questioning of the official story of the shared benefits of trade. Mainstream economists bear their part of the responsibility for the current state of affairs. Ignoring their own theoretical subtleties and the nuances of economic history, they remain biased in favour of *unqualified free trade* when it comes to communicating with policymakers and broader audiences. The mainstream narrative pitches "comparative advantage" as a "win–win" boost to economic efficiency and social welfare, without specifying the conditions under which such beneficial outcomes can occur or how any negative effects could be reduced.

There is no doubt that the new protectionist tide, together with the declining spirit of international cooperation, poses significant challenges for governments around the world. However, doubling down on business as usual is not the right response. Resisting isolationism effectively requires recognizing that many of the rules adopted to promote "free trade" have failed to move the system in a more inclusive, participatory and development-friendly direction.

This means that it is now essential to introduce a more evidence-based and pragmatic approach to managing trade as well as to designing trade agreements. The narrative around trade should abandon unrealistic assumptions – such as full employment, perfect competition, savings-determined investment or constant income distribution – that have underpinned the dominant policy discourse on trade policy. Instead, recognition of the lessons from successful export economies and the insights of new trade models that acknowledge the impact of trade on inequality need to be combined with an assessment of the causal relationship between rising inequality, corporate rent seeking, falling investment and mounting indebtedness.

UNCTAD has argued consistently in the past few years that a new international compact is required – a Global New Deal – that would aim for international economic integration in more democratic, equitable and sustainable forms. Specifically, with reference to strategies for international trade and the architecture that sustains it, there is a strong case, on its seventieth anniversary, for revisiting the Havana Charter for an International Trade Organization, which emerged – albeit ephemerally – from the original New Deal and can still provide important pointers for our contemporary concerns.

First of all, the Havana Charter looked to situate trade agreements in an expansionary macroeconomic setting, noting that "the avoidance of unemployment or underemployment, through the achievement and maintenance in each country of useful employment opportunities for those able and willing to work and of a large and steadily growing volume of production and effective demand for goods and services, is not of domestic concern alone, but is also a necessary condition for the achievement of the general purpose… including the expansion of international trade, and thus for the well-being of all other countries". This focus on full employment has been abandoned in the period of hyperglobalization, both at the national level and in the "trade" and "economic cooperation" agreements that have dominated the landscape. It should be revived if the widespread backlash against trade is not to gather more strength.

Secondly, the Havana Charter recognized the links between labour market conditions, inequality and trade, calling for improvements in wages and working conditions in line with productivity changes. It also aimed to prevent "business practices affecting international trade which restrain competition, limit access to markets or foster monopolistic control", and dedicated an entire chapter to dealing with the problem of restrictive business practices. Revisiting these goals in light of twenty-first century challenges, including those of the digital economy, should be a priority.

Thirdly, the Havana Charter insisted that there were multiple development paths to marry local goals with integration into the global economy, and that countries should have sufficient policy space to pursue pragmatic experimentation to ensure a harmonious marriage. This need for policy space also brings to the forefront the matter of negotiating "trade" agreements that have in recent decades privileged the requirements of capital and limited the possibilities for development in line with social priorities.

A decade after the collapse of Lehman Brothers, the global economy has been unable to establish a robust and stable growth path. Instead, weak demand, rising levels of debt and volatile capital flows have left many economies oscillating between incipient growth recoveries and financial instability. At the same time, austerity measures and unchecked corporate rentierism have pushed inequality higher and torn at the social and political fabric. As the drafters of the Havana Charter knew from experience, tariffs are treacherous instruments for dealing with these problems and if a vicious cycle of retaliation takes hold only make matters worse. But trade wars are a symptom not a cause of economic morbidity. The tragedy of our times is that just as bolder international cooperation is needed to address those causes, more than three decades of relentless banging of the free trade drum has drowned out the sense of trust, fairness and justice on which such cooperation depends. ∎

CURRENT TRENDS AND CHALLENGES IN THE GLOBAL ECONOMY

A. Making sense of global economic trends

1. The Panglossian disconnect

At some point in the past year, signs of a synchronized pick-up in growth, which began in early 2017, changed the global economic mood music to a generally more upbeat tempo.[1] Positive assessments of future growth prospects from leading forecasting institutions have led central bankers and macroeconomic policymakers in advanced economies to accept that the time has come to end the easy money policies in place for the past decade. The debate is now about when a "monetary reversal" should begin, and how fast and how far the process should proceed.

But there are already signs that the band members are not fully in step with the new score. Recent growth estimates have been more mixed than forecast and show growing unpredictability. For example, eurozone growth (EU-19) in the first quarter of 2018 is estimated to have decelerated to 0.4 per cent relative to the previous quarter, the slowest rate since the third quarter of 2016 (Eurostat, May 2018).[2] In the United States, annualized GDP growth for the first quarter has been revised down 2.2 per cent, lower than the previous three quarters, while second quarter growth rebounded spectacularly to 4.1 per cent, thanks to increased household spending and a sharp rise in export earnings. In G20 countries as a group, year-on-year growth in the first quarter of 2018 at 3.9 per cent was still much lower than the 5.4 per cent rates recorded in the middle of 2010, during the short-term recovery just after the crisis (figure 1.1). All this suggests that the recovery observed since 2017 remains uneven and its trajectory uncertain.

More significantly, despite the optimism surrounding the official discussion on economic prospects, there is a growing sense of uncertainty, driven both by recent evidence and by a more sober assessment of

medium-term trends, of not knowing exactly what is going on in the global economy, or the direction that it is taking. The uncertainty is compounded by the multiple disconnects between what is officially projected and announced, and what people around the world are experiencing: wage stagnation and rising inequality despite falling unemployment; excessive asset-price inflation and volatile currency movements despite a financial system deemed safer, simpler and fairer; depressed real investment despite high corporate profits; and ratios of debt to income that are close to or even higher than those that prevailed just before the global crisis a decade ago.

In this context, talk of an accelerating pace of economic recovery, tighter labour markets and emerging inflationary pressures serves to make the shift to tighter monetary policy more palatable to an anxious

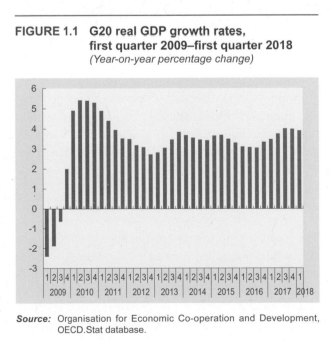

FIGURE 1.1 G20 real GDP growth rates, first quarter 2009–first quarter 2018
(Year-on-year percentage change)

Source: Organisation for Economic Co-operation and Development, OECD.Stat database.

public. It also dampens calls for fiscal expansion. As discussed in *TDR 2017*, fiscal austerity has been the norm in the advanced economies since 2010[3] but current projections warn against a more proactive fiscal stance. Rather, the prevailing view is that fiscal deficits should continue to be suppressed and public debt reduced. The recent measures adopted by the United States Administration (which are otherwise favoured by private capital), such as the tax cuts announced in 2017 and plans to enhance infrastructure spending (albeit with the vaguest of financial commitments), are being viewed with suspicion, since they would widen the fiscal deficit of the United States.

The conventional position, therefore, is that fiscal consolidation must remain the order of the day, notwithstanding the potential benefits of public spending for reducing inequalities and imparting greater cyclical stability to economies. This leaves monetary policy as the only active macroeconomic instrument available to policymakers – and in a context of economic revival, the consensus is that such policy should now gradually wind down and begin to tighten. The difficulty with this position is that it involves walking a knife-edge between overheating and potential recession, even as it sidesteps the continuing problems of insufficient good quality employment generation and rising inequality. In addition, this policy stance creates financial bubbles in the form of asset-price appreciations, volatile cross-border capital flows and – perhaps most important of all – unsustainable build-up of debt in both advanced and emerging market economies.

In many senses, different parts of the global economy are as, if not more, vulnerable than they were in 2007 and 2008 prior to the global panic created by the collapse of Lehman Brothers. In such a context, attempting to resolve the disconnect between real and financial movements in the economy through monetary policies alone may well precipitate another painful episode of restructuring through crisis.

2. Asset market surges

The monetary policy reversal in advanced countries begs a question. If the recovery is not robust, why are central banks and governments fixated on withdrawing the one measure that has kept their economies afloat since the crisis? Standard explanations such as the threat of inflation cannot really provide the answer, since inflation in advanced economies is tepid and still below (the very low) target rates, and cost push pressures are generally weak as wages are not rising significantly, if at all.

The more plausible explanation is a concern with overheating in asset markets in both advanced and developing economies. The cheap and readily available liquidity in developed country markets has enabled investors to engage in various forms of the carry trade, which have fuelled asset-price spirals in two ways. First, the low cost of capital has encouraged speculators to invest in a range of asset markets in anticipation of high returns. The resulting surge of capital flows to bond, equity and property markets in many different countries has driven prices up and ensured the realization of investors' expectations, generating more such investment. Second, the infusion of liquidity triggered credit expansions, once banks had partially corrected their post-crisis balance sheets with government and central bank support. The result is improved access to credit for households and corporates, even though many of them still have large volumes of legacy debt on their balance sheets. Some of that credit was in turn used for investments in assets, which strengthened the price spiral. The resulting price inflation in asset markets is increasingly seen as both unwarranted and unsustainable, a symptom of "financial euphoria" in a Minsky-type cycle.

This boom in asset markets as growth remained sluggish, is indicative of the persistent disconnect between trends in the real economy and financial sectors.

The impact of the liquidity surge on equity markets has been marked, as valuations touched levels not warranted by "fundamentals" or by potential earnings. This is widely accepted; but, as long as the music plays, those in the markets have to keep dancing – and with few players willing to exit, the boom has continued. Figures 1.2 and 1.3 present long-term trends in markets in some developed economies and some emerging markets in Asia. A noteworthy tendency is the growing synchronization of movements across both sets of markets both during the boom and when markets collapsed during the 2008/09 crisis.

Such synchronization did not exist during the early hyperglobalization years. At the time of the 2001 dot-com bust, for example, while equity markets experienced downturns in the Western developed countries like France, Germany, the United Kingdom

FIGURE 1.2 Stock market, selected developed economies, January 1990–March 2018
(Index)

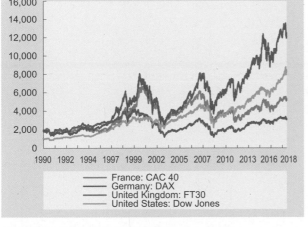

Source: CEIC Data's Global Database.

FIGURE 1.3 Stock market, selected developed and emerging Asian economies, January 1990–March 2018
(Index)

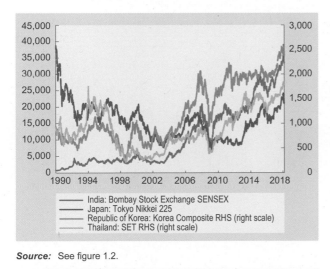

Source: See figure 1.2.

FIGURE 1.4 Change in stock market indices, selected economies, 2009–2018
(Percentage)

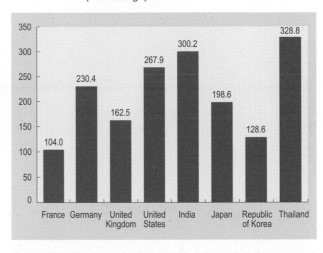

Source: UNCTAD secretariat calculations, based on CEIC Data's Global Database.

example, the increase was 230 per cent in Germany, 163 per cent in the United States, 300 per cent in India and 329 per cent in Thailand (figure 1.4).

Property prices took longer to adjust after the 2008 crash, but even in real estate markets, buoyancy returned with the surge in liquidity, even if to a lesser extent than was true of equity markets. In both the United States and the euro area (figures 1.5 and 1.6) property prices have risen significantly in recent years – since 2012 in the case of the United States and 2014 in the case of the European Union. However, synchronization has been far less pronounced even across the advanced country property markets. Within Europe, for example, real residential property prices have been stagnant in France, falling in Italy and rising in Germany (figure 1.7).

3. Asset markets and income inequality

Sharp price increases in asset markets have aggravated the inequalities associated with growth during the hyperglobalization years. Figure 1.8, which compares the increases in average nominal wages between 2009 and 2015 (the last year for which data are currently available) and stock market appreciation, shows the substantial differences in the increases of the two in a set of advanced and developing economies. The gap is likely to have grown further since then in all of these countries. This underlines the regressive redistribution of wealth in favour of the financial

and the United States, and in Japan and the Republic of Korea in Asia, those in emerging markets like India and Thailand performed reasonably well. But after 2003, stock markets have moved in tandem to a far greater degree. In particular, after adoption of policies that infused cheap liquidity into the advanced countries in response to the global crisis, markets across the world have been buoyant. However, although the rise in the equity market index between March 2009 and March 2018 was high across the board, the extent of increase varied significantly across countries. For

FIGURE 1.5 United States residential property prices, first quarter 2005–fourth quarter 2017
(Real price index, 2010=100)

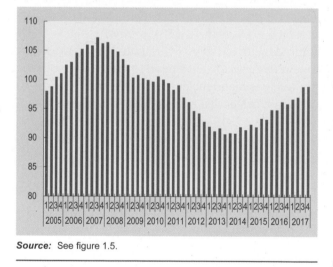

Source: Bank for International Settlements (BIS), property price statistics.

FIGURE 1.7 Residential property prices, selected European economies, first quarter 2005–fourth quarter 2017
(Real price index, 2010=100)

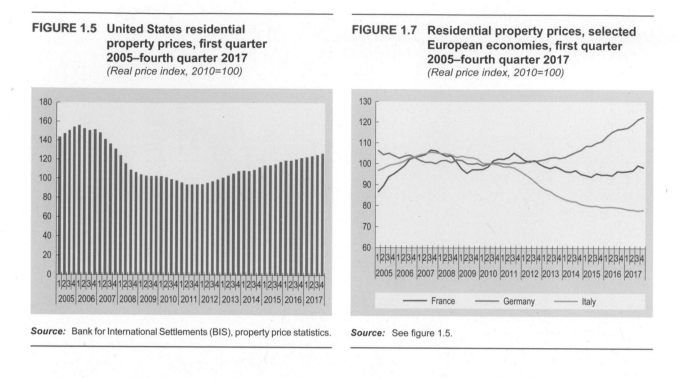
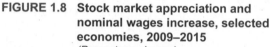

Source: See figure 1.5.

FIGURE 1.6 Euro area residential property prices, first quarter 2005–fourth quarter 2017
(Real price index, 2010=100)

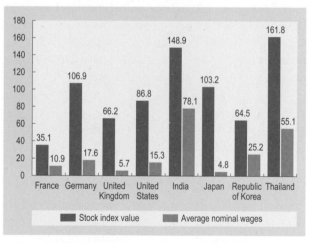

Source: See figure 1.5.

FIGURE 1.8 Stock market appreciation and nominal wages increase, selected economies, 2009–2015
(Percentage change)

Source: UNCTAD secretariat calculations, based on CEIC Data's Global Database; and International Labour Organisation (ILO), *Global Wage Report.*
Note: The latest available data on nominal wages allow for comparisons only through 2015.

elite that has resulted from the disconnect between the real and financial economies.

The increase in inequality is a continuation of a long-term trend, as noted in *TDR 2017*. The sharp increase in inequality associated with hyperglobalization has been reflected inter alia in declining shares of wages in national income. Even during the "boom" years between the early 2000s and 2007, the share of wages fell from 57.5 per cent to less than 55 per cent in developed countries, and from 53 to 49.5 per cent in developing countries, which until then were

the lowest points on record.[4] Thereafter, the decline has continued in advanced economies, and while the wage share has recovered somewhat in developing and transition economies, it remains significantly below the levels of the 1990s or even the early 2000s.

One consequence of that trend has been potentially sluggish growth in household demand, which could be sustained, if at all, only on the basis of debt. This was the trajectory in the developed world before the global crisis; what is alarming is that a similar trajectory is now evident in many developing countries as well. The next subsection describes how this is playing out and creating extreme vulnerabilities in many parts of the world.

4. Volatile capital flows

A clear sign of vulnerabilities accumulated during the easy money years is that as the United States Federal Reserve and other central banks began the process of tentatively unwinding their easy money and low interest rate policies, the environment for capital flows to developing countries, especially the emerging market economies, became extremely uncertain and volatile. From 2010, with quantitative easing under way, net private capital flows to developing regions surged. Investors faced with dramatically lowered yields on financial assets in the main financial centres restructured their portfolios favouring carry trades and, more generally, higher yield emerging market assets (*TDR 2016*, *TDR 2017*). But when developed country governments signalled an anticipated return to more conventional monetary policies, net private capital flows to all developing regions turned steeply negative, beginning late in 2014 and remained in negative territory through 2016 (figure 1.9).

However, 2017 saw a return to modestly positive overall net capital inflows mainly to developing Asia (excluding China), high-income Latin American economies and some transition economies. This upward trend is unlikely to last in the wake of adverse current account trends and currency volatility in several large developing countries, including Argentina, Brazil, India, Indonesia and Turkey. Recent estimates from the Institute of International Finance (IIF) suggest that, starting in February 2018, there has been a reversal of portfolio capital flows to emerging economies. According to IIF data for 25 emerging economies, sales of bonds and equities by foreign investors exceeded purchases in April 2018 by $200 million, which was the largest outflow since November 2016 (Otsuka and Toyama, 2018). The figure for sales of bonds and equities rose to $12.3 billion in May led by outflows of $8 billion in Asia and $4.7 billion in Africa and the Middle East (Jones, 2018). However, since foreign direct investment held up, the IIF estimated net capital flows to emerging markets at a positive $32 billion in April, as

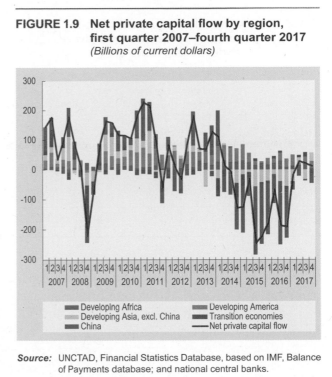

FIGURE 1.9   Net private capital flow by region, first quarter 2007–fourth quarter 2017
(Billions of current dollars)

- Developing Africa
- Developing Asia, excl. China
- China
- Developing America
- Transition economies
- Net private capital flow

Source: UNCTAD, Financial Statistics Database, based on IMF, Balance of Payments database; and national central banks.

compared to a monthly average of $7 billion in 2017. This has been corroborated by the IMF Emerging Markets Capital Flows Monitor (Koepke and Goel, 2018), according to which, while net capital flows to emerging markets had been positive in the first quarter of 2018, there was a reversal of portfolio capital flows to these markets starting mid-April through to late May. However, strong foreign direct investment flows have made up for the decline in portfolio flows.

5. The global explosion of debt

In this context, the continued dependence of even limited global growth on debt remains a core concern. By the third quarter of 2017, global debt stocks had risen to close to $250 trillion – or to more than three times global output – from less than $150 trillion at the onset of the global financial crisis. The most recent estimate by UNCTAD for the ratio of global debt to GDP puts this at nearly one third higher now than in 2008. One implication is that even the current modest global recovery rides on a credit bubble. But the "wealth effect" that appreciation in asset values has in the form of enhanced consumption has been much weaker during the asset-price boom experienced after 2012 as compared to the run-up to the global financial crisis. This is partly because the burden of legacy debt accumulated during the previous boom had not been

TABLE 1.1 Completed and pending mergers and acquisitions deals worldwide, 2016–2018

	Value (Millions of current dollars)	Number
H1 2016	1,793,769.6	24,510
H2 2016	2,287,519.7	25,058
H1 2017	1,858,420.4	26,134
H2 2017	2,069,205.3	26,415
H1 2018	3,031,137.9	23,777

Source: Thomson Reuters.

substantially undone, dampening household spending. When a bubble rides on the unresolved remnants of a previous bubble, its effectiveness as a stimulus for private spending is much reduced.

Moreover, in keeping with the disconnect between the financial and real realms spoken of earlier, debt expansion has not financed increased investment. The ratio of investment to GDP for emerging markets and developing economies, which stood at 30.4 per cent in crisis year 2008, was only marginally higher at 32.3 per cent in 2017, according to the IMF World Economic Outlook database. In the advanced economies, the figure fell from 22.8 to 21.2 per cent.

On the other hand, encouraged by appreciated equity values and access to cheap and easy money, corporations have opted for mergers and acquisitions (M&A). According to Thomson Reuters data, the value of completed and pending M&A deals worldwide crossed $3 trillion in the first half of 2018, rising by close to 65 per cent compared with the first half of 2017 (table 1.1). These M&A, which often require buying up rivals in an oligopolistic context, have taken company valuations even higher, completely delinking them from either current fundamentals or possible future earning streams. High profits also allowed large corporates to use the cash reserves they held to buy back their own stocks at high value, boosting the value of the stockholding of promoters and incumbent managers. This too has added to the fragility and uncertainty characterizing the current environment.

At the same time, the economic dynamics driving ballooning debt burdens and potential debt crises have changed. A decade ago, unsustainable household debt in the United States and excessive borrowing by financial institutions triggered disaster. With core banking sectors in lead economies having deleveraged – to an extent and not least due to tighter regulatory measures – the biggest worry at present is corporate debt, with corporate bond markets and non-bank intermediaries playing an increasingly important role relative to core banking sectors. By some estimates, globally, over a third of non-financial corporations are now highly leveraged, with debt-to-earnings ratios of 5 and above, while noninvestment-grade corporate bonds have quadrupled since 2008 (Standard & Poor Global, 2018; Lund et al., 2018). In the United States, the ratio of credit to non-financial corporations to GDP, which had fallen from 69.7 per cent in 2007 to 66.1 per cent in 2011, has since risen to 73.5 per cent in 2017.[5]

In this context, the debt vulnerabilities of developing countries have built up on several fronts (United Nations, forthcoming 2018a). While the bulk of global debt stocks is still held in advanced economies, the share of developing countries in these stocks increased from around 7 per cent in 2007 to around 26 per cent a decade later. Total external debt stocks of developing countries and economies in transition are estimated to have reached $7.64 trillion in 2017, having grown at an average yearly rate of 8.5 per cent between 2008 and 2017. This substantially reverses the achievements of the 2000s, during which many developing economies managed to stabilize and improve their debt positions because of the combination of a favourable external economic environment, international debt relief and strong domestic growth performance. The principal difficulty faced by developing countries in regard to maintaining debt sustainability has been their hastened and often premature integration into rapidly expanding international financial markets, and the concomitant much larger presence of private lenders in developing country liabilities. For developing countries as a whole, the share of public and publicly guaranteed (PPG) external debt owed to private creditors increased from 41 per cent in 2000 to over 60 per cent in 2017. In sub-Saharan Africa alone, the share of private non-guaranteed external debt (PNG) in overall external debt rose from a low of around 6 per cent in 2000 to about a quarter by 2015. This has entailed important structural shifts in external balance sheets, from debt to equity and towards bond- rather than bank-related finance.

Least developed economies have mostly been affected in terms of their external public debt positions and associated rising debt service costs in the wake of sudden reversals of procyclical inflows of cheap credit from the international financial markets. Median levels of external public debt for this group of countries increased from 33 per cent of GDP in 2013 to 47 per cent in 2017. As a result, the number of low-income developing economies facing significant debt challenges has increased from 22 to 35, with countries in sub-Saharan Africa accounting for most of this increase (United Nations, 2018b). Between 2014 and 2017, the number of developing countries for which debt service represents more than 15 per cent of government revenues has increased from 21 to 29.

The explosion of non-financial corporate debt over recent years has more directly affected emerging market economies, where the ratio of credit to non-financial corporations to GDP went up from 56.3 per cent in 2008 to 104.6 per cent in 2017. Where emerging market corporates face difficulties in appropriately hedging their exposures, this represents a worrying vulnerability to private sector debt crises that, if systemic enough, can easily spill over into public sector debt crises. More generally, in many emerging market economies, changes in their external balance sheets from debt to equity (on the asset as well as the liability side) between 2000 and 2016, promoted by governments as a way of lowering external debt vulnerabilities, have only served to heighten other financial vulnerabilities, such as a large and volatile foreign presence in local equity markets (Akyüz, forthcoming 2018). In addition, a more recent feature of portfolio capital flows to these economies is a renewed high share of flows through debt instruments rather than equity (van Dijkhuizen and Neuteboom, 2018).

B. Emerging policy challenges

At the global level, excess liquidity has rendered the system vulnerable to crises. This is causing central bankers in developed countries to look for opportunities to unwind their unconventional monetary measures, to prevent further build-up of fragility. But the moment central banks made clear their intention to allow rates to rise and drawback the monetary lever, markets turned unstable, as such measures would undermine the basis on which carry trade-type investments were undertaken. As central banks, using the justification of a (still uncertain) synchronized global recovery, decide to unwind balance sheets and raise rates, investors will turn bearish.

As we have seen, vulnerabilities are particularly serious in the emerging markets. The large foreign capital inflows that drove asset-price inflation also led to the accumulation of stocks of foreign financial capital, brought in by investors with short-term interests, who are likely to exit when access to cheap money in developed countries comes to an end. If and when they do, the resulting capital flight will have destabilizing effects in not just stock, but also currency markets, with attendant external effects (on firms that have foreign currency borrowings on their books, for example). Countries that have been most favoured by foreign investors and experienced the largest spike in asset prices, like India and Thailand, would likely be most vulnerable.

This creates a dilemma for central bankers. If they do not reverse the easy money regime, the collapse in asset markets, when it occurs, will be steeper and more damaging. On the other hand, reversing the policy regime would abort the halting recovery that is under way. There are no clear responses to this dilemma, especially as (other than in the United States) there are no plans for any compensating fiscal stimuli to cover for the possible instability. So, even with the more optimistic assessments of future economic prospects, considerable uncertainty prevails. The real issue now is how hard the landing in asset markets is likely to be and the implications that would have for the real economy. The landing is likely to be harder, and the external effects more damaging, the more prolonged the speculative spiral.

Current conditions clearly seem to be pointing to a crisis of some kind. However, a situation of heightened volatility and uncertainty around a weak and erratic growth path can persist for quite some time, especially if accommodating monetary policy is further extended, and the proposed sequence of interest rate increases in the major economies is softened.

In the interim, flows of easy money will continue to support asset appreciation worldwide, including through outflows to developing countries, at least for some more time.

There are other measures that could add further froth to financial markets. For example, the recent tax reform in the United States (which represents a net private windfall gain of nearly 1 per cent of GDP per annum going predominantly to the wealthy, and a corresponding loss for the government), together with similar transfers of wealth into the hands of the corporate sector and wealthy individuals in other developed economies (through privatization and similar measures) could continue to support financial innovation and speculation, as well as activities such as M&A, stock buy-backs and other portfolio operations. These contribute to increased financial concentration and political leverage, even as they provide a temporary boost to growth; they also add to the forces potentially creating future instability in financial markets.

But policymakers face other factors that are potent sources of instability. Navigating these requires both astute planning and a much greater degree of international cooperation and coordination than is currently evident. Two in particular deserve closer attention: the revival of global oil prices, which were depressed over recent years, and their likely effects on inflation and balance of payments in oil-importing countries; and the possible impacts of the protectionist pressures that now appear to be building between the major trading partners.

1. The oil price hike

Since mid-May 2018, the price of Brent crude has been hovering close to the $80 per barrel mark. That was a $47 per barrel (or 64 per cent) rise compared to the previous low recorded in June 2017. This increase in price occurred despite the absence of any major revival in global demand for oil. It has been driven largely by two factors operating on the supply side. One is the success of what has been termed "OPEC-plus" in curtailing global oil supplies, which began with a change in stance by Saudi Arabia. In 2014, Saudi Arabia, which accounted for nearly a third of OPEC production, resisted production cuts to stall the oil price decline, on the grounds that this would render shale producers competitive and increase their market share at the expense of its own. However, this

position changed over time, as the low oil prices hit the Saudi Government's finances, requiring unpopular subsidy cuts and heavy borrowing by the state. Therefore, it agreed to control supply to raise prices, and OPEC went even further in December 2016 by striking a deal with the Russian Federation and other non-OPEC oil producers to cut their supplies to the global market by 558,000 barrels of crude a day. These cuts were on top of the 1.2 million barrels a day in cuts already agreed to by OPEC members. In total, this amounted to a reduction equal to almost 2 per cent of the then global oil supply. As a result of these cuts oil inventories have fallen sharply and oil prices have risen.

Other measures that are more geopolitical in nature (such as the decision of the United States to withdraw from the nuclear deal with the Islamic Republic of Iran and reimpose sanctions) are likely to worsen the oil supply shortfall, and have affected expectations accordingly. The net result was a sharp rise in world oil prices. To the extent that this increase contributes to overall inflation, the justification being provided by central banks to unwind their easy money policies would be validated and rate rises are likely to follow. But, as noted earlier, that move could have unintended effects that abort the incipient recovery.

2. United States protectionism and potential trade wars

Another factor intensifying uncertainty is the protectionist turn in the United States. From January 2018 the United States Administration has announced various measures that have come close to triggering what many are calling a "trade war", beginning with quotas and tariffs on solar panels and washing machine imports from China, and then moving onto steel and aluminium for a wider set of countries, as well as investigating United States car imports.

The tariffs were imposed under a World Trade Organization (WTO) clause relating to imports that threaten national security, though the idea is to curb competition from "cheap metal that is subsidized by foreign countries", which amounts to a "dumping" charge. Subsequently, further trade sanctions were imposed on China, on the grounds that it was using unfair tactics such as hacking commercial secrets and demanding disclosure of "trade secrets" by United States companies in return for access to the Chinese market. Those measures included investment restrictions and tariffs on other Chinese exports to be imposed in stages.

These measures – and other tariffs imposed on other trading partners such as the European Union, Canada and Japan – are being contested at the WTO, but the consequences of such a move are not clear and will anyway be drawn out. The other response has been in the form of announcing retaliatory tariffs, targeted at specific activities and exports of the United States. The European Union announced duties on a series of United States imports totalling over $3 billion and Canada has countered with tariffs on over $16 billion worth of imports. The initial response from China was measured. In an early April 2018 statement, the Chinese Government announced tariffs on United States imports worth around $3 billion, which included a 15 per cent duty on 120 American products such as fruits, nuts, wine and steel pipes and a 25 per cent tax on eight others, like recycled aluminium and pork. This was seen as a symbolic gesture indicating that China would respond when necessary. In June 2018 the United States announced the launch of substantially enhanced tariffs on imports from China, the first tranche of which was a 25 per cent tariff on 818 products, imports of which into the United States were valued at $34 billion. And in early July 2018 President Trump threatened to impose an additional $200 billion of tariffs on Chinese goods. This triggered a more concerted response from China on imports from the United States. There are further lists of products to be taxed that are pending as at the time of writing. A tit-for-tat process is already under way.

The impact of such a wave of protectionism is uncertain. It is true that the United States aggregate trade deficit increased by close to 13 per cent to $568 billion in 2017. Of that, around $375 billion was on account of the deficit between China and the United States. The point, however, is that imposing these unilateral tariffs, is not going to help in reducing these deficits, which reflect macroeconomic imbalances, and things could get even worse with retaliatory action. Moving in this direction would likely disrupt prevailing global value chains around which much of trade is now built. Such disruption would, in the first instance, affect the profits of multinational operations rather than national output, but with a likely adverse knock-on impact on investment given the heightened level of uncertainty. However, over time it could encourage relocation or 'reverse' relocation in some areas in order to jump tariff barriers, thereby partially arresting the process of globalization. On the other hand, to the extent that it increases government revenues and therefore expenditures in individual nations, it could drive growth based on domestic demand with reduced leakages in the form of imports. So the effect on global growth and its distribution is not easily predicted. But so long as trade continues, which it would since factors other than tariffs drive trade, trade deficits and surpluses would persist.

In sum, while unilateral protectionist actions by the United States may or may not help strengthen its domestic producers, they are unlikely to make a significant difference to the size of its external deficit. Moreover, they are likely to introduce disruptions to trade patterns and add to uncertainty, which in the absence of expansionary macroeconomic measures will probably damage world trade. They will also have distributional consequences which are likely to weaken growth (see appendix I.A below). The Trump Administration sees its protectionist actions as a way of escaping the long years of relative stagnation. What it may actually get is more of the same.

C. Global trade patterns

1. Signals from global trade

World merchandise trade has picked up recently but still remains below recent highs. World merchandise exports amounted to $17 trillion in 2017, higher than the $16 trillion recorded in the previous year, but below the $19 trillion level recorded in 2013 and 2014, though this partly reflects the decline of commodity prices from the pre-2014 highs.[6]

Trade measured in volume terms is also showing signs of losing momentum. In 2017, the volume of world merchandise trade grew at 4.6 per cent, up from 1.5 per cent in 2016. However, trade is estimated to grow at 4.2 per cent in 2018. So, while merchandise trade growth is off its post-crisis lows, the recovery, even before the recent rise in trade tensions, shows signs of tapering off. This means that unless there are substantial cross-country variations in trade

**FIGURE 1.10 World trade volume trends,
January 2008–April 2018**
(Index numbers, 2010 = 100)

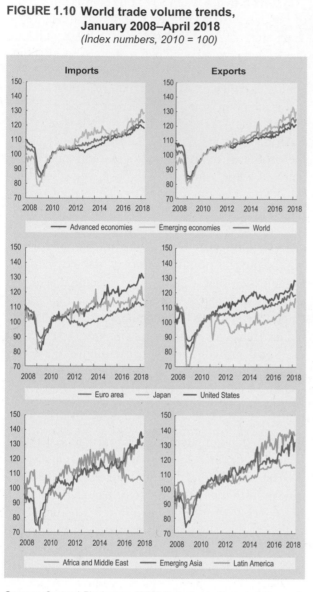

Source: Centraal Planbureau (CPB) Netherlands Bureau of Economic Policy Analysis, World Trade database.
Note: Country groupings are those used by the source.

3.5 and 2.1 per cent. Second, Asia, Latin America and the United States led the table in terms of import volume growth, with Asia (8.8 per cent growth) well ahead of Latin America (6.2 per cent) and the United States (4 per cent). Euro area imports grew at a much slower rate of 3.1 per cent. Asia, according to the WTO, contributed 2.9 percentage points to world import growth, or 60 per cent of the overall increase.

However, the evidence for the first four months of 2018 suggests that after what appeared to be a revival, import demand from some of the post-crisis growth poles in the world economy is slowing (figure 1.10). For the world as a whole, year-on-year growth rates of import volumes during the first four months of 2018 stood at 4.7 per cent as compared with 4.8 per cent in the corresponding period of the previous year. But import growth had come down from 6.9 per cent to 5.9 per cent in the case of the emerging economies.

Asia's retreat as a source of demand was partly led by China, which besides experiencing a slowdown in output growth is simultaneously engaged in an effort at rebalancing growth away from investment to consumption. Investment, which accounted for 55 per cent of GDP growth in 2013, contributed only 32 per cent in 2017, resulting in a decline in imports of capital goods that may not have been compensated by additional imports of consumption goods. Given that development, the continued presence of the United States as a contributor to growth in global demand is even more crucial for global trade buoyancy. This makes the United States Administration's threat of raising broad protectionist walls potentially even more detrimental to growth in the rest of the world, coming as it does at a time when global demand is already subdued. While Asia's role as a growth pole has been dampened, the contribution of the United States is increasingly uncertain.

2. Commercial services trade

Services trade, by contrast, does not show such loss of momentum. World services exports, which fell in 2015 and were sluggish in 2016, registered a significant revival in 2017, from a little less than $5 trillion to $5.3 trillion. However, the value of services exports was not very much higher than the $5.1 trillion registered in 2014.[8] The shift to higher growth in 2017 characterized all groups: developed countries, developing countries and transition economies, which after consecutive years of negative or

performance underlying the aggregate trends, individual countries cannot expect trade to serve as the lead stimulus to growth. A critical issue is the extent to which subdued trade growth affects the performance of China as a significant driver of global demand, because if this is adversely affected, other countries would face sluggish demand for their exports.

According to disaggregated figures from the CPB database,[7] there were two noteworthy features of the recovery in world trade in 2017. First, the largest increases in import demand came from emerging economies, which saw imports grow at 6.9 per cent in 2017 compared with 0.6 per cent in 2016. The corresponding figures for the developed countries were

TABLE 1.2   World primary commodity prices, 2008–2018
(Percentage change over previous year, unless otherwise indicated)

Commodity groups	2008	2009	2010	2011	2012	2013	2014	2015	2016	2017	2018[a]
All commodities[b]	33.5	-31.6	24.7	28.6	-3.0	-3.8	-7.9	-36.1	-9.7	17.8	17.1
Non-fuel commodities[c]	22.9	-18.2	27.3	18.7	-12.8	-6.6	-7.8	-19.0	2.8	10.2	0.4
Non-fuel commodities (in SDRs)[c]	19.0	-16.2	28.7	14.7	-10.1	-5.8	-7.8	-12.1	3.5	10.5	-5.5
All food	32.6	-9.9	12.3	24.0	-6.5	-10.0	-0.1	-16.1	4.1	-0.6	-4.0
Food and tropical beverages	31.8	-2.3	12.3	24.1	-9.8	-9.4	3.8	-14.1	2.7	-1.1	-5.4
Tropical beverages	19.4	1.2	19.6	31.0	-22.2	-19.7	23.7	-11.0	-3.0	-3.1	-6.3
Food	35.9	-3.3	10.1	21.8	-5.4	-6.4	-1.2	-15.1	4.6	-0.4	-5.2
Vegetable oilseeds and oils	33.9	-22.5	12.3	23.9	0.3	-11.0	-7.3	-20.4	7.5	0.4	-1.0
Agricultural raw materials	8.1	-16.1	38.9	23.1	-19.4	-8.8	-11.8	-13.3	-0.2	5.3	-4.8
Minerals, ores and metals	20.8	-13.8	34.8	20.5	-7.0	-9.3	-13.0	-17.1	4.9	12.2	6.7
Minerals, ores and non-precious metals	19.2	-26.9	41.4	12.1	-16.9	-1.7	-15.0	-24.6	2.2	27.8	7.2
Precious metals	23.4	7.5	27.5	30.8	3.4	-15.8	-11.0	-9.9	7.1	0.4	6.1
Fuel commodities	37.9	-38.5	23.3	32.2	-0.4	-1.2	-7.5	-44.2	-18.2	26.1	27.3
Memo item:											
Manufactures[d]	4.9	-5.6	1.9	10.3	-2.2	4.0	-1.8	-9.5	-1.1	4.9	..

Source: UNCTAD secretariat calculations, based on UNCTAD, Commodity Price Statistics Online; and United Nations Statistics Division (UNSD), Monthly Bulletin of Statistics, various issues.
Note: In current dollars unless otherwise specified.
   a Percentage change between the average for the period January to May 2018 and January to May 2017.
   b Including fuel commodities and precious metals. Average 2014–2016 weights are used for aggregation.
   c Excluding fuel commodities and precious metals. SDRs = special drawing rights.
   d Unit value of exports of manufactured goods of developed countries.

low growth recorded growth rates of 7.1, 7.9 and 12.2 per cent respectively.

Quantity data available for the two largest components of trade in services – maritime transportation and tourism – offer additional insight on trends in the trade in services. World seaborne trade gathered momentum in 2017, with volumes expanding by 4 per cent, the fastest growth in five years. Within this, containerized trade and dry bulk commodities recorded the fastest rates of expansion. Following the relatively weak performances of the two previous years, containerized trade increased by a firm 6 per cent and dry bulk commodities trade increased by 4.4 per cent in 2017 (UNCTAD, forthcoming 2018).

International tourism performed poorly in 2016, when international tourist arrivals grew at only 3.9 per cent, the lowest rate since 2009. However, international tourist arrivals rose by 7 per cent in 2017, the strongest growth registered in seven years. The United Nations World Tourism Organization estimates that this buoyancy would be sustained with arrivals rising by 4 to 5 per cent in 2018. Growth rates rose across all regions, with Europe and Africa registering 8 per cent growth in arrivals, Asia-Pacific 6 per cent, the Middle East 5 per cent and the Americas 3 per cent (in which South America recorded 7 per cent).

3. Commodity price trends

A return of buoyancy to commodity markets is likely to benefit some developing country commodity exporters. The prices of a broad range of commodities are set to rise over 2018, continuing (with some exceptions) the trend observed since January 2016, which is when the decline in commodity prices from 2011 was reversed. That rising price trend gathered momentum and spread to a larger range of commodities during the first half of 2018. Overall, according to the World Bank,[9] commodity prices in the first quarter of 2018 rose in three fourths of the commodities covered by it. However, in the case of more than 80 per cent of these commodities, prices are still below their 2011 peaks.

There are two other noteworthy features in these trends. First, for one large group of commodities, consisting of agricultural food products, the price decline of 2017 intensified in the first half of 2018 (table 1.2). The All Food Index fell by 4 per cent in

FIGURE 1.11 Monthly commodity price indices by commodity group, January 2002– May 2018

(Index numbers, 2002=100)

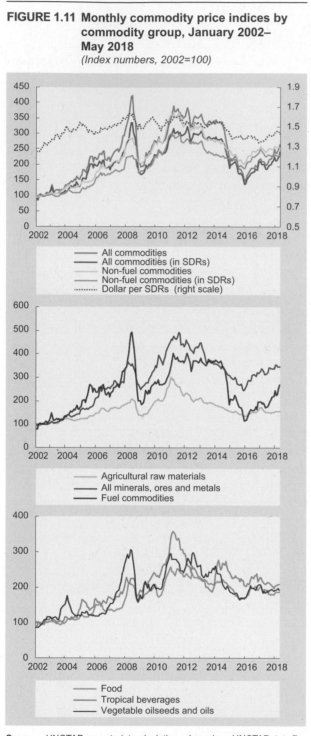

Source: UNCTAD secretariat calculations, based on UNCTADstat. For more details on the data sources see http://unctadstat.unctad. org/wds/TableViewer/summary.aspx?ReportId=140863.

the first half of 2018 relative to the same period of the previous year. All categories (food, tropical beverages, and vegetable oilseeds and oils) reflected this tendency. Second, it appears that commodity price movements are being determined less by strengthening demand conditions and more by developments on the supply side. The case of oil (discussed in section B) is striking in this regard, with production cuts not just by OPEC countries but others like the Russian Federation and many non-OPEC producers, and supply disruptions resulting from sanctions and political unrest, underlying the recent sharp price increases. But even in the case of metals, supply-side factors – such as measures to address pollution – held back production in China, which is a leading commodity importer. The consequent substitution of domestic production with imports rather than additions to demand increased imports, affecting steel, aluminium and iron ore. In the case of commodities for which supply was easy, prices were stable or even fell.

Overall, prices of metals seem to be losing momentum. As compared to an increase of 27.8 per cent in 2017, the index of prices of minerals, ores and non-precious metals rose by just 7.2 per cent in the first half of 2018 relative to the same period of the previous year. The continued buoyancy of prices was true mainly of oil and the precious metals.

From a medium-term perspective, while the commodity price cycles for the major groups of commodities were more or less similar (figure 1.11), within the non-fuel group there were significant differences between agricultural raw materials, on the one hand, and fuel commodities and minerals, ores and metals on the other. For a considerably long period since early 2011, the prices of agricultural commodities have been declining or stagnant. Food price indices for major crops and food crops as a whole have fallen by more than a third relative to their recent peaks (Bellmann and Hepburn, 2017). While supplies have been plentiful, the major reason is depressed demand, aggravated by the slowdown in China.

D. The drivers of growth

As noted earlier, the decade-long strategy of reviving growth through unorthodox monetary means ("quantitative easing") in the advanced economies has had only limited success in spurring income and employment growth. The persistent weakness of effective demand, compounded by post-crisis deleveraging by households and firms, dampened productive investment, while higher income inequality and lower employment rates prevented a strong rebound of consumption. It does not help that governments remain reluctant to spend to support growth. The result is a new normal of low growth.

In the two decades prior to the global crisis, in a context of financial liberalization and tight fiscal policies, two means of stimulating growth operated to differing degrees in the various regions of the world: debt-fuelled consumption expansion and export expansion. A mapping of global growth shows that these have continued to be the major strategies in the post-crisis period. However, both options tend to increase vulnerabilities and fail to generate robust global growth.

Table 1.3 shows the configuration of demand in selected countries and regional groups across the world economy. The categorization is derived from a model-based analysis of different forms of expansion and contraction of demand in the global system.[10] In this framework, domestic output increases in response to increased demand through private investment, government spending and exports, and shrinks because of subtractions from aggregate demand in the form of private savings, taxes and imports. Private saving is part of income, but when it is not equally compensated by investment, it drops out from the flow of effective demand. Taxes represent income diverted to the government, which if not spent by the public sector becomes "government saving". Imports represent income spent on output generated abroad. Accordingly, the growth rate of aggregate supply can be decomposed into its three main demand components or "growth drivers":

1. private demand, whose growth rate depends on investment, savings and the tax, saving and import rates;

2. government demand, whose growth rate depends on government spending on goods and services, taxes and the tax, saving and import rates;

3. external demand, whose growth rate depends on exports, imports and the tax, saving and import rates.

Based on this framework, table 1.3 presents the results of an analysis of the drivers of global growth in the current year.[11] The average rate of growth of aggregate supply over the two-year period 2017–2018 is estimated, along with the relative contributions of each of its components.[12] The countries or country groups in the table are classified according to which growth driver is dominant. Within each category, countries are ranked by the relative importance of that particular driver.[13] A ranking of economies in this way sheds light on the character of the growth strategy per se (how the observed growth of output is achieved), rather than on how fast that economy is growing.

A striking result in table 1.3 is that in 19 out of 30 cases, growth relies more strongly on net exports than on domestic demand, whether private or public. This raises a number of concerns. First, an economy that shows a relatively strong dependence on net export demand, as defined above, must record stronger growth of exports than of imports. This can result from either a successful strategy of increasing exports over time, or a successful strategy of containing domestic demand for imports relative to demand for exports, or a combination of the two.

Countries showing a tendency towards a relative reduction of imports are likely to be those dealing with current account deficits, such as France, India, Turkey, the United Kingdom and some countries in Central America and the Caribbean. In these and similar cases, increases in net export demand result from containing imports, through reductions of government demand (possibly because of fiscal austerity measures that constrain public spending) or private demand (possibly because of reductions in workers' real incomes that erode consumption and by extension private investment). Either way, the result is a shrinking current account deficit. This creates an underlying bias that depresses global demand in the aggregate, particularly if a considerable number of relatively large countries choose such a macroeconomic strategy.

An obvious alternative way for these countries to reduce their external deficits would be for other

TABLE 1.3 Drivers of demand in different countries, 2017–2018

	Aggregate supply	Fiscal	Private	External	Relative strength
External demand is main driver					
United Kingdom	1.7	-0.5	0.1	2.1	***
Other transition economies	6.6	0.8	0.8	5.1	***
North Africa	6.9	0.6	1.0	5.4	***
Other East Asia	3.9	0.6	0.4	2.9	***
Republic of Korea	3.6	0.1	0.8	2.7	***
Other West Asia	5.9	1.3	0.4	4.3	***
Non-European Union Europe	2.4	0.2	0.5	1.7	***
Russian Federation	3.4	-0.3	0.9	2.8	***
Mexico	3.1	-0.1	1.1	2.1	***
Japan	1.5	-0.9	0.8	1.6	***
Germany	2.3	-0.1	0.9	1.5	**
Italy	2.0	-0.2	0.8	1.4	**
Caribbean	3.1	0.8	0.9	1.5	**
Other European Union	2.9	0.4	0.9	1.6	**
France	2.2	0.4	0.7	1.1	**
Turkey	6.4	1.4	2.3	2.9	*
Indonesia	5.4	1.0	2.0	2.5	*
Other developed countries	3.6	1.3	0.8	1.5	*
India	7.4	1.5	2.9	3.2	*
Private demand is main driver					
Other South America	0.2	-0.5	1.2	-0.5	***
Argentina	4.5	0.3	3.0	1.2	***
Canada	2.5	0.7	1.6	0.2	***
United States	2.7	0.7	1.2	0.8	**
Australia	2.7	1.0	1.3	0.5	**
Brazil	1.8	-1.0	1.5	1.3	*
China	6.6	1.9	2.5	2.4	*
Government demand is main driver					
Other sub-Saharan Africa	3.0	2.3	0.1	0.6	***
Saudi Arabia	0.2	2.6	-3.5	1.0	***
Other South Asia	5.0	3.1	1.4	0.5	***
South Africa	1.4	0.7	0.5	0.2	**

Source: United Nations Global Policy Model.

Note: Stars indicate the relative strength of the main driver of aggregate demand with respect to the second strongest driver (* if difference is smaller or equal to 30 per cent of main driver, ** if difference is greater than 30 per cent and smaller or equal to 50 per cent of main driver, *** if difference is greater than 50 per cent of main driver). Country groups are as follows: *Other East Asia* includes the Democratic People's Republic of Korea, Hong Kong (China), Malaysia, Mongolia and Singapore; *Non-European Union Europe* includes Norway, Serbia and Switzerland; *Caribbean* includes Costa Rica, the Dominican Republic and Jamaica; *Other European Union* includes Croatia, Estonia, Greece, the Netherlands, Norway, Portugal, Spain and Sweden; *Other West Asia* includes Iraq, Lebanon and the United Arab Emirates; *North Africa* includes Algeria, Egypt, Libya, Morocco and Tunisia; *Other transition economies* includes Georgia, Kazakhstan and Ukraine; *Other developed countries* includes Israel and New Zealand; *Other South America* includes Chile, Colombia, Ecuador and Peru; *Other South Asia* includes Afghanistan, Bangladesh, the Islamic Republic of Iran and Pakistan; *Other sub-Saharan Africa* includes Angola, the Democratic Republic of the Congo, Kenya, Nigeria and most sub-Saharan African countries excluding South Africa.

trading countries that consistently run surpluses to increase their domestic demand and thus their imports, which would in the process contribute to an addition to global demand for exports. Besides helping other countries, this would also facilitate a recovery of global growth. Indeed, in the economies in the upper section of table 1.3, for whom the main driver of aggregate supply growth is net export demand, and which are known as "surplus" economies, the contribution of domestic demand to growth of either the public or the private sector (or both), is considerably weak, if not negative, and so there is considerable scope for expansion.

A second cause for concern is with respect to economies whose aggregate supply growth is mostly driven by net external demand. Nearly half of them rely heavily on commodity or oil exports. (This includes Saudi Arabia, for which government demand is a strong driver, but where there is also a role for external demand.) These economies tend to be large importers of manufactures from their main export markets. Since global commodity demand tends to be procyclical, rising during the booms and falling during slowdowns, the "strong exporters" in this group as a whole are likely to be vulnerable to, and contribute to, boom–bust growth cycles. The growth dynamics of this group therefore have a considerable bearing on the potential instability of global growth.

The middle section of table 1.3 includes six economies (and one country group) for whom the strongest demand driver is the private sector. Among these, a noteworthy case is China. First, despite running a current account surplus, net external demand is not its main growth driver. As a matter of fact, relative to its own GDP, its current account surplus is shrinking, to just above 1 per cent, as compared with about 9 per cent of GDP in 2007. Second, the contributions to growth of the three components (public, private and external) are remarkably similar. This reflects some success in rebalancing the economy, as well as in contributing to global demand to the extent that the domestic growth drivers are strong, with respect to its own economy as well as relative to world output. While debt levels in China have been increasing, this was partly the result of a planned credit expansion seeking to rebalance growth away from external sources; and there have been recent moves to reduce domestic debt, especially that held by corporations. However, the other five economies in the group where private sector demand is stronger than the other two drivers (Argentina, Australia, Brazil, Canada and the United States) are experiencing rising financial vulnerability, since the growth of private demand has been accompanied by increasing levels of debt. As discussed earlier in section A, in some cases the debt burden is carried by the corporate sector, and in other cases it is with households. Corporate debt increases have been mostly fed by two factors. Some corporate borrowing has been directed towards activities like M&A and "share buy-backs", which have led to unsustainable increases in stock valuations. There is also a link between corporate indebtedness and capital flows, because of the carry trade possibilities enabled by loose monetary policies in advanced economies and liberalized capital accounts in recipient economies. The debt accumulation of private households is also strongly associated with price appreciation in real estate and stock markets, as occurred before the 2008 crisis.

It should be noted that private sector debt burdens are also high in other economies that do not currently exhibit a strong role for private demand, such as India, Turkey and the United Kingdom. As noted above, these economies seem to be experiencing domestic demand deflation, which weakens growth prospects even as it does not resolve issues of financial vulnerability.

Finally, there are four countries / country groups where the government is the main growth driver. Of these, as noted above, in Saudi Arabia the contribution of external demand feeds the strong role of public sector demand, and fiscal expansion has been strongly dependent on oil revenues. Patterns like this, which can also be found among other commodity and oil exporters (such as those in sub-Saharan Africa included in this section of the table, as well as other developing countries in Asia and Latin America) reflect "windfall gain cycles" where the inflows from abroad are partly channelled to pay for increases in government spending. In "normal" times, the actual contribution of the public sector to growth is moderate or low in the economies in this section of the table, as it is in those in other sections, except for a couple of cases where the contribution to growth is above 2 per cent. This confirms the observation made in *TDR 2017* about the unjustifiable shift to continuing fiscal austerity in many countries, precisely in a period when other growth drivers have been weak or contribute to greater financial vulnerability.

E. Regional growth trends

1. Developed countries

Amid signs of a loss of momentum in the global economy, the United States is a partial exception. Europe and Japan, after showing promise of consistently positive and significant rates of growth, have seen growth rates fall. But the United States appears to be staying on course. Although the latest annualized growth estimates for the first quarter of 2018 have been revised down to 2.2 per cent, second quarter estimates show growth rebounding to 4.1 per cent. By May 2018, the United States economy had experienced the second-longest phase of expansion since the 1850s, according to figures released by the National Bureau of Economic Research. However, even in the United States, the 16 quarters of uninterrupted positive GDP growth had not yet restored the quarterly growth rate to its previous post-crisis high. Moreover, the pace of the expansion was slower than in many expansionary episodes in the past, and the slowest in the post-war period. The current Administration's ambition is to use tax cuts to the tune of $1.5 trillion, higher import tariffs and a promised increase in infrastructural spending to raise the rate of growth from around 2 to 3 per cent per annum.

The sharp fall in the unemployment rate in the United States, from close to 10 per cent in the middle of the crisis to 4.0 per cent in June 2018, is seen as evidence of the strength of recovery. This is significantly below the 5 per cent level recorded in January 2008, before the onset of the crisis, and the lowest since 2000. However, doubts have been expressed about the meaning of these figures, since the definition of employment is such that even the underemployed, or workers employed for less than the 40 hours a week they are willing to work, are treated as employed.[14] Furthermore, paradoxically, the low unemployment rate also decreased as a result of the deterioration

FIGURE 1.12 United States private-sector nominal average hourly earnings, 2007–2018
(Year-on-year percentage change)

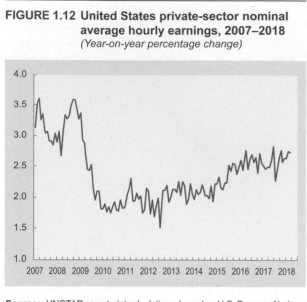

Source: UNCTAD secretariat calculations, based on U.S. Bureau of Labour Statistics, nominal wage data.

of the labour market during the crisis: facing long-term unemployment, many workers abandoned the search for a job, leaving the labour force. This drove down the unemployment rate. Confirming this trend, the employment rate – which measures the ratio of employed workers to total population – is still lower than before the crisis (at 59 per cent in 2017, compared to 61 per cent in 2005). Recent data indicate that this trend is reversing as formerly "discouraged" workers re-enter the labour market attracted by its improved conditions. How this will impact the unemployment rate remains to be seen.

Nominal wage growth in the United States has been well below its pre-crisis high and the pick-up in wage growth from early 2015 lost momentum from the second half of 2016 (figure 1.12). Together with cheap imports and subdued oil prices, this has kept the inflation rate in the United States low. As noted by the Economic Policy Institute, "Until nominal wages are rising by 3.5 percent to 4 percent, there is no threat that price inflation will begin to significantly exceed the Fed's 2 percent inflation target."[15] Overall, the assessment that the United States is on a new robust growth path which would raise wages and trigger inflation is not grounded in the data.

Beyond the United States, optimism about the global economy was related to expectations that Europe would begin to experience a robust recovery as well – but such expectations have been muted because of

the slowdown in growth in the first quarter of 2018. Growth in the euro area, which rose from 1.8 to 2.5 per cent per cent between 2016 and 2017, is projected to drop to 1.9 per cent in 2018 (table 1.4). Explanations for faster growth in 2017 flagged the unconventional monetary easing measures adopted by the European Central Bank since early 2015 and the beneficial effects on trade of higher growth in China, India and the United States. Conversely, the slowdown is attributed to the blunting of the stimulus offered by quantitative easing, depressed wage growth (Jezard, 2018), and the inadequacy of external demand to make up the shortfall.

Within the eurozone, there is generalized evidence of a slowdown, including in the largest two economies, Germany and France. Germany (accounting for 30 per cent of the zone's output) saw quarter-on-quarter growth rates falling from 0.6 per cent in the last quarter of 2017 to 0.3 per cent in the first quarter of 2018, according to figures from the Federal Statistical Office in early May. Slower trade growth played a role there. France also suffered a setback. GDP grew by only 0.2 per cent in the first and the second quarters of 2018, after expanding 0.6 per cent in the last quarter of 2017. Elsewhere, Italy and Spain saw economic performance affected by extremely high bond yields, resulting from investor fears triggered by adverse economic and political developments. These psychological effects contributed to the persistence of austerity policies in the two countries. Overall, therefore, the news from Europe is looking less rosy after the optimism generated by the performance in 2017.

Growth in the United Kingdom is expected to be lower in 2018 compared to 2017, with uncertainty over Brexit negotiations adding to structural weaknesses reflected in weak productivity growth and sluggish business investment. Even more pessimistic news came from Japan, which had appeared to be finally coming out of a long recession because of a combination of fiscal stimuli and aggressive monetary easing. When the Japanese economy grew by 0.6 per cent in the last quarter of 2017, that was the eighth straight quarter of positive growth, marking the longest expansionary stretch in 28 years. However, the optimism that was generated thereby was dashed when estimates for the first quarter of 2018 showed that the Japanese economy had contracted by 0.2 per cent over the three months ending March 2018. Expectations now are that lower than expected consumption spending and exports will

TABLE 1.4　World output growth, 1991–2018
(Annual percentage change)

Country or area	1991–2000[a]	2001–2008[a]	2008	2009	2010	2011	2012	2013	2014	2015	2016	2017	2018[b]
World	**2.8**	**3.5**	**1.9**	**-1.8**	**4.3**	**3.1**	**2.5**	**2.6**	**2.8**	**2.8**	**2.5**	**3.1**	**3.1**
Developed countries	**2.6**	**2.2**	**0.1**	**-3.6**	**2.6**	**1.5**	**1.1**	**1.2**	**1.9**	**2.3**	**1.7**	**2.3**	**2.1**
of which:													
Japan	1.3	1.2	-1.1	-5.4	4.2	-0.1	1.5	2.0	0.4	1.4	1.0	1.7	0.9
United States	3.6	2.5	-0.3	-2.8	2.5	1.6	2.2	1.7	2.6	2.9	1.5	2.2	2.7
European Union (EU-28)	2.2	2.2	0.5	-4.4	2.1	1.7	-0.4	0.3	1.7	2.3	2.0	2.5	2.0
of which:													
Eurozone	2.1	1.9	0.5	-4.5	2.1	1.6	-0.9	-0.2	1.3	2.1	1.8	2.5	1.9
France	2.0	1.8	0.2	-2.9	2.0	2.1	0.2	0.6	0.9	1.1	1.2	2.2	1.5
Germany	1.7	1.3	1.1	-5.6	4.1	3.7	0.5	0.5	1.9	1.7	1.9	2.5	2.0
Italy	1.6	1.0	-1.0	-5.5	1.7	0.6	-2.8	-1.7	0.1	1.0	0.9	1.6	1.3
United Kingdom	2.7	2.5	-0.5	-4.2	1.7	1.5	1.5	2.1	3.1	2.3	1.9	1.8	1.2
European Union Member States after 2004	1.9	5.0	3.7	-3.4	1.7	3.1	0.6	1.2	3.0	3.8	3.1	4.6	4.0
Transition economies	**-4.9**	**7.2**	**5.3**	**-6.6**	**4.8**	**4.7**	**3.3**	**2.0**	**1.0**	**-2.2**	**0.3**	**2.1**	**2.2**
of which:													
Russian Federation	-4.7	6.8	5.2	-7.8	4.5	4.3	3.5	1.3	0.7	-2.8	-0.2	1.5	1.7
Developing countries	**4.8**	**6.3**	**5.5**	**2.6**	**7.8**	**6.1**	**5.0**	**5.0**	**4.5**	**4.0**	**3.9**	**4.4**	**4.6**
Africa	2.6	5.8	5.5	3.4	5.4	1.3	5.9	2.3	3.7	3.3	1.7	3.0	3.5
North Africa, excl. the Sudan and South Sudan	2.9	5.0	6.4	3.6	4.3	-6.1	9.7	-3.5	1.3	4.2	3.1	5.2	4.6
Sub-Saharan Africa, excl. South Africa	2.7	7.0	6.0	5.3	7.0	5.0	5.3	5.4	5.6	3.6	1.3	2.6	3.8
South Africa	2.1	4.4	3.2	-1.5	3.0	3.3	2.2	2.5	1.7	1.3	0.6	1.2	1.1
Latin America and the Caribbean	3.1	3.8	4.0	-1.9	5.9	4.4	2.8	2.8	1.0	-0.3	-1.1	1.1	1.7
Caribbean	2.2	5.1	2.6	-0.9	3.0	2.2	2.2	2.7	2.8	3.9	1.5	2.1	2.7
Central America, excl. Mexico	4.4	4.5	4.3	-0.7	3.9	5.4	4.8	3.7	4.0	4.1	3.9	3.7	3.7
Mexico	3.2	2.2	1.1	-5.3	5.1	3.7	3.6	1.4	2.8	3.3	2.7	2.3	2.1
South America	3.0	4.3	5.0	-1.0	6.4	4.7	2.6	3.2	0.3	-1.7	-2.6	0.6	1.4
of which:													
Brazil	2.8	3.7	5.1	-0.1	7.5	4.0	1.9	3.0	0.5	-3.5	-3.5	1.0	1.4
Asia	6.3	7.5	6.1	4.3	8.8	7.4	5.6	6.1	5.7	5.4	5.7	5.5	5.5
East Asia	8.7	9.0	7.7	7.0	9.9	8.3	6.7	6.8	6.5	5.9	5.9	6.2	6.0
of which:													
China	10.6	10.9	9.7	9.4	10.6	9.5	7.9	7.8	7.3	6.9	6.7	6.9	6.7
South Asia	4.8	6.7	4.5	4.1	8.8	5.3	2.6	4.8	6.3	5.8	8.4	5.7	6.1
of which:													
India	6.0	7.6	6.2	5.0	11.0	6.2	4.8	6.1	7.0	7.6	7.9	6.2	7.0
South-East Asia	4.9	5.6	4.4	2.0	7.8	4.9	5.9	5.1	4.5	4.6	4.6	5.2	4.8
West Asia	4.1	5.7	4.1	-1.9	6.0	8.6	4.9	6.2	3.4	4.2	3.1	3.0	3.3
Oceania	2.7	2.8	0.3	2.0	5.8	1.7	2.4	2.6	6.9	5.2	2.4	2.3	2.4

Source:　UNCTAD secretariat calculations, based on United Nations, Department of Economic and Social Affairs (UN DESA), National Accounts Main Aggregates database and World Economic Situation and Prospects: Update as of mid-2018; ECLAC, 2018; OECD.Stat, available at : https://stats.oecd.org/Index.aspx?DataSetCode=EO (accessed 18 June 2018); IMF, 2018, Economist Intelligence Unit, EIU CountryData database; J.P.Morgan, *Global Data Watch*; and national sources.

Note:　Calculations for country aggregates are based on GDP at constant 2010 dollars.

　a　Average.

　b　Forecasts.

reduce Japanese growth closer to 1 per cent in 2018 as compared to 1.7 per cent in 2017.

As noted earlier, despite the signs of a loss of momentum that challenge the claims of a robust growth path in the advanced nations, central banks in most of these countries are choosing to withdraw the easy money and low interest policies that they have pursued for such an extended period. This has affected the extent to which the hesitant recovery in some advanced nations and the accompanying commodity price increase can deliver a return to stable growth in the rest of the world.

2.　Transition economies

The transition economies that are members of the Commonwealth of Independent States (CIS) have been recovering from two years of no or negative growth. They recorded a strong rebound in 2017, with growth of 2 per cent, as compared with 0.2 per cent in 2016. That figure is expected to marginally improve in 2018. An important factor underlying the recovery was an increase in commodity prices, especially of oil, which accounts for close to 60 per cent of merchandise exports from the Russian Federation. The spike in oil prices improved both the current account on the balance of payments and the revenues of the Government in the Russian Federation. The result was a transition from recession (contraction of 2.8 per cent in 2015 and 0.2 per cent in 2016) to recovery in 2017, when growth was 1.5 per cent. This is likely to move closer to 1.7 per cent in 2018.

That recovery should benefit the whole of the CIS, as the Russian Federation accounts for 80 per cent of GDP of the region and is its principal growth driver as a major source of import demand and remittances for other countries in the CIS. The other CIS countries are also likely to benefit from loan-financed infrastructure spending under the Belt and Road Initiative in China. However, dramatic improvements in performance on the back of higher oil prices are unlikely, because of the dampening effects of austerity programmes of some of these economies.

The growth dynamics of the transition economies in South-Eastern Europe is determined by the performance of the European Union, which consumes anywhere between half and 80 per cent of exports from these economies. Uncertainties in Europe can affect the pace of GDP growth in this region. Still expectations are that growth would accelerate from 2.3 per cent in 2017 to around 3 per cent in 2018.

While oil-exporting countries have obtained a temporary reprieve from balance-of-payments difficulties and currency depreciations, current account deficits persist in many countries such as Georgia and Ukraine. Since these deficits are financed by capital inflows, increases in global interest rates can reduce flows, increase balance-of-payments stress and trigger currency depreciation. Vulnerability persists within the improved growth scenario.

3. Latin America

Having benefited from the recovery from recession in two large economies in the region (Argentina and Brazil), the rise in commodity prices, and a consequent 3 per cent improvement in the terms of trade, Latin American economies recorded higher growth in 2017, especially in relation to the slowdown starting 2015. The recovery is expected to continue with GDP growth in Latin America and the Caribbean projected at around 1.7 per cent in 2018, compared to 1.1 per cent in 2017 (table 1.4). All countries benefited from the higher prices, though price increases were particularly sharp in the case of hydrocarbons and oil derivatives, iron ore and soya bean.

The biggest economy in the region, Brazil, recorded positive expansion of 1 per cent in 2017, after contraction amounting to 7 per cent of GDP over the previous two years. This growth from a low base persisted in early 2018, although signs of deceleration (partly precipitated by a truckers' strike) appeared in the second quarter, creating uncertainties about the pace of recovery for the remainder of the year. The year-on-year growth in 2018 is projected to be around 1.4 per cent.

Until recently, Brazil was attracting attention because of the weakness of its currency. The real depreciated significantly over the first six months of 2018. The pace of depreciation was moderated only by the issue of currency swaps by the central bank (under which investors receive interest at the benchmark Selic rate, but are promised compensation for any fall in the value of the real against the dollar). This combination of a hedge against currency depreciation and a reasonable Selic interest rate kept investments flowing in, especially given the carry trade opportunities that exist when the spread between United States rates and the Selic is high. However, low inflation rates encouraged the Government to bring down the Selic rate from 14.25 per cent in October 2016 to 6.5 per cent in March 2018, at a time when interest rates in the United States were being nudged upward. In addition, lower volatility encouraged the central bank to reduce the volume of swaps issued, from well over $100 billion to less than $25 billion. Once these measures that supported the carry trade were diluted, the *real* could not hold and even became the target of a speculative attack. The fall of the currency stalled only when the central bank president declared that he could "intensify" the use of swaps. A sharp depreciation of the currency can trigger a currency crisis and destabilize financial markets with adverse external effects on the real economy. Particularly hard hit would be firms with debt denominated in foreign currencies, with bankruptcies and asset-price deflation which could hold back investment. And if the central bank decides to hike interest rates sharply to prevent foreign investor exit and capital flight, the investment climate would worsen further. But the low deficit on the current account, not-too-high external debt and significant foreign reserves of around $380 billion give Brazil some ammunition to weather possible external turbulence in the second half of 2018.

External vulnerability appears greater in Mexico, which experienced a drop in the GDP growth rate to 2.3 per cent in 2017 from 2.7 per cent in 2016, partly because of the adoption of a conservative fiscal stance and partly because of the uncertainties surrounding NAFTA. However, seasonally adjusted GDP growth in the first quarter of 2018 accelerated recording a 1.1 per cent increase relative to the previous quarter. This may be under challenge because of the imposition of higher tariffs by the United States on a range of imports from Mexico. Growth can also be adversely affected because of an increase in interest rates from already high levels, necessitated by rising interest rates in the United States and a substantially depreciated currency. If rates are not raised, capital flight could severely damage the currency. However, a more proactive fiscal stance on the part of the newly elected Government could increase domestic demand.

The Central American countries have performed reasonably well in terms of growth. While the GDP growth rate of the subregion came down marginally from 4.1 to 3.9 per cent between 2015 and 2016, it dropped to 3.7 per cent in 2017 and is estimated to be at that level in 2018 as well. The Caribbean, on the other hand, has seen a rise in growth rates from 1.5 to 2.1 per cent between 2016 and 2017, and is projected to grow at a significantly higher 2.7 per cent in 2018.

Interestingly, the danger of retreat by foreign investors seems to affect almost all emerging market economies, irrespective of their recent economic performance. In some countries where the effects on the currency have already been significant, interest rates have been hiked up – to as much as 40 per cent for foreign investors in Argentina. The damaging effects this can have on domestic investment and growth should be obvious.

4. West Asia

Growth in West Asia in 2017 was at its lowest in the post-crisis period, as low oil prices and voluntary production restraints affected income growth in the oil-producing countries, and political conditions adversely affected economic performance in countries like the Syrian Arab Republic and Yemen. Strikingly, GDP in Kuwait and Saudi Arabia contracted by 3.2 and 0.7 per cent respectively. This, however, is likely to change in 2018, given the sharp

increase in oil prices and the positive effect that would have on budgetary revenues and expenditures. However, such gains may be partly neutralized by the need to keep production low to prevent oil prices from returning to their earlier lows. Overall, growth is likely to accelerate in all member states of the GCC (Cooperation Council for the Arab States of the Gulf), namely Bahrain, Kuwait, Oman, Qatar, Saudi Arabia and the United Arab Emirates. This would have knock-on effects on other countries in the region as well, through increased trade flows, remittances and capital flows.

In Turkey, however, growth is likely to decelerate. The Turkish lira depreciated by more than a third over the year ending mid-June 2018, as foreign investors began to pull out capital from the country. Turkey, like Argentina, illustrates the dangers associated with an open capital account. The Government and central bank have responded by repeatedly raising interest rates, which touched 17.8 per cent in June 2018, the highest since the financial crisis a decade back. Yet depreciation has continued, with potentially damaging consequences. Turkish private sector companies that are reportedly saddled with close to $340 billion of foreign currency debt in mid-2018 are being severely hit by the sharp deceleration of the lira, threatening bankruptcies and slowing investment and growth. Investment is also likely to be held back by the high interest rates following hikes of as much as 500 basis points over a short span of less than two months.

In the Islamic Republic of Iran, the decision of the United States to withdraw from the nuclear deal and reimpose sanctions is likely to adversely affect economic performance, as the country had just managed to move to steady growth after suffering many years of sanctions. Importers of oil from the Islamic Republic of Iran are likely to shift to other sources, affecting revenues and foreign exchange availability. Sanctions on the Iranian energy sector halved the country's oil exports, to around 1.1 million barrels per day, in 2013. After the easing of sanctions, the Islamic Republic of Iran currently exports around 2.5 million barrels daily. That trend may well be reversed. Imports into the Islamic Republic of Iran are also likely to be hit. Meanwhile, uncertainty has seen the rial depreciating. While the official rate is around 42,000 rials to the dollar, the black market rate was reportedly ruling at more than double that at the end of June 2018.

5. Developing Africa

After having experienced a rise in the average growth rate from 1.7 to 3.0 per cent between 2016 and 2017, developing countries on the African continent are projected to grow at 3.5 per cent in 2018. A major factor in this recovery is the reversal of the commodity price decline, which is crucial for this set of countries given their dependence on commodity exports. The rise in oil prices particularly benefits countries like Algeria, Angola, the Democratic Republic of Congo, Ghana and Nigeria.

Growth rates and growth drivers varied across the continent, with the less resource-dependent East African subregion continuing to record higher annual rates of growth of more than 5 per cent, largely because of performance in countries such as Djibouti, Ethiopia, Uganda and the United Republic of Tanzania. The other two subregions with comfortable growth rates are Northern Africa, helped in large measure by growth in Egypt, and Western Africa with many economies, such as Benin, Burkina Faso, Côte d'Ivoire, Ghana and Guinea, recording reasonably high growth. The two worst performing subregions are Middle Africa and Southern Africa.

Factors driving growth included, besides increased commodity prices, increased infrastructure investments. However, much of the expenditure driving growth was funded with borrowing from abroad in many cases, resulting in a return of the "high indebtedness" problem. By the late 2000s, debt relief programmes had substantially reduced the debt burden of African countries. But since then, countries have accumulated new debt and a number of African countries are currently being identified as being debt-distressed. With international interest rates set to rise, the health of these economies could deteriorate quickly.

Nigeria, the largest economy in Africa, saw a return to moderate growth in 2018, after two years of contraction and stagnation. Growth in 2018 is projected at 2.5 per cent as compared with negative 1.6 per cent in 2016 and 0.8 per cent in 2017. When oil prices collapsed after 2014, Nigeria was badly hit, with falling state revenues (as oil accounts for 90 per cent of federal revenues), rising fiscal and trade deficits, and a recession. The reversal of the oil price decline has restored growth and improved conditions, with the volatility pointing to the need for economic diversification. However, while growth in the first quarter

of 2018, at 1.95 per cent, was a major improvement over the 0.91 per cent contraction in the first quarter of 2017, it was a dip from the 2.11 per cent year-on-year growth recorded in the fourth quarter of 2017, pointing to the tenuous nature of the recovery.

South Africa, the second largest economy in Africa, saw an improvement in its low rate of growth last year, with GDP increasing from 0.6 per cent in 2016 to 1.2 per cent in 2017, but growth is projected at 1.1 per cent in 2018 (table 1.4). The fact that the economy is not out of the woods was brought home when GDP contracted by 2.2 per cent in the first annualized quarter of 2018. Agricultural GDP contracted by 24.2 per cent, which reportedly was the largest quarter-on-quarter fall in 12 years. Manufacturing GDP also contracted by 6.4 per cent. Underlying this volatility is low growth in the medium term, with GDP growth rates never exceeding 2.5 per cent in any quarter over the last four years, and touching zero or negative levels in two, and around 1 per cent in many quarters.

A fundamental and well-recognized failure of South Africa is its inability to diversify out of mining into manufacturing. In fact, gross value added in manufacturing fell from around 21 per cent in the early 1990s to around 13 per cent in 2016. While the ratio of gross value added in mining to GDP declined, the sector that has gained is Finance, Real Estate and Business Services, in the case of which the ratio of gross value added to GDP rose from close to 16 to 23 per cent. Underlying this increase is a sharp increase in capital flows into the country, facilitated by an increasingly open capital account. Between 2008 and 2016 foreign investment flows into South Africa rose (in rand terms) by 250 per cent, because of a 230 per cent increase in direct investment and a 350 per cent increase in portfolio inflows. One consequence was a relative strengthening of the South African rand, which appreciated (while fluctuating) from 15.1 rand to the dollar in June 2016 to 11.8 in March 2018 (or by more than 20 per cent). This underscores the dilemma of developing countries in currency markets: both appreciation and depreciation bring with them different problems. In South Africa, the recent appreciation is hardly conducive to the growth of production in either agriculture or manufacturing, and so the result has been slow and volatile output growth.

Egypt, the third largest economy in Africa, was rescued from a crisis because of the benefits of increased production and exports of natural gas, especially from new fields such as the Zohr gas field. Egypt claims to have completed four important gas extraction projects in 2017 to add 1.6 billion cubic feet of gas per day to its production. Partly as a result of that, despite being faced with a balance-of-payments crisis and a collapse of its currency which forced it to approach the IMF for a $12 billion line of credit in November 2016, Egypt has been registering reasonable rates of growth of 4.3 and 5.1 per cent in 2016 and 2017 and is expected to grow at 5.4 per cent in 2018.

In 2016, the Egyptian Government was faced with a current account deficit of 7 per cent of GDP and foreign reserves were running out. While the Government sought to keep the exchange rate of the Egyptian pound stable, black markets rates relative to the dollar rose, and remittances fell sharply in the expectation of a devaluation. Between 2011 and 2014 the growth rate hovered at around 2 per cent and the unemployment rate was more than 12 per cent, with the figure at more than 40 per cent among the 15–24 age group who constituted one fifth of the population in 2010. The external economic crisis forced the Government to turn to the IMF, which focused on the fiscal deficit of 12 per cent, the public debt to GDP ratio, and the pegged exchange rate. In return for an IMF loan, Egypt agreed to cut fuel, electricity and food subsidies sharply and float the Egyptian pound (which depreciated from 8.8 to the United States dollar in October 2016 to 16 in November and 18.5 by January 2017). Fiscal austerity increased unemployment and the currency float triggered inflation of more than 25 per cent early in 2018, but growth was buoyed by the discovery of gas reserves and increased exports of gas and petroleum products. Rising oil prices and a devaluation-supported increase in non-petroleum exports helped as well, to some extent concealing a situation of continuing economic vulnerability.

6. Developing Asia

After recording GDP growth rates of 5.7 and 5.5 per cent in 2016 and 2017, the developing countries in Asia are expected to sustain that rate in 2018 as well. This is partly because while growth in China is expected to decelerate from 6.9 in 2017 to 6.7 per cent in 2018, in India it is expected to rise from 6.2 to 7 per cent. However, first quarter growth in China beat expectations, coming in at 6.8 per cent – the third straight quarter of growth at that rate. Growth in the

second quarter was marginally lower at 6.7 per cent. The deceleration in China was in substantial measure the result of the process of deleveraging pushed by the Government to address the credit bubble. Total social financing, or the sum total of official and shadow bank lending, reportedly fell by 14 per cent (or by $110 billion) in the first four months of 2018. This is reflective of a medium-term trend. This is because of a fall in lending by the shadow banking sector, the share of which in total social financing came down from close to 50 per cent to 15 per cent. It had been 8 per cent in 2002. Shadow bank lending fell by 64 per cent in yuan renminbi terms during January to April 2018 as compared to the same period the previous year (by $274 billion in United States dollar terms). Total social financing which averaged two times GDP in the period from 2002 to 2008, rose to 3.2 times in the context of the post-crisis stimulus. It fell to 2.4 times GDP over 2014 to 2017 (Hodges and van Scheltinga, 2018). An example of what this does to demand comes through from the evidence that automobile loans that grew by more than 50 per cent in 2009 and around 33 per cent in 2010, had risen by just 3 per cent in the first four months of 2018.

An important driver of the deleveraging process has been the adoption of a strategy of rebalancing that reduces the role of public and private investment financed by debt in driving growth. The ratio of gross capital formation to GDP, which peaked at 48 per cent in 2011 had come down to 44.4 per cent by 2017. Rebalancing has also reduced the role of net exports in driving GDP growth. The ratio of net exports to GDP came down from 8.6 per cent in 2007 to 1 per cent in 2014, rose to 3.4 per cent in 2015 and fell again to 0.7 per cent in 2017. The result has been a slowing of growth in China, as a result of which growth in East Asia that rose from 5.9 to 6.2 per cent between 2016 and 2017 is expected to fall back to its 2016 level in 2018. Similarly, growth in South-East Asia is expected to drop from 5.2 per cent level recorded in 2017 to 4.8 per cent this year.

Meanwhile, with a GDP growth of 7.7 per cent year-on-year in the first quarter of 2018, India is currently among the world's fastest growing economies. The year-on-year quarterly growth rates have risen from 5.6 per cent in the first quarter of financial year (April–March) 2017/18 to 6.3, 7.0 and 7.7 per cent in the subsequent three quarters pointing to an acceleration of growth. But this is at variance with the story emerging from the annual figures. If annual rates are considered, the GDP growth rate fell from 7.1 per cent in 2016/17 to 6.7 per cent in 2017/18. Growing demand for exports has led to a moderate recovery in industrial production, although the effects of demonetization are still evident in private consumption trends within the economy. The resulting increase in capacity utilization in manufacturing along with a recapitalization of public banks has enabled a rise in investment for the first time in several years. But at the same time, a disconcerting feature is the deceleration of growth in the primary sectors. The service sector is expanding with trade, hotels, transport and communication leading the way.

A lending spree by the banking system during the high growth years has led to the accumulation of large volumes of bad debt or non-performing assets in the balance sheets of leading banks. This, besides threatening financial stability, is curbing credit expansion and is likely to adversely affect investment and growth. Further, the Indian rupee is under pressure on foreign exchange markets. Over the first five months of 2018 the currency had depreciated by more than 7.5 per cent relative to the dollar. Depreciation relative to other major currencies like the British pound, the euro and the yen, has been much less. Yet, the fall vis-à-vis the dollar is of significance, especially since much of the trade and foreign debt of India is denominated in dollars. A leading determinant of the depreciation is the rise in the current account deficit on the balance of payments of India intensified by the sharp rise in the international price of oil.

A similar picture is emerging in Pakistan. Despite robust growth, the currency has lost a quarter of its value against the dollar since the beginning of the year. Higher oil prices have led to a widening trade deficit and foreign exchange reserves have dropped sharply. A widening external debt position, currently standing at $92 billion or 31 per cent of GDP has raised concerns about its sustainability. Expectations are that the new government has no choice but to turn to the IMF for a large loan, which would require adopting austerity measures that are likely to affect growth adversely. Over the medium term, much will depend on whether large infrastructure projects will support a stronger export push.

Growth in ASEAN countries remains stable in the light of strong domestic demand, rising private consumption, and infrastructure investments (especially in countries such as Indonesia and the Philippines). But concerns are rising that these trends can be overshadowed by sluggishness in the global economy

and the worsening of trade relations between the United States and China, both of which are key export markets for many countries in the region. In addition, as elsewhere in emerging markets, the build-up of household and corporate debt is a source of vulnerability. Since 2010, Cambodia, Indonesia, Malaysia, Myanmar, the Philippines and Thailand have increased their non-financial sector debt ratios by an average of almost 20 percentage points. Growth in Indonesia which stood at a comfortable 5.1 per cent in 2017, is officially estimated at 5.1 per cent in the first quarter of 2018 as well. The effects of monetary tightening in the United States and elsewhere threaten the sustainability of this pace of growth, despite the benefits from improved commodity prices.

Benefiting from a revival of exports of information technology products, especially memory chips, the Republic of Korea registered improved export growth in the first quarter of 2018, which helped take GDP growth to 1.1 per cent, as compared with a contraction of 0.2 per cent in the last quarter of 2017. The new Government elected in 2017 on a redistributive platform has raised the minimum hourly wage by 16 per cent and promises to create more jobs, reduce working hours and push for permanency for contract workers. This could trigger some wage-led expansion, which, combined with the pick-up in exports, can raise growth even more. Similar growth trends are visible elsewhere in South-East Asia. Thailand, too, has registered a better-than-expected 4.8 per cent GDP growth rate in the first quarter of 2018, after having grown at 3.9 per cent in 2017, which was the highest since 2013. Here, too, improved exports and increased tourism revenues played a role.

On the whole, across Asia the problem is not so much a weakening of growth, as fear that interest rate increases and monetary tightening could trigger capital outflows, leading to financial and currency instability. Combined with the effects of rising protectionism in the United States and possible responses, this could adversely impact growth resulting in levels lower than initially predicted.

7. Growth in an environment of instability

Across the transition, emerging market and developing countries, two tendencies are visible. First, there are some positive trends in some countries, in the form of the probable continuation during 2018

BOX 1.1   Global scenarios: From toiling to troubling

In the baseline projections for the global economy all countries are assumed to keep their current policy stances unchanged through to 2023. Based on information available in 2018, fiscal policy is assumed to remain as observed in section D, with notable trends towards tightening in France, Brazil and Indonesia and moderate expansion in the Republic of Korea and the United States. Expansionary monetary policy (both in the form of low interest rates and quantitative easing) is expected to continue, although at a more moderate pace, as renewed financial instability – possibly triggered by international disputes over trade and exchange rates – threatens global growth. In this baseline scenario, global GDP growth is projected to slow down to 2.9 per cent in 2018 and hover around this rate through to 2023 (see appendix I.A for details).

The "trade war" scenario explores the consequences for the global economy of an escalation of recent tariff increases. It is generally recognized that the immediate impact of tariffs on growth, through lower trade volumes, is unlikely to be very large but that greater damage can come from increased uncertainty and the possible disruption to global supply chains (Eichengreen, 2018). In fact, ubiquitous calls to preserve or expand international market shares suggest that trade volumes might not significantly fall. However, even if trade volumes are unaffected, higher tariffs could still have serious consequences for global growth through their impact on income distribution and aggregate demand. To highlight this possibility, the scenario assumes that the government of each opposing party reimburses its exporters for any tariffs paid to foreign governments, thereby keeping exports and domestic prices at "pre-war" levels.

In this scenario, confrontation unfolds under four assumptions. First, three country blocs are assumed to face off; the United States is assumed to impose a 20 per cent tariff on all its imports from China and two thirds of its imports from Canada, Japan, Mexico, the Republic of Korea and the European Union. It is assumed that all countries retaliate with equivalent tariffs, dollar for dollar.

Second, all countries are assumed to fully indemnify their exporters for the tariffs paid to foreign governments, using the revenue obtained by taxing imports and, where this is not sufficient, general tax revenue. If this set of measures generates a positive net revenue, this is used towards principal payments on sovereign debt. For example, under the given assumptions it is estimated that in 2019 the United States Government will gain approximately \$280 billion in tariff revenues and will transfer to United States exporting businesses an amount equal to \$181 billion to compensate for the higher tariffs paid by them in Canada, China, Japan, Mexico, the Republic of Korea and the European Union – a version of the border adjustment tax. The net revenue for the United States will be \$99 billion.

While trade flows remain unchanged, a large redistribution of resources is projected to take place: businesses will transfer resources to foreign governments (in the form of tariffs) and these will transfer them to their exporting businesses (in the form of reimbursements). Globally, the result of these flows is a transfer of resources between governments with some obtaining a net revenue and others a net loss.

Third, countries that suffer a net fiscal loss are assumed to resort to exchange rate depreciation in an attempt to gain competitiveness and increase their international market shares, expecting to compensate some of the tariff losses. In recent years, exchange rate targeting has been achieved through a variety of actions, including "managed floating", quantitative easing and other forms of policy driven liquidity expansions.

Fourth, labour shares are assumed to fall slightly as a form of "wartime" economic mobilization undercuts wage claims. Since the assumed policy mix of tariffs and export subsidies does not influence domestic prices, any changes in labour shares will be achieved through nominal wage cuts and increases of productivity passed through to profits.

The direct result of the redistribution of income towards profits will be a loss of domestic demand as workers' reduced purchasing power forces them to cut consumption. But the fall of the labour share will also undermine domestic demand indirectly by sapping business confidence. Fearing more policy changes that may further compress private consumption (and corporate sales), businesses become less willing to invest.

A "trade war" is projected to damage growth and employment and to increase income inequality in the countries involved, even in the case in which trade flows do not change. Moreover, in the current context of increasing financial fragility in several developing countries, a trade war may lead to even more serious consequences, through unruly capital movements. For example, increased exchange rate volatility could induce risk aversion and trigger capital flight as lenders and portfolio managers, following a well-rehearsed script, seek safer assets and higher margins of safety. This could lead to severe currency depreciations in a number of financially vulnerable developing countries and activate a spiralling sequence of declining investment, hikes in unemployment, falling consumption, inflating sovereign debts (when denominated in foreign currencies) and falling government spending. Full-blown financial panic would only be a few steps away. The global consequences would then depend on contagion forces which continue to be difficult to predict.

of the higher growth recorded in 2017, and, in some cases, an improved current account situation at least until the recent spike in oil prices. Oil exporters have benefited significantly from the sharp rise in oil prices. By contrast, oil importers, including those that gained from the rise in non-oil commodity prices, are increasingly under stress.

Second, there has already been depreciation of the value of national currencies, triggered by net capital outflows, especially in the so-called emerging markets. As discussed, these net capital outflows appear to have been precipitated by interest rate increases in the developed countries, as a result of which the carry trade investments that had been undertaken in recent years are being unwound. A combination of interest rate increases and currency depreciations would subject the firms in countries that are exposed to foreign currency debts to considerable stress. These could even lead to bankruptcies and asset-price deflation, with substantial adverse external effects on financial stability and growth.

The scenario then is one of instability in many forms. The likely emerging scenario, in the absence of quick proactive macropolicy measures by governments, is as follows:

1. Net outflows of capital, especially of portfolio capital, from emerging markets, are triggered largely by monetary tightening and increases in interest rates in the United States and other advanced countries.

2. The consequent depreciation of currencies is then worsened by speculative attacks, even as domestic inflation is triggered by the depreciation.

3. Debt service payments valued in domestic currency, on substantially increased corporate debt, rise sharply, precipitating default and bankruptcies.

4. This further depresses investment precisely at a time when it was expected to revive.

As long as the medium-term scenario is one shaped by fiscal conservatism which depresses economic activity, governments in both developed and developing countries are then left hoping for a robust recovery – but never experiencing one. Instead, they are more likely to face a repeat of the instability and crises of a decade ago. This could be made even worse by ongoing tensions in the trading system (box 1.1 and appendix I.A). In an interdependent global economy, inward-looking policies do not offer a way forward; substantial and coordinated shifts in macroeconomic strategy appear to be the only way out of this trap. ∎

Notes

1. The January 2018 edition of the IMF *World Economic Outlook* noted: "Some 120 economies, accounting for three quarters of world GDP, have seen a pickup in growth in year-on-year terms in 2017, the broadest synchronized global growth upsurge since 2010." By April 2018, when the IMF issued the next edition of the *World Economic Outlook*, the prognosis was even better.

2. htpp://ec.europa.eu/eurostat/documents/2995521 /8897618/2-15052018-BP-EN.pdf/defecccc-f9 d9-4636-b7f8-d401357aca46.

3. The average growth of real government expenditure of developed countries during the post-crisis period (excluding the extraordinary stimuli of 2009/10) was a mere 0.6 per cent, far short of the pre-crisis figure.

4. Figures are derived from the United Nations Global Policy Model and based on national statistics and United Nations Statistics Division records.

5. Bank for International Settlements (BIS) statistics obtained from: https://stats.bis.org/statx/srs/table/ f4.1.

6. Figures from the WTO database at: https://www.wto. org/english/res_e/statis_e/merch_trade_stat_e.htm.

7. Centraal Planbureau, The Netherlands, https://www. cpb.nl/en/data.

8. Data on trade in services described in this paragraph come from UNCTADstat and correspond to the concepts and definitions in IMF, 2009.

9. http://databank.worldbank.org/data/databases/ commodity-price-data.

10. The notion of "aggregate supply" (X) is derived directly from the main national accounting identity that defines gross domestic product (GDP):
   $GDP = C + I + G + E - M => $ *"Aggregate Supply" (X)*
   $= GDP + M = C + I + G + E$
   where C stands for consumption, I private investment, G government spending, E exports and M imports.
   This expression can be rearranged by replacing consumption with "disposable income minus savings", where disposable income is GDP minus taxes. Further, using t to denote the average aggregate tax

rate, *s* to denote the private saving propensity and *m* the import propensity, the expression for aggregate supply growth reduces to:

$$\hat{X}=\left[\dot{\gamma}_t+\gamma_t(\hat{G}-\hat{t})\right]\frac{G}{T}+\left[\dot{\gamma}_s+\gamma_s(\hat{I}-\hat{s})\right]\frac{I}{S}+\left[\dot{\gamma}_m+\gamma_m(\hat{E}-\hat{m})\right]\frac{E}{M}$$

where: $\gamma_t=\dfrac{t}{t+s+m}$; $\gamma_s=\dfrac{s}{t+s+m}$; $\gamma_m=\dfrac{m}{t+s+m}$

Dots denote variations over time and hats denote growth rates. See Godley, 1999; and Berg and Taylor, 2001.

11 The data in the table is generated using the United Nations Global Policy Model, which is based on historic data sets from official statistics up to the year 2016, and on an "alignment" tool that uses most current information up to the first and second quarter of 2018 and projects results to the end of the current year as a "model solution". Hence, the table should not be taken as a forecast, but as a conditional model projection subject to the most current information.

12 A two-year period is chosen because such drivers are either directly or indirectly influenced by policy, the effects of which usually take a couple of years to materialize.

13 For example, the United Kingdom is at the top of the section where net external demand is the strongest. The average growth of aggregate supply during these two years is 2.1 per cent, of which the estimated average contribution of net exports is 2.6 per cent. This is followed by a meagre 0.1 per cent contribution of private demand and by a negative 0.6 contribution of government demand. The relative gap between the first and the second growth drivers is the largest for the United Kingdom relative to countries in this section. By contrast, Indonesia shows a growth of aggregate supply of 5.5 per cent, with a 2.3 per cent contribution of external demand, which is only slightly above the contribution of the second strongest driver, private demand.

14 For further discussion see Valletta, 2018 and Polychroniou, 2018.

15 Economic Policy Institute, "Nominal Wage Tracker", https://www.epi.org/nominal-wage-tracker/, accessed 23 June 2018.

16 https://www.un.org/development/desa/dpad/publication/united-nations-global-policy-model/.

17 This is captured in the underlying behaviour of the model and is not an explicit assumption.

References

Akyüz Y (2018, forthcoming). External balance sheets of emerging economies: Low-yielding assets, high-yielding liabilities. South Centre. Geneva.

Bellmann C and Hepburn J (2017). The decline of commodity prices and global agricultural trade negotiations: A game changer? *International Development Policy*. Articles 8.1. Available at: https://journals.openedition.org/poldev/2384.

Berg J and Taylor L (2001). External liberalization, economic performance and social policy. In: Taylor L, ed. *External Liberalization, Economic Performance and Social Policy*. Oxford University Press. Oxford: 11–56.

Eichengreen B (2018). The economic consequences of Trump's trade war. *Project Syndicate*. 12 July. Available at: https://www.project-syndicate.org/commentary/economic-consequences-of-trump-trade-war-by-barry-eichengreen-2018-07.

Godley W (1999). Seven unsustainable processes: Medium-term prospects and policies for the United States and the world. Special Report. Jerome Levy Economics Institute of Bard College. Available at: http://www.levyinstitute.org/publications/seven-unsustainable-processes.

Hodges P and van Scheltinga D de B (2018). China's lending bubble history. *Financial Times*. 22 May.

Available at: https://www.ft.com/content/45bd8052-59dc-11e8-bdb7-f6677d2e1ce8.

IMF (2009). *Balance of Payments and International Investment Position Manual*. International Monetary Fund. Washington, D.C.

Jezard A (2018). Where in Europe have wages fallen most? *World Economic Forum*. 3 April. Available at: https://www.weforum.org/agenda/2018/04/where-in-europe-have-wages-fallen-most/.

Jones M (2018). Foreign investors dumped $12.3 bln in emerging market assets in May – IIF. *Reuters*. 5 June. Available at: https://www.reuters.com/article/emerging-markets-flows/update-1-foreign-investors-dumped-123-bln-in-emerging-market-assets-in-may-iif-idUSL5N1T729D.

Koepke R and Goel R (2018). EM capital flows monitor. Monetary and Capital Markets Department. International Monetary Fund. 4 June.

Lund S, Woetzel J, Windhagen E, Dobbs R and Goldshtein D (2018). Rising corporate debt: Peril or promise? McKinsey Global Institute Discussion Paper. Available at:. https://www.mckinsey.com/~/media/McKinsey/Business%20Functions/Strategy%20and%20Corporate%20Finance/Our%20Insights/Rising%20corporate%20debt%20Peril%20or%20promise/Rising-corporate-debt-peril-or-promise-web-final.ashx.

Otsuka S and Toyama N (2018). Indonesia and Brazil fall off easing track as capital bleeds out. *Nikkei Asian Review*. 18 May. Available at: https://asia.nikkei.com/Economy/Indonesia-and-Brazil-fall-off-easing-track-as-capital-bleeds-out.

Polychroniou CJ (2018). Misleading unemployment numbers and the Neoliberal Ruse of "labor flexibility". Interview with Robert Pollin. *Truthout*. 6 June. Available at: https://truthout.org/articles/misleading-unemployment-numbers-and-the-neoliberal-ruse-of-labor-flexibility/.

Standard & Poor Global (2018). *Global Corporate Leverage Trends*. February. Standard & Poor. New York, NY.

UNCTAD (2018, forthcoming). *Review of Maritime Transport 2018* (United Nations publication. New York and Geneva).

UNCTAD (*TDR 2016*). *Trade and Development Report, 2016: Structural Transformation for Inclusive and Sustained Growth* (United Nations publication. Sales No. E.16.II.D.5. New York and Geneva).

UNCTAD (*TDR 2017*). *Trade and Development Report, 2017: Beyond Austerity: Towards a Global New Deal* (United Nations publication. Sales No. E.17.II.D.5. New York and Geneva).

United Nations (2018a, forthcoming). *Secretary General Report on External Debt Sustainability and Development to the 73nd Session of the UN General Assembly*. United Nations, New York.

United Nations (2018b). *Report of the Inter-agency Task Force on Financing for Development 2018* (Sales No. E.18.I.5. New York).

Valletta RG (2018). Involuntary part-time work: Yes, it's here to stay. SF Fed Blog. 11 April. Federal Reserve Bank of San Francisco. Available at: https://www.frbsf.org/our-district/about/sf-fed-blog/involuntary-part-time-work-here-to-stay/.

van Dijkhuizen A and Neuteboom N (2018). Emerging Markets Watch – EM capital flows: Singling out the weakest links. ABN Amro Insights. Available at: https://insights.abnamro.nl/en/2018/05/emerging-markets-watch-em-capital-flows-singling-out-the-weakest-links/.

Appendix I.A: A "trade war" scenario

This appendix presents model projections of an escalation of trade tensions between the United States, and Canada, China, Japan, Mexico, the Republic of Korea and the European Union.

The direct impact of actual tariff increases on the economies involved appears negligible – for example, recent United States tariffs hit $34 billion of imports from China, or less 0.02 per cent of the GDP of the United States. However, the indirect consequences of a "trade war" have raised more serious concerns, with most assessments focusing on supply-side effects such as the possible disruption of global supply chains and the risk that technology flows across countries may become restricted. By contrast, there has been comparatively little recognition of the macroeconomic mechanisms that may play out in a trade war, especially in terms of distributional and financial imbalances and their impact on aggregate demand. The projections presented here address this gap.

Seen through the lens of these projections the most serious effect of a trade war may be to trigger a fall in aggregate demand, regardless of the extent to which trade volumes initially suffer. Consequently, the projections remain relevant even if the current trade tensions are eventually defused. In fact, the impact of trade policy cannot be seen in isolation from the distributional conflicts, inadequate aggregate demand and rising financial vulnerabilities that have become centrepieces of today's global economy.

The projections are calculated with the United Nations Global Policy Model (GPM),[16] a dynamic macroeconomic model based on a globally consistent database of macrofinancial variables. A distinguishing feature of the GPM is its demand-driven character, implying that it does not assume full employment or constant income distribution (as is often the case in other global models). While the GPM is not a trade model (therefore it contains no details on tariffs and limited details on trade of specific merchandises) it provides an aggregate picture in which trade is linked to macroeconomic features, including growth and income distribution.

Two scenarios are presented here: a baseline scenario, which charts out the path the global economy would take without a trade war or any exogenous shocks, and the trade war scenario.

Country grouping

For the purpose of these projections the global economy is divided into 30 countries/groups, including 19 individual countries (Argentina, Australia, Brazil, Canada, China, France, Germany, India, Indonesia, Italy, Japan, Mexico, the Republic of Korea, the Russian Federation, Saudi Arabia, South Africa, Turkey, the United Kingdom and the United States) and 11 aggregated groups (Other European Union, Other Europe, Other Developed Countries, Other Transition Economies, Other East Asia, Other West Asia, Other South Asia and Pacific, Other South America, Caribbean, North Africa and Other Africa).

For ease of presentation only, the 30 blocs are rearranged into six blocs. Three of these are participants in the trade war: China, the United States and Other Warring Countries (Canada, Japan, Mexico, the Republic of Korea and the European Union). The other three blocs contain the "non-belligerent" countries: Other Developed Countries, Other Developing Countries and a bloc of Vulnerable (developing) Countries (Argentina, Brazil, Indonesia, South Africa and Turkey) characterized by volatile growth rates, persistent current-account imbalances, large accumulation of net external liabilities and significant exchange rate fluctuations.

The challenges of the Vulnerable Countries are, to a lesser extent, shared by many other economies, both developed and developing. Hence, as noted further below, depending on the gravity of such vulnerabilities several of these economies may be subject to major macrofinancial adjustments in the event the trade war escalates.

Baseline scenario

Projected outcomes of the trade war are assessed in comparison with projected outcomes in the baseline scenario, a scenario with no trade war or any exogenous shocks. But while a no-shock baseline scenario is the standard term of comparison in model projections, it is not necessarily the most likely future scenario. In fact, as this chapter has argued, the global economy exhibits unsustainable trends (in policies, indebtedness, asset prices etc.) that cannot deliver reasonable growth for the next five years. Several crisis scenarios may be more likely but are less useful as terms of comparison for another crisis scenario, such as a trade war. In this sense, a no-shock baseline scenario is inevitably ambiguous but provides an informative comparison.

In the baseline projections, all countries are assumed to keep their current policy stances unchanged through 2023. Based on information available in 2018, fiscal policy is expected to reflect the discussion in section D of this chapter, with a trend towards moderate relaxation of the fiscal deficit in the United States (following the tax reform that has taken effect in 2018) and towards moderate tightening in China, Other Warring Countries and Vulnerable Countries. The group of Other Developed Countries is projected to keep its fiscal stance unchanged at the current level. It has been clearly stated in the corpus of the chapter that such a configuration of policies is neither conducive to a sustained and inclusive pattern of growth, nor sustainable to the extent that imbalances would tend to implode in the form of financial crises. The experience of the years before the Great Recession are painful testimony of such concern. However, it can also be observed by looking at the data from this period that it is difficult, if not impossible, to forecast the timing and concrete manifestations of such a kind of crisis, just as it is also impossible to predict the nature of the policy responses.

The external imbalance of the United States is expected to worsen, given the larger fiscal deficit and moderate "releveraging" by the private sector (responding to asset appreciations and financial deregulation). Under such conditional projections the deficit of the current account of the United States will rise from about 3.4 per cent of GDP in mid-2018 to about 4.5 per cent in 2023. China is assumed to continue its shift towards greater reliance on domestic demand, with the external balance stabilizing around a surplus of about 2 per cent of GDP, close to the average for the period after the Great Recession. The group of Other Warring Countries has recorded rising external surpluses in the recent past, which are likely to continue over this period. The group of Other Developed Countries is projected to experience a moderate rise of their export surplus, along with moderately expansionary domestic demand. Other Developing Countries as a group will experience robust growth (though at a more moderate pace than in the past) and a balanced external sector. By contrast, the set of Vulnerable Developing Countries

are projected to remain in deficit and further increase their external debt.

Real exchange rate changes during 2018 are estimated to continue along the trajectory of 2017, implying nominal appreciations of the euro, the United States dollar and the British pound and, conversely, some degree of nominal depreciation in many other countries, including China, Japan and Mexico which are singled out as being involved in the simulated trade war. Throughout the years 2019 to 2023 the inherited trends are maintained at a more moderate pace, both for nominal and real exchange rates. By contrast, many economies in the developing world have experienced sharper depreciations in the years 2016 and 2017 and, more recently, in 2018. Hence a relatively protracted period of weaker currencies is projected for these groups, even though the tendency to devaluation will reduce over time.

The labour income share of GDP has been on a declining path for nearly two decades or more in almost all developed countries and in numerous developing countries. This trend has meant a massive transfer of income from wage earners to profit earners since the early 1990s (4 per cent of GDP in the United States, 5 per cent in Germany, 10 per cent in France, 12 per cent in Italy). In China, the sharply falling trend that characterized the period of insertion in global trade was reversed from 2007 to 2015. It has since stabilized after recovering almost half of the previous years' losses. The picture has been more varied for the other sets of countries assumed here to be directly involved in the trade conflict. Despite such varying trends, for the purpose of this exercise labour shares are assumed to remain relatively stable in China and in the United States while they are assumed to decrease only slightly in Other Developed Countries, Other Developing Countries and Vulnerable Countries.

As also stressed graphically for the groups involved in the trade war (see figure 1A.1), the trends in labour income shares have been closely related to the growth of consumption in real terms (with the usual caveat, discussed in this and other *TDR*s, that economies with considerably deregulated financial markets can maintain rapid increases in debt-driven consumer spending, usually supported by asset appreciations). Such a correlation, which denotes the known causality from income, spending/saving behaviour of wage earners and consumption, plays a meaningful role in the outcome of the trade war scenario described below.

FIGURE 1A.1 Labour income share and consumption in countries involved in the trade war, 2003–2023
(Labour income as a percentage of GDP; consumption in annual growth rates)

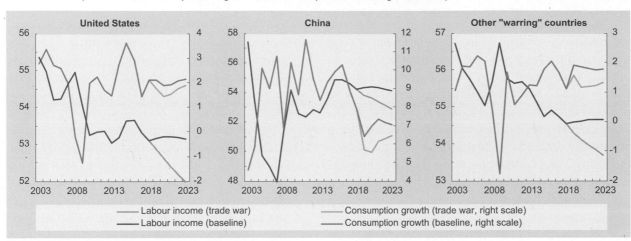

Source: United Nations Global Policy Model and World Database.

Expansionary monetary policy (in the form of both low interest rates and quantitative easing) is expected to continue in all developed countries, although at a more moderate pace, as renewed financial instability – possibly triggered by international disputes over trade and exchange rates – threatens global growth.

In the baseline scenario global GDP growth is projected to slow down to 2.9 per cent in 2018 and hover around this rate through to 2023.

Trade war scenario

The trade war scenario is based on the view that the major consequences of a tariff escalation would come from macroeconomic adjustments rather than a change in trade volumes. To explore these consequences, governments are assumed to fully compensate their exporters for any tariffs paid to foreign governments, so that tariffs will not have any immediate impact on trade volumes. Trade volumes are projected to change eventually because of changes in national incomes (which affect import demands) rather than tariffs.

While short-term exchange rate fluctuations are generally reflected in changes in profit markups, in a trade war policymakers are more likely to be proactive. On the one hand, governments are typically sensitive to the requests of exporters. On the other hand, multilateral discussions on policy

coordination have emphasized growth strategies that are still based on increasing most countries' export shares, notwithstanding the inconsistency of that position. Assuming that all participants in the trade war will try to preserve their export shares reflects this reality.

From the perspective of an importing economy it should be clear that the network of production and specialization cannot be rebuilt domestically from one day to the next. An existing domestic structure of production, as well as consumption patterns that depend heavily on acquired technologies and preferences, do not change drastically. From the perspective of producers in the exporting country, the implication of shutting down the entire market of the importing country because of the "cost of the tariff" would certainly have more severe implications in terms of employment and social stability in the originating country than the "price cost" for the exporter itself. In other words, the domestic implication of the tariff faced abroad becomes a far greater social and economic concern for the policymaker than what the tariff actually represents. In sum, this assumption simply reflects the known historical experience that when the corporate sector faces financial difficulties, the government usually steps in with support mechanisms.

At the same time, producers, and especially the large companies that have been increasing their market shares over the past two decades, are assumed to continue to exercise their leverage in labour markets to lower wage costs in response to a more challenging trading environment.

In a nutshell, the scenario presents a situation where increased tariffs will lead to the government of each belligerent party reimbursing its exporters, so as to retain global export shares and avert employment collapses, while in the receiving economy domestic prices will remain, in principle, at previous levels. This effectively implies transfers (even if these are small compared with the sizes of these economies) from surplus economies to the United States. Additionally, some countries will allow their real exchange rates to depreciate marginally to maintain global market shares.

In the trade war scenario, the tariff escalation triggers downward pressures on wages and generates uncertainty around the path of economic policy. This damages aggregate demand, economic growth and, ultimately, trade activity and financial stability. More specifically, the scenario is defined by the following four assumptions:

1. *Tariffs*

   The United States is assumed to impose a 20 per cent tariff on all its imports from China and two thirds of its imports from Canada, Japan, Mexico, the Republic of Korea and the European Union. It is assumed that China and these other countries retaliate with equivalent tariffs, dollar for dollar. No country is assumed to impose higher tariffs than those it was targeted by or impose them on a larger trade volume.

2. *Tariff revenues*

   Warring governments fully compensate their exporters for the tariffs paid to foreign governments, using the revenue obtained by taxing imports and, where this is not sufficient, general tax revenue. If this combination of tariffs and transfers produces a net revenue, this is used to reduce the government's deficit and debt. For example, in 2019 the United States government is projected to gain approximately $280 billion in tariffs and to transfer to United States exporting businesses $181 billion for the tariffs paid to Canada, China, Japan, Mexico, the Republic of Korea and the European Union – a version of the border adjustment tax. The United States government is projected to gain a net $99 billion in revenue that it then uses to reduce its deficit and debt.

Under this assumption, a redistribution of resources is projected to take place: businesses will transfer resources to foreign governments (in the form of tariffs) and these will transfer them to their exporting businesses (in the form of reimbursements). Globally, the result of these flows is a transfer of resources between governments, with some obtaining a net revenue and others a net loss. The largest transfer will be from China to the United States, and it will be in the order of 0.5 per cent of the GDP of China. The other countries estimated to experience net losses are Japan, Mexico and the Republic of Korea, to degrees significantly lower than those of China, both absolutely and relative to GDP (see figure 1A.2, which shows the net international transfer in nominal terms).

3. *Currency devaluation*

   Countries that suffer a net fiscal loss resort to exchange rate devaluation in an attempt to increase their export shares and gain additional export revenue. In recent years, exchange rate targeting has been achieved through a variety of actions, including "managed floating", quantitative easing and other forms of policy-driven liquidity expansion.

   For the purpose of this simulation, China, Japan, Mexico and the Republic of Korea, which are the countries that eventually make a net tariff payment to the United States, are assumed to let their currencies depreciate approximately 2 per cent below the baseline. As noted above, the depreciation trend is partly embedded in the fact that the main reserve currencies are projected to strengthen in the coming years in the wake of the normalization of monetary policy.

4. *Labour shares*

   Labour shares of national income are assumed to fall as the trade war is used in the public discourse to justify calls for (more) wage moderation. Projected decreases are approximately half of those observed during the recessions and economic slowdowns of the last two decades. The decline will deepen real exchange depreciations, which depend not only on the nominal rate but also on domestic inflation, of which unit labour costs are the main factor.

The direct result of the redistribution of income towards profits will be a weakening of domestic demand, as workers' relatively reduced purchasing

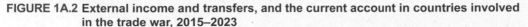

FIGURE 1A.2 External income and transfers, and the current account in countries involved in the trade war, 2015–2023
(External income and transfers in billions of dollars; current account as a percentage of GDP)

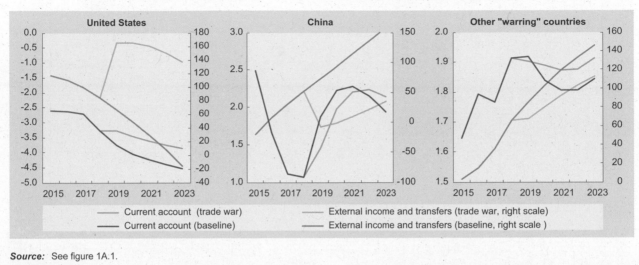

Source: See figure 1A.1.

power causes consumption to decelerate. This is observed in all warring countries, with the largest impacts projected in China and Other Warring Countries, especially Germany, Japan and the Republic of Korea (see figure 1A.1 and table 1A:1). The dynamics of wage-share compression and weaker aggregate demand will have a spillover effect on other countries as well, observed in the form of slight falls in their wage shares (this being entirely an outcome, not an assumption).

The impacts of the distributional shifts will eventually be felt by investors, despite the implied rising profit shares. The model estimates that dampening effects on investment may be significant in all warring countries. In China, the United States, the European Union and Other East Asia, the growth rate of private investment is projected to decrease by approximately 1 percentage point per year through 2023, leading to cumulative drops of about 6 per cent or more (see table 1A.1). Other countries will also experience declines of investment, because of the global impact on aggregate demand emanating from the countries in litigation, as well as on confidence. The impact of the deceleration of investment trends on economic growth is in this case considerably more noticeable than in other circumstances. In this case, investment in practically all economies highlighted has been experiencing a relatively declining trend in the last years (among those, the case of China reflects an intended domestic restructuring effort). Moreover, as has also happened in earlier periods of economic deceleration triggered

initially by consumer demand, the deceleration or decline in consumption and investment demand affect growth in obvious ways (see figure 1A.3).

The combined effects of monetary policy normalization in reserve currency economies, with partial devaluations in affected economies paying net tariffs, and the overall effects of slowdown of unit labour costs (in the wake of wage-share compressions) will lead to a slight decline of real exchange rates in China (see table 1A.1) as well as in Japan, Mexico and the Republic of Korea.

A trade war is projected to damage growth, income distribution and employment, in all countries, though this will be more marked in the countries assumed to be involved in the tariff skirmishes. Admittedly, the United States will experience a decline in the current-account deficit, while China and, to a lesser degree, other warring countries will experience the opposite effect of reduced surpluses. For the United States and China, this will be almost entirely the result of the tariff transfer and not because of a change in the configuration of global production and demand (see figure 1A.2). Taking away such tariff changes, the deficit in the United States could be comparable to the baseline, since there will be both a deceleration in imports due to the changes in domestic consumption and investment, as well as a deceleration of United States exports in response to the changes in global demand. Indeed, the shocks to distribution, consumption and investment at a global level will

TABLE 1A.1 Outcomes for countries/other groups
(Constant dollar prices, annual percentage changes)

	United States			China			Other "warring" countries			Vulnerable developing economies			Other developed economies			Other developing economies		
	2018	2023	Cum. change over 5 years	2018	2023	Cum. change over 5 years	2018	2023	Cum. change over 5 years	2018	2023	Cum. change over 5 years	2018	2023	Cum. change over 5 years	2018	2023	Cum. change over 5 years
GDP growth *(percentage)*																		
Baseline	2.7	2.2		6.7	5.8		1.8	1.8		2.8	3.2		2.5	2.3		3.7	4.1	
Trade war scenario		1.8	-2.5		5.3	-3.9		1.3	-2.9		2.9	-1.5		2.0	-1.6		3.7	-2.2
Private investment *(percentage)*																		
Baseline	6.1	2.7		3.8	3.9		2.7	1.9		2.9	2.2		3.4	2.9		4.8	4.1	
Trade war scenario		1.9	-5.8		2.9	-6.3		0.9	-5.9		1.7	-2.1		2.4	-2.2		3.5	-2.9
Consumption growth *(percentage)*																		
Baseline	2.1	2.2		7.9	7.1		1.1	1.8		4.5	3.5		2.4	2.4		5.6	4.4	
Trade war scenario		1.9	-1.9		6.5	-6.2		1.3	-2.8		3.3	-1.0		2.3	-0.9		4.3	-1.3
Labour income share *(percentage of GDP)*																		
Baseline	53.1	53.1		54.2	54.1		54.6	54.7		50.6	50.6		56.3	55.8		48.2	48.2	
Trade war scenario		54.1	-2.5		54.7	-4.2		55.8	-4.1		48.2	-0.3		50.6	-0.1		48.2	0.0
Real exchange rate *(index: world = 1)*																		
Baseline	1.341	1.350	–	0.831	0.854	–	1.197	1.256	–	0.842	0.779	–	1.507	1.476	–	0.661	0.657	–
Trade war scenario		1.372	–		0.821	–		1.257	–		0.790	–		1.496	–		0.665	–
Current account balance *(percentage of GDP)*																		
Baseline	-3.3	-4.5		1.1	1.9		1.9	1.8		-3.1	-2.0		1.6	2.9		0.6	0.5	
Trade war scenario		-3.9	4.5		2.1	-0.9		1.9	0.2		-2.4	-0.5		2.3	-0.5		-0.2	-1.6
Balance of income and transfers *(billions of current dollars)*																		
Baseline	83.6	-16.3		51.6	158.2		65.6	145.2		-91.7	-145.9		-0.2	-7.3		-108.9	-133.8	
Trade war scenario		137.2	641.3		34.5	-518.9		112.2	-131.8		-144.6	2.5		-8.0	-1.6		-131.4	8.6
Export volume growth *(percentage)*																		
Baseline	3.7	2.3		7.1	7.9		5.0	2.9		3.9	4.8		3.2	3.2		1.3	4.4	
Trade war scenario		1.5	-4.8		7.8	-2.4		2.2	-4.9		4.2	-4.1		2.6	-4.3		3.8	-4.7

Source: See figure 1A.1.

FIGURE 1A.3 Growth of GDP and investment, 2015–2023
(Annual percentages)

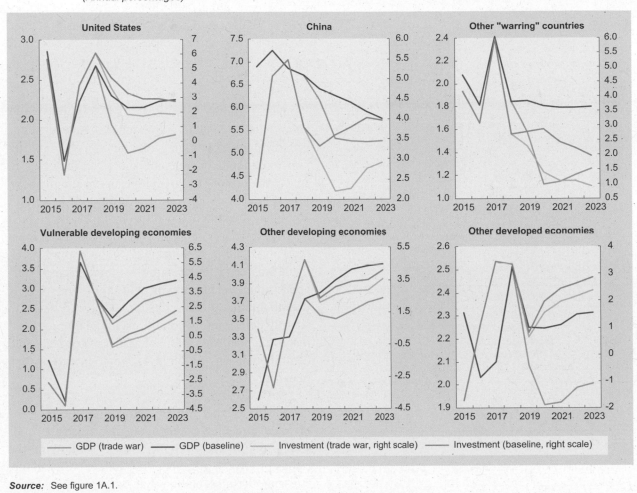

Source: See figure 1A.1.

result in sizeable slowdowns in global demand, and hence export and import growth (see figure 1A.4 and table 1A.2). On account of the export slowdown, China and Other Developing Countries will suffer real losses in their current account. China, however, will manage to regain most of its external net position after four years, resulting from the real exchange rate adjustment and presumably from the persistent structure of trade linkages with other partners not directly involved in the trade dispute. The historical data on bilateral manufacture exports and imports suggest that when China experiences a slowdown of its exports to a particular set of countries outside its region, it can resort to cutting regional imports in a commensurate way.[17]

In the current context of increasing financial fragility in several developing countries, a hypothetical trade war of the kind simulated in this exercise may lead to even more serious consequences for such countries. The main channels involve currency depreciations, unruly capital movements and deflationary policy responses. For example, the higher projected exchange rate volatility could affect investors' confidence and trigger capital flights as lenders and portfolio managers, following a well-rehearsed script, seek safer assets and higher margins of safety. This could exacerbate and activate a spiralling sequence of falling investment, spiking unemployment, falling consumption, inflating sovereign debts (especially the liabilities denominated in foreign currencies) and falling government revenue and spending.

It should be clear, though it is not empirically projected in this model simulation, that several developing countries experiencing increasing financial and distributional imbalances can be shaken by events of even minor significance for the global economy. In particular, for approximately a decade, the set of "vulnerable" countries singled out in this exercise

FIGURE 1A.4 World gross product and trade volume growth rates, 1990–2023
(Annual percentages)

Legend:
- World gross product (trade war)
- World gross product (baseline)
- Trade volume (trade war, right scale)
- Trade volume (baseline, right scale)

Source: See figure 1A.1.

TABLE 1A.2 World variables
(Constant dollar prices; annual percentage changes)

	2018	2023	Cumulative change over 5 years
World gross product (WGP) growth			
Baseline	2.9	2.9	
Trade war scenario		2.4	-2.7
Private investment growth			
Baseline	4.0	3.2	
Trade war scenario		2.3	-5.0
Consumption growth			
Baseline	3.7	3.6	
Trade war scenario		3.2	-2.5
Trade volume growth			
Baseline	4.1	3.8	
Trade war scenario		3.2	-4.6
Labour income share of WGP			
Baseline	52.3	52.3	
Trade war scenario		51.6	-2.2

Source: See figure 1A.1.
Note: WGP is calculated weighing country blocs based on 2005 GDP.

accumulated negative balances on external assets and liabilities. They have also all experienced depreciating real exchange rates that have not helped their external balances recover (either because a "trade recovery" did not materialize because of structural constraints, or because the external debt payments have been larger than the trade revenues).

As noted above, however, such vulnerabilities should not be considered unique to countries in this group. Many developing and developed countries may experience unwelcome shocks in the event of severe disruptions of direct investment and financial flows. For all countries, any further weakening of aggregate demand in developed countries, triggered by a tariff struggle or any other spark in global markets, combined with more wage compression, fiscal austerity and related factors that discourage productive investment and employment, may lead to another global crisis or, at the very least, to sharply deteriorating conditions in the international macrofinancial environment, with governments and central banks having far less room to intervene than in earlier crises.

Chapter II of this *Report* shows that the patterns of trade flows have been changing since the mid-1990s. Figure 1A.4 highlights this by showing the trends of growth of global GDP and export volume, stressing the dissociation that starts after the Great Recession. It is apparent that the changes estimated to affect global trade in this simulation, resulting not from tariffs per se but from more fundamental macroeconomic effects, are not significant compared with changes in other recent periods, when global aggregate demand has fluctuated more severely than is projected in this scenario.

As is discussed in this *Report*, there is no doubt that global trade, even before the slowdown after the crisis, has fallen short of its promise to promote higher value added activities more evenly across the world economy. Still, after decades of experiencing the limits of "free trade", it would be tragic to embrace the opposite excess – a trade-tariff war – rather than to consider what governments could do, through global policy coordination, to avert the continuing deterioration of income distribution and employment that are at the root of most recent economic crises. ■

have all experienced deceleration or high fluctuations of GDP growth and persistently negative current-account balances. Over time, these countries have

THE SHIFTING CONTOURS OF TRADE UNDER HYPERGLOBALIZATION

A. Introduction

The backlash against hyperglobalization is gaining momentum with the international trading system on the front line. This is a surprising turn of events. As discussed in previous *Report*s, the roots of the heightened insecurity, indebtedness and inequality that are hallmarks of the current era stem more from the workings of the financial system than the trade regime; and that regime proved robust in the face of the economic fallout from the global financial crisis. Moreover, using tariffs to mitigate the problems of hyperglobalization will not only fail to do so but runs the danger of adding to them, through a vicious circle of retaliatory actions, heightened economic uncertainty and slower growth.

Still, it would be foolish to dismiss the constituency in advanced economies worried about trade shocks as simply ignorant of the subtleties of Ricardian theory or misguided victims of populist politicians. Indeed, in addition to discontent in the North, there are numerous and long-standing concerns that developing countries have been raising about the workings of the international trading system which have also intensified in this century.

In reality, the lived experiences of each and every constituency at the local level reflects the intertwining of trade, financial and technological forces operating through national, regional and global markets and managed by policies, regulations and institutions designed to govern those markets and interactions.

The dominant narrative of the current era equates globalization with the growing reach (and porosity) of markets and an accelerating pace of technological change. It employs the language of "free trade" to promote the idea of a harmonious (win-win) world governed through clear rules and greater competition. But hyperglobalization has as much to do with profits and mobile capital as with prices and mobile phones and it is governed by large firms that have established increasingly dominant market positions. Indeed, while trade and technology, through both destructive as well as creative impulses, have, no doubt, had an impact on the way we go about organizing our lives, in the end it is social and political initiatives in the form of rules, norms and policies that matter most for the outcomes of an interdependent world. And, as described in previous *Report*s, the hyperglobalized world is one where money and power have become inseparable and where capital – whether tangible or intangible, long term or short term, industrial or financial – has extricated itself from regulatory over-sight and restraint and muted the voice and influence of other social stakeholders with an interest in the direction of public policy.

As a result, it is hardly surprising that heightened anxiety among a growing number of casualties of hyperglobalization has led to much more question-ing of the official story of the shared benefits of trade. Trade sceptics now have substantial political constituencies across the world, in both developed and developing countries.

Mainstream economists bear part of the responsibil-ity for the current state of affairs. Ignoring their own analytical nuances and the subtleties of economic history, they remain biased in favour of unqualified free trade when it comes to communicating with poli-cymakers and broader audiences (see e.g. Driskill, 2012; Rodrik, 2017, 2018).[1] The mainstream narra-tive pitches "comparative advantage" as a "win-win" boost to economic efficiency and social welfare, without specifying the conditions under which such beneficial outcomes can occur or how any negative effects could be abrogated.

There is no doubt that the new protectionist tide, together with the declining spirit of international cooperation, poses significant challenges for governments around the world. However, the call to double down on "free trade" provides a cover for a regime of footloose capital, concentrated market power and the capture of public policy by powerful economic interests. Fighting isolationism effectively requires recognizing that many of the rules adopted to promote "free trade" have not promoted a rules-based system that is inclusive, transparent and development friendly. Reviving optimism about trade and multilateralism must go beyond simply promoting trade for trade's sake and pitching multilateralism as the last line of defence against an autarchic Hobbesian dystopia. A more positive narrative and agenda is required.

The 2030 Agenda for Sustainable Development offers such an agenda but it lacks a clear accompanying narrative, simply stating that "[i]nternational trade is an engine for inclusive economic growth" (United Nations, 2015). This is unfortunate, because the case for international trade and its implications for growth, employment and distributive justice and social norms is a subtle one that depends heavily on context (Rodrik, 2011).

In the context of hyperglobalization, this chapter addresses the following questions: To what extent has trade promoted structural change? Which countries and/or social groups have benefited from deeper trade integration? Under what conditions can trade have positive developmental and distributive effects? It provides new evidence that the governance of international trade in the era of hyperglobalization has contributed to increasing domestic inequalities in many countries. This has in part reflected the way in which trade is governed in global value chains (GVCs), which has heightened the bargaining power of footloose capital, including through job offshoring to poorer countries (or simply the threat of that), as well as market concentrating and rent-seeking practices of large firms that effectively weaken competition. This is partly because international trade is increasingly governed by "free trade" agreements that empower global firms. For example, services derived from intangible assets whose geographical location can be determined by firms almost at will – such as financial assets or intellectual property rights (IPR) – can now be "traded" more freely between higher-tax and lower-tax jurisdictions and within transnational corporations (TNCs) themselves. Overall, these processes have tilted the distribution of value added in favour of capital, especially transnational capital, whose owners remain mostly headquartered in developed countries.

The chapter is structured as follows.[2] Section B reviews some stylized facts on the shifting dynamics of world trade since the Second World War, highlighting some key patterns that have shaped this changing landscape. Section C assesses to what extent trade has promoted structural change in developing countries. Section D examines the effects of trade on inequality. Section E discusses the macroeconomic relevance of the trade and development challenges and lays out some policy recommendations.

B. Trade dynamics after the Second World War

Between the end of the Second World War and the global financial crisis (GFC), the growth of world trade consistently outpaced that of global output albeit with significant differences in the gap across subperiods (figure 2.1). The gap has persisted since 2008, just as both trade and output growth have been low by historical standards. However, there are other significant changes in trade dynamics over the last 70 years, particularly with respect to developing country participation, that it is important to flag.

1. The rise and fall of the Golden Age: 1950–1986

Between 1950 and 1973, world trade grew at an average annual rate of nearly 8 per cent, amid strong declines of trade costs of all kinds resulting from peace dividends, improvements in transport, a fast pace of investment and rapid productivity growth, a measured drop in tariffs, and a stable international monetary system. Rapid recovery in Western Europe,

FIGURE 2.1 World trade, global output and related elasticities, selected country groups and periods, 1870–2016

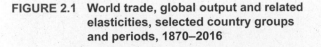

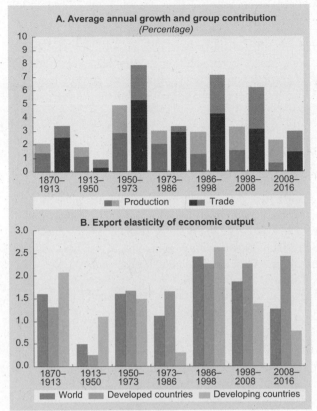

Source: UNCTAD secretariat calculations, based on Maddison (2006) tables 1–3 and F-3 for data until 1973 and UNCTADstat afterwards.

Note: The darker areas in panel A represent the contribution of developed countries to the corresponding world aggregates. Data in panel A represent real annual compound growth rates, computed using constant 1990 dollars between 1870 and 1973 and constant 2010 dollars between 1973 and 2016.

FIGURE 2.2 Share in global merchandise exports, 1948–2017
(Percentage)

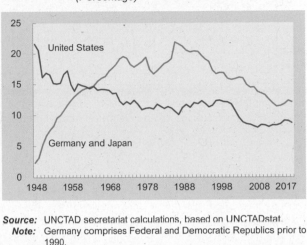

Source: UNCTAD secretariat calculations, based on UNCTADstat.
Note: Germany comprises Federal and Democratic Republics prior to 1990.

tolerance of the trade practices of (mainly developing) countries who were not part of the club but with little concern to address their particular challenges.

In the South, growth rates of output and trade during the "Golden Age" were consistently higher than in previous periods but persistently lower than those in advanced economies. Moreover, developing countries' structure of trade remained highly unbalanced, dominated by primary exports to Northern markets, which on average still accounted for two thirds of developing country exports at the end of the Golden Age.

Figure 2.3 shows the sharp asymmetry, in terms of world tonnage, in the participation of developing

solid growth in the United States and stellar growth in Japan, along with continuing industrialization in the Soviet Union and the emergence of first-tier newly industrializing economies (NIEs) towards the end of this period also contributed to this process. Developed countries accounted for two thirds of the growth of world trade during this period with the big change being the steady decline of the United States as a trading hegemon and its replacement by the Federal Republic of Germany and Japan (figure 2.2).

Most of the increase in trade flows reflected rising intra- and inter-industry trade among developed countries and with a strong regional dimension. Trade rules, consequently, were designed by a small club of relatively wealthy converging economies, to consolidate broad economic gains coming from outside the trading system (Rose, 2004), and with a degree of

FIGURE 2.3 Developing economies' share of trade by weight, 1970–2016
(Percentage)

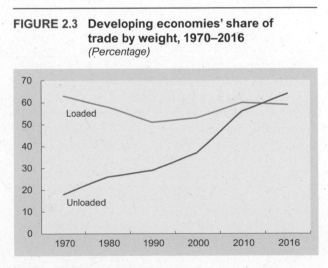

Source: UNCTAD, 2017a: figure 1.4 (b).
Note: Data reflect share of total tonnage in world seaborne trade.

BOX 2.1   Measurement challenges in mapping international "trade"

The statistical recording of "trade" has become increasingly complex, as more production across the world is organized by GVCs and so parts and components of products, as well as the services that are embedded in traded products, cross borders several times.[a] Moreover, a growing share of traded services (particularly services deriving from intangible assets with no determined geographical location, such as financial loans or IPR licensing) represent intra-firm trade, much of which used for tax optimization strategies of firms. Unlike regular trade between distinct firms, such trades often do not generate any production, employment and labour income in the low-tax jurisdictions where they are recorded, even as they siphon capital income and profit out of higher-tax jurisdictions. These distortions are most visible in offshore financial centres, but they also occur in a less perceptible manner in much larger countries.

Such processes create obstacles to a mapping of world trade that accurately reflects production, employment, and capital and labour incomes. At present, the basic principle for the compilation of trade statistics is the crossing of a border, following recommendations made by the United Nations Statistical Commission. Because trade in goods necessarily involves crossing a border at a customs checkpoint, merchandise trade has long been reasonably accurately registered, at least to the extent that states properly performed their core functions. However, as production has fragmented along GVCs, the growing trade in intermediate goods and services embedded in final goods as well as reimports tend to exaggerate the trade performance of countries with large processing trade sectors, such as China. This can distort the mapping of global trade, which is why statistical offices and researchers have created and are using trade in value added databases, such as TiVA or WIOD (which are also used in this *Report*). Even though such value added data rely on input–output tables and reductionist assumptions, such as the reliance on a representative firm for each industry-country (e.g. see discussion in Koopman et al., 2014; Johnson, forthcoming 2018), these efforts represent an improvement over gross trade data.

But trade in services creates additional complications and difficulties for the measurement of cross-border trade. This is essentially because of the non-tangible nature of most services: unlike merchandise trade, these services do not cross borders in physical forms that enable classification according to commodity codes, quantity, origin and destination. They do not have to go through the customs procedures that are crucial for collecting merchandise trade data. So trade in services is not recorded in customs-based data. Effectively it only exists in the balance-of-payments accounts, which consider only whether there was a change in the country of residence of the owner of the goods and services that are exchanged, rather than whether and how they crossed borders.[b]

However, services now account for the bulk of global GDP, and their share in international trade is growing. In the past, some economists may have labelled all services as "non-tradable", but the growing importance of services in recent trade negotiations and in the new generation of trade agreements (box 2.2) show that this approach is obsolete. According to some estimates, the share of services in total trade in value added exceeds 50 per cent in many developed countries and could now have reached 40 per cent at the global level, compared to 30 per cent in 1980 (World Bank et al., 2017). The rising share of traded services in value added terms stands in contrast with the share of traded services in gross terms, which remained unchanged at about 20 per cent of total (goods and services) gross trade since 1980. This difference arises from the embedding of intermediate services into final goods, which tends to inflate the relative magnitude of gross trade in goods.

Data on trade in value added may correct to some extent the biases created by production fragmentation along GVCs, but they do not address the fundamental difficulty of assessing the real or fictive nature of reported flows of trade in services. As noted above, unlike physical goods, services are intangible and their official geographical location is determined not by which borders they may have crossed, but by the residence of the owner of exchanged services. The measurement of some services, such as tourism, may not be affected by this problem, but only because it involves the travel of a natural person, who needs to physically pass through a customs checkpoint to cross a border. Many internationally traded services, however, do not involve international travel, and in an increasing share of cases, they do not even involve natural persons but only intangible exchange between companies. Such international transactions often represent fictitious intra-firm accounting techniques aiming at avoiding taxation, which biases the measurement of the "actual" amount of international trade in services. Contrary to a widely shared belief, almost no trade in goods is taking place within multinational firms, whose boundaries are increasingly determined by the use of a common set of intangible inputs, knowledge and the transfer of capabilities rather than by the transfer of goods (Ramondo et al., 2016; Atalay et al., 2014).

The growing significance of intangible assets, such as financial assets, patents, trademarks, rights to design, corporate logos, etc., has important implications for how companies behave as well as how economists and trade analysts consider international trade. Mainstream trade economists still tend to believe that "[t]he decision about whether and where to build a foreign plant is quite separate from how and where to raise the financing for that plant" (Markusen, 2004: xii), and that the latter can simply be analysed as part of the traditional theory of capital flows. But multinational companies tend to treat issues of "residency" quite differently. For them, the location of intangible assets is one of the most significant instruments for minimizing tax liabilities, and therefore they can and do choose to locate their intangible assets in jurisdictions that minimize their aggregate tax payments. This can create "phantom trade flows" that do not represent genuine movements of services at all. As Lipsey (2009) has noted, economists therefore need to accept that there has been a change in the reality they are attempting to measure, rather than get fooled into believing that the recorded data represent the reality in such circumstances.

The extent to which this is a problem is easily seen from the example of TNCs of the United States, evident in figure 2.B1.1. The large and exploding incomes from investments abroad (much of which is in the form of intangible investment in IPR of various kinds, valued by the firms themselves) in low-tax or no-tax jurisdictions that do not constitute large markets in themselves, shows how important this strategy has become for the overall profitability of these large TNCs. Obviously this affects tax collection by government; but it also distorts our understanding of global trade in services.

FIGURE 2.B1.1 Income of the United States on direct investment abroad, selected countries, first quarter 2000 to first quarter 2018
(Billions of dollars)

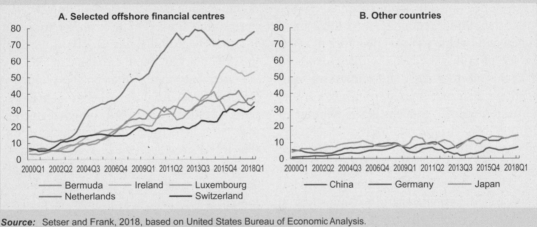

Source: Setser and Frank, 2018, based on United States Bureau of Economic Analysis.
Note: Data correspond to the four-quarter trailing sum.

One solution for disentangling growing flows of fictitious intra-firm trade in services from genuine trade in services would be for national statistical offices to produce accounts based on ownership rather than residency. Such accounts would net out the effects of phantom intra-firm transactions and provide a more accurate picture of trade in services. So far, the Bureau of Economic Analysis (BEA) of the United States is the only statistical office that regularly publishes an ownership-based current account for that country.[c] There have been several attempts by civil society to push for country-by-country reporting of TNCs accounts, and the United Nations has also called for this in the discussions on financing for development (UNCTAD, 2017b). These proposals are very important not only for more transparency about intra-firm trade flows, and better knowledge about the true nature of trade in services, but also for raising the fiscal resources required by governments to meet the Sustainable Development Goals.

---

[a] See e.g. Lipsey, 2009 and Feenstra et al., 2010 for a detailed discussion of the main issues at stake.

[b] The concern of public authorities with the residency of the holders of goods and services has its origin in the gold standard monetary regime, which incentivized countries to track how much gold was in the hands of their nationals as a proxy for the demand for their national currency at a time when monetary authorities were constrained by the need to preserve fixed exchange rates.

[c] Research by Ramondo et al., 2016 and Atalay et al., 2014 cited above are based on these BEA data.

economies in world seaborne trade, the main vector for shipping goods. In 1970, almost two thirds of world tonnage were loaded in (i.e. exported from) developing countries, whereas less than one fifth was unloaded (i.e. imported into) there. This gap contrasts with developing countries' exports and imports measured in nominal terms, which were roughly equivalent. This difference is a reminder of the unfavourable terms of trade and the balance of payment constraints that prevailed during that era due to developing countries' relatively constrained role as providers of primary commodities.

The asymmetric structure of international trade and lagging growth performance of most developing countries fuelled growing concerns among many of their policymakers over biases in the rules of the trading system. It also underpinned the idea of "unequal exchange", which argued that the structure of world trade was responsible for the persistent inequality between developed and developing economies. The worries that developing economies would remain marginalized and unable to take advantage of international trade provided the basis for the creation of UNCTAD in 1964, to renegotiate trade rules so as to loosen the constraints on catch-up growth and to redirect international cooperation in support of diversification away from commodity dependence. However, signs of the success of the export-oriented growth model in the East Asian NIEs started to show in the late 1960s, with a more dramatic acceleration, demonstrated by their sharply rising share in global merchandise exports, from the mid-1970s (*TDR 2016*).

Under pressure from a series of internal and external shocks, the 1973–1986 period was difficult for advanced and developing countries alike, except for oil exporters, who enjoyed significant terms-of-trade gains, as well as for first-tier NIEs, whose market shares in manufacturing exports expanded. In part as a result of the slowdown in advanced country growth, and the (short-lived) recycling of petro-dollars to emerging economies, a discussion of southern markets replacing northern markets for each other exports (so-called South–South trade) briefly emerged (Lewis, 1979) but was abruptly cut short by the debt crisis in the early 1980s and subsequent structural adjustment programmes which further repressed growth, particularly in Africa and Latin America. As a result, the annual growth of trade almost halved in the 1973–1986 period compared to 1950–1973. Meanwhile, the annual growth of global

output decreased from about 5 per cent to 3 per cent. During this period, the South contributed a little over one tenth of global trade expansion, but to one third of the growth of world income.

2. Hyperglobalization: 1986–present

Starting from the mid-1980s, a new phase of trade expansion took place. In contrast with the two previous post-war periods included in figure 2.1 – the Golden Age and the subsequent turbulent decade – this new round of globalization was marked by very fast acceleration of trade, especially in some parts of the developing world. Until the GFC, the growth of world trade in real terms rebounded to an annual average of more than 6 per cent, with the contribution of the South peaking at about half of this figure in the 2000s. This new era was also marked by a further increase in the elasticity of world trade to global output, which peaked at 2.4 during the 1986–1998 period and then remained close to 2 during the following decade (figure 2.1.B). Interestingly, the growth of global output remained much lower (about 2 percentage points) than in the Golden Age era, which reflects the shift in the broad macroeconomic policy framework that led to higher unemployment and lower investment in developed economies, and thus lower growth (see e.g. *TDR 1995*: part three).

The metamorphosis of trade started around 1986, though significant measurement challenges remain in properly mapping international "trade" (box 2.1). This period coincides with the beginning of the Uruguay Round and came in the wake of several important political shifts. It occurred when many developing countries were still adjusting to the debt crisis by abandoning import-substitution industrialization (ISI) and turning to more export-oriented strategies based on liberalized imports. It also coincided with the end of the East–West divide and the rise of a "new world order" dominated by liberal ideology. On the supply side, the erosion of organized labour and the flexibilization of labour markets, along with the continued spread of technological progress (containerization, information and communication technology (ICT), etc.), facilitated the fragmentation of production along GVCs and the coordination of complex processes across long distances, with the resulting cross-border movement of inputs instrumental in boosting trade. This was supported by the proliferation of free trade agreements (FTAs) and bilateral investment treaties (BITs) (box 2.2) and subsequently by the accession of China to the World Trade Organization (WTO) in 2001, which lowered the cost of labour by enlarging the globally available reserve army of workers. On the demand side, the end of full employment and the growing deregulation of financial markets encouraged a shift from wage-driven to debt-driven aggregate demand in large advanced economies; that, in turn, eased the balance-of-payments constraint, allowing some economies, including in the developing world, to prolong asset booms for longer and, in turn, for other economies to tap into external demand to maintain growth (*TDR 2016*: chap. I.C).

The trade acceleration was particularly strong in East and South-East Asia, based on mutually reinforcing dynamic interactions between profit, investment and exports in state-targeted industrial sectors; within this subgroup, the share of first-tier NIEs in world exports reached about one tenth of world trade in the mid-1990s and stabilized at this level thereafter (figure 2.4). This successful profit–investment–export nexus was accompanied by specific policy measures aiming at promoting structural changes, from resource-based to labour-intensive and subsequently to technology-intensive production and exports, and by increased penetration of northern markets (*TDR 1996*: chap. II; *TDR 2003*: chap. IV). With some lag, China followed broadly the same strategy, although on a scale and speed never achieved before and with a stronger presence of state-owned enterprises (SOEs). Chinese exports increased from less than 2 per cent of world trade in the mid-1980s to more than 13 per cent in 2016. This increase in China (on top of the first-tier NIEs) was associated with a reduction in developed countries' share in world exports, from nearly three quarters of gross merchandise exports in 1986 to just over one half in 2016.[3] This decline was almost entirely due to the relative decline of North–North trade, which decreased from more than 60 per cent of global trade to less than 40 per cent over the same period. Nevertheless, in most of the rest of the developing world, export shares remained roughly constant or sometimes even declined, except during the rising phase of the commodity price supercycle when major commodity exporters registered a temporary increase of their market shares.

This mirrored changes in the destination of exports, which progressively shifted to developing countries. Between the mid-1980s and 2016, the share of world exports to developing and transition economies rose from roughly one quarter to one half. South–South

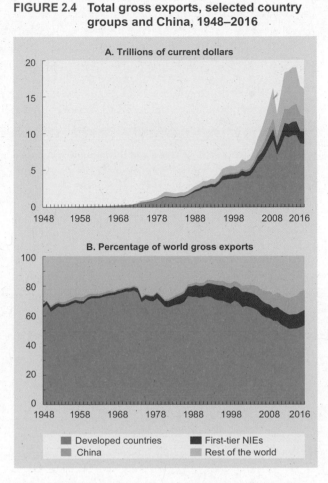

FIGURE 2.4 Total gross exports, selected country groups and China, 1948–2016

Source: UNCTAD secretariat calculations, based on UNCTADstat.

trade accounted for more than 50 per cent of this increase, from a base of only one quarter of exports to the South in 1986. Since these data include trade in intermediate goods, these changes partly reflect the expansion of GVCs, which have had significant impacts on the geography of production of manufactured products. While gross trade data show that developing countries' gross revenues from manufacturing as a share of their total exports increased from about one half in 1995 to two thirds in 2016, this may overestimate the rise of the manufacturing in developing countries' exports, partly because of double-counting problems arising in the context of GVCs (see box 2.1).[4]

Figure 2.5 provides four snapshots of the global network of merchandise trade at 10-year intervals from 1986 onwards. The 1986 figure illustrates the limited trade flows outside the developed economies, at a time when developing countries mostly provided raw material and energy sources to developed economies. In 1996, the increased role played by the most

BOX 2.2   Using laws not wisely but too well: The international legal framework in the era of GVCs

The expansion of GVCs has been closely connected with changes in the legal architecture of the international trading system. The number of trade agreements and other kinds of international economic treaties (such as bilateral agreements on investment protection, avoidance of double taxation, etc.) rose exponentially after 1990. In this process, TNCs headquartered mostly in developed countries found themselves in a privileged position to influence rule-making and to reorganize large swathes of world production, thereby creating possibilities of expanding their cost-minimizing strategies on a global scale.

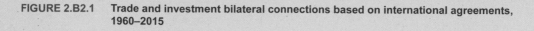

FIGURE 2.B2.1   **Trade and investment bilateral connections based on international agreements, 1960–2015**
(Number of country pairs)

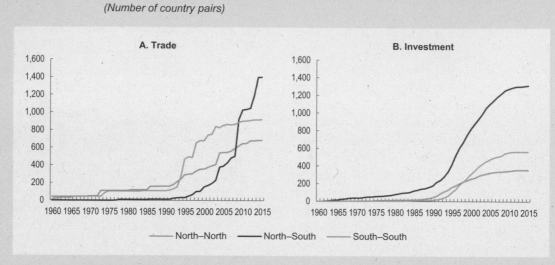

Source: UNCTAD secretariat calculations, based on de Sousa, 2012, and UNCTAD International Investment Agreements Navigator.
Note: Investment category does not include trade treaties with investment provisions (TIPs).

Between 1990 and 2015, the number of trade agreements increased from 50 to 279, with many of them plurilateral and therefore involving a larger number of country pairs (figure 2.B2.1.A). Bilateral investment treaties (BITs) grew almost tenfold from 238 to 2,239 over the same period (figure 2.B2.1.B). These legal changes were designed to enhance international economic integration, boosting trade and cross-border investment. However, they also greatly eased the possibilities for tangible asset acquisition, intangible asset shifting and financial speculation. As a result, the main actors and beneficiaries of this metamorphosis of "trade" were not necessarily the populations in the concerned countries, but rather the largest corporate players that were involved in lobbying for and shaping the rules of international trade and finance.

Trade agreements prior to 1990 were mostly between neighbouring countries sharing comparable levels of economic development and labour protection, with the objective of promoting regional integration through trade (figure 2.B2.1.A). However, post-1990 agreements were more about increasing economic integration across regions and between developed and developing countries, promoting both more open trade (including processing trade) and liberalized capital flows. At the same time, the "depth" of such agreements kept increasing, bringing under their discipline many policy areas that had thus far been excluded from trade negotiations. Historically, trade agreements focused on issues pertaining mostly to tariffs and quotas. After 1995, so-called "WTO-plus" provisions included in most trade agreements (figure 2.B2.2.A) also covered customs regulations, export taxes, anti-dumping measures, countervailing duty measures, technical barriers to trade, and sanitary and phytosanitary standards. Other agreements further committed signatories to enforce provisions liberalizing financial services or public procurement, with far-reaching implications for public policy, employment and income distribution. As to "WTO-extra" provisions (figure 2.B2.2.B), which are not discussed under the WTO umbrella, they include a wide-ranging and expanding set of policy areas, which often further reduced developing countries' policy space.

So-called "core" provisions are defined as the set of WTO-plus provisions and four WTO-extra provisions (competition policy, movement of capital, investment and investor rights protection, and IPR protection), because they are economically more meaningful, at least from the perspective of non-financial and financial TNCs alike. Interestingly, trade agreements between developed and developing countries cover on average almost as many policy areas (20) as those among developed countries (22) and thus have equivalent "depth". This reflects the ability of developed country TNCs to insert provisions dear to their interests in agreements negotiated by their governments. By contrast, South–South trade agreements (13) are considered more "shallow".

Almost 90 per cent of trade agreements include at least one of the core WTO-extra provisions and one third include all of them (Hofmann et al., 2017). By contrast, policy areas of great importance for social actors with much lesser voice in opaque closed-door trade negotiations, such as the protection of labour rights, consumers and the environment or provisions preventing corporate tax avoidance, are barely included or remain legally unenforceable. If negotiators genuinely want "trade" and related agreements to become vehicles for more inclusive and sustainable development, they must begin by correcting this glaring asymmetry (Namur Declaration, 2016; Kohler and Storm, 2016; Piketty, 2016).

It has been noted that the expansion of trade agreements and their increasing depth after 1990 are a testimony to greater leverage of large exporters in trade negotiations, which exceeds the leverage of importers (Rodrik,

FIGURE 2.B2.2   WTO-plus and WTO-extra policy areas included in trade agreements
(Number of treaties)

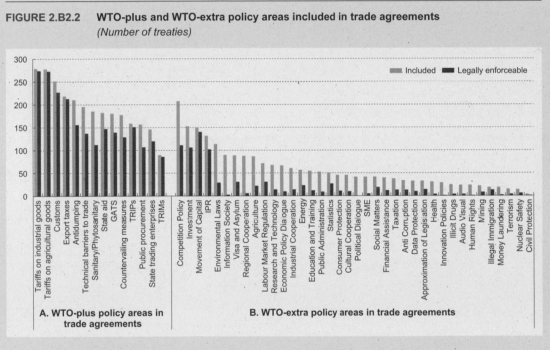

Source: UNCTAD secretariat calculations, based on Hofmann et al., 2017.

2018). Hence, it is likely that such agreements are increasingly becoming a mechanism for promoting rent-seeking by large exporting firms, especially through provisions pertaining to IPR, cross-border capital flows, investor–state dispute settlement procedures and the harmonization of regulatory standards, etc., which have little to do with "trade" in the strict sense.

As the meaning of "trade" is increasingly adrift, what economists commonly label as "trade agreements" should rather be properly designated as "comprehensive economic and trade agreements". Accordingly, their impact on distribution, jobs and welfare should be assessed using more comprehensive models including macrofinancial linkages, rather than narrow trade models, which incorporate many flawed assumptions, such as full employment of production factors of constant distribution, thus ruling out a priori any risks and costs associated with deeper "trade" liberalization (Kohler and Storm, 2016). In addition to ensuring greater voice to civil society and to concerned stakeholders in the process of negotiating these legal agreements, it is important to incorporate into such treaties both greater accountability and flexibility to change clauses in the light of experience.

FIGURE 2.5 Global network of merchandise trade, selected years, 1986–2016

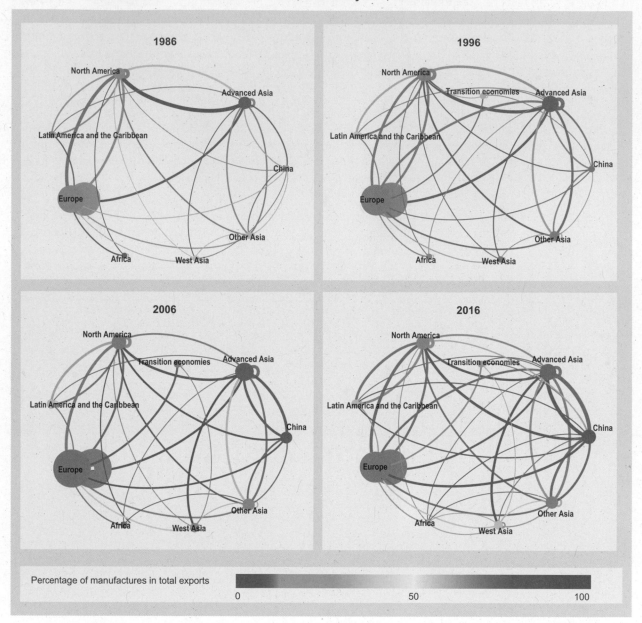

Source: UNCTAD secretariat calculations, based on the United Nations Comtrade database.
Note: The node size and edge width depict export flows as a share of world gross product. The node/edge colour reflects the commodity versus manufacture intensity. The direction of edges is clockwise. When the exports of a given node are less than 5 per cent of its total exports, the edges are not reported. "Advanced Asia" refers to Australia, Japan, New Zealand, the Republic of Korea, Singapore, Hong Kong (China) and Taiwan Province of China.

advanced economies in Asia was already evident, as was the shift in this region away from commodity-based exports. Ten years later, the significant change was the increased significance of China, even as intra-European trade strengthened further. Around this time, there had been a gradual shift within Asia, as China overtook Japan as the largest exporter from the region in 2004, and then became the world's largest exporter in 2007.[5] Overall, this strengthened the East Asian hub in the global trade network. Finally,

by 2016, China registered an even greater share in world exports, together with other advanced Asian economies.

Beyond the rise of South–South flows depicted by the increased links between developing regions over the decades, what figure 2.5 shows is the restructuring of the Asian pole in global trade, most of all the growth acceleration and structural transformation in China. This then spilled over to the rest of the developing world, mainly in the form of boosted demand for raw materials. Consequently, apart from some successful cases in Asia, there has been very little evidence of broad-based trade-induced structural change in other parts of the developing world regions. Hyperspecialization has in fact accompanied the acceleration of trade from the 1990s, including with the rise of South–South trade (Hanson, 2012; Escaith and Gaudin, 2014). This, in part, reflects the reversion in many developing countries to primary export dependence against the backdrop of rising commodity prices from the start of the millennium but it is also

a reflection of asymmetric power relations between lead firms and suppliers in manufacturing value chains and weak bargaining positions for developing countries. The experiences of Mexico and Central American countries as assembly manufacturers, for example, have been linked to the creation of enclave economies, with few domestic linkages and limited, if any, upgrading (Gallagher and Zarsky, 2007; Paus, 2014). The same can be said about the electronics and automotive industries in Eastern and Central Europe (Plank and Staritz, 2013; Pavlínek, 2016; Pavlínek and Ženka, 2016).

C. Trade-charged structural change: Diverging paths among developing regions

The "rise of the South" in international trade has been a much-cited feature of hyperglobalization, disrupting the dominant pattern of North–North trade in the previous era of managed globalization, and establishing a landscape in which North–South and South–South trade have assumed greater weight. BRICS[6] have become symbolic of this changing landscape but GVCs are seen as its great disruptors.

On closer examination, the gap between BRICS and RIBS[7] is a significant one (figure 2.6) and the rise of the South refers primarily to the singular experience of some Asian countries in trading manufactured products. As discussed in *TDR 2016*, these economies (beginning with the first-tier NIEs followed, albeit more restrained, by a second tier in South-East Asia, and then more dramatically by China) have managed to narrow the income gaps with richer countries based on the establishment of leading industrial sectors, along with related technological and social capabilities that have promoted upgrading, and, through a series of linkages, diversification into new sectors. On this basis, these tiger economies (albeit with variation across them) were able to combine a strong rise in the share of manufacturing output and employment with strong labour productivity growth. In most cases, a rapid pace of investment helped to tap both learning and scale economies, sustaining rapid productivity growth. Yet, a rise in exports – due to a robust investment–export nexus – was also key to this pattern of expansion. In the absence of such linkages in other developing regions, the export of manufactures has been a poorer predictor of productivity growth during this period.

As a result, in 2016, Asia alone accounted for about 88 per cent of developing country gross exports of manufactures to the world, and for 93 per cent of South–South trade in manufactures, while East Asia alone accounted for 72 per cent of both.[8] To a lesser extent, the increase of the South's share in global exports in this century was also the result of increased export revenues of commodity exporters during the 2000s supercycle.

Trade in Value-Added (TiVA) data show the evolution of exports in both developed and developing countries (figure 2.7). In value added terms, developing

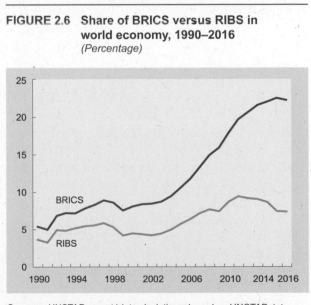

FIGURE 2.6 Share of BRICS versus RIBS in world economy, 1990–2016
(Percentage)

Source: UNCTAD secretariat calculations, based on UNCTADstat.
Note: Underlying data corresponds to the sum of GDP in current dollars.

FIGURE 2.7   World trade in value added by sectors, selected country groups, 1995–2011

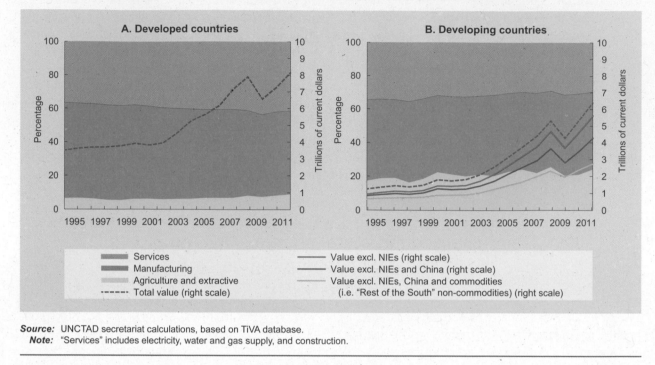

Source: UNCTAD secretariat calculations, based on TiVA database.
 Note: "Services" includes electricity, water and gas supply, and construction.

countries' exports in 2011 were still smaller than those from developed countries: $6.4 trillion versus $8.2 trillion. Figure 2.7.B also indicates the rapid development of China and first-tier NIEs in manufactured products, along with the increasing export share of the extractive industries in the rest of the developing world. The increase in exports from the remaining sectors of the rest of developing countries was far less significant: amounting to only $2.7 trillion in 2011, compared to $6.4 trillion worth of exports from China and the first-tier NIEs (all three sectors) along with other developing countries' exports of extractive industries.

Similar conclusions arise by looking at the country level. Table 2.1 shows how China has been more of an outlier, one of very few countries that have managed to increase their shares of manufacturing domestic value added in gross exports (an 11.9 percentage point increase between 1995 and 2014). The trajectory of China has benefited from a well-calibrated industrial policy to help exploit growing demand from developed countries (e.g. Poon, 2014). This experience was not common: out of 27 developing entities recorded in TiVA, only 6 others experienced increases, albeit of much smaller magnitudes: the Philippines, 7.4 percentage points (from a very low starting point); Indonesia, 4.3; Argentina, 2.3; Viet Nam, 2.1; Turkey, 1.8; and Mexico, 0.4.

Instead, for many developing countries, trade under hyperglobalization strengthened the economic weight of extractive industries, whose share in aggregate domestic value added exported by developing countries (not their gross exports as shown in table 2.1) rose from 1995 by almost nine percentage points to reach 21.5 per cent in 2011. Eighteen out of 27 developing and emerging market economies experienced increases in the shares of extractive industries in export value added. Some like the Russian Federation, Brazil, Colombia, Peru and Brunei Darussalam (along with the "rest of the world", which covers many African and smaller developing countries), showed increases of more than 10 percentage points.[9] This may partly reflect price effects during the commodity boom, but the persistence of such effects over many years has strengthened incentives for investment in extractive industries, private and public, resulting in higher volumes. In the long run, this is likely to further entrench dependence on extractive industries, with adverse implications for structural change.

Table 2.1 shows that production fragmentation along GVCs also resulted in a declining share of domestic value added in gross exports, also known as vertical specialization (Hummels et al., 2001), in both developed and developing countries.[10] This share dropped in developed countries by 7 percentage

TABLE 2.1 Value added shares in gross exports of developing economies, level and changes, 1995–2014

| | Level of domestic value added in gross exports in 2014 (Percentage) | Changes in value added shares in gross exports since 1995 (Percentage points) | | | |
| | | FOREIGN | DOMESTIC | | |
			Agriculture and extractives	Manufacturing	Services[a]
Argentina	87.5	6.8	1.0	2.3	-10.1
Brazil	87.6	4.7	17.6	-16.5	-5.8
Brunei Darussalam[b]	95.7	-3.0	15.5	-2.6	-9.8
Cambodia	61.6	25.6	-32.4	-3.2	10.0
Chile	81.1	4.8	1.5	-2.7	-3.6
China	70.7	-1.7	-2.8	11.9	-7.4
Colombia	91.1	0.5	9.0	-1.2	-8.3
Costa Rica	73.5	4.4	-9.7	-2.3	7.6
India	79.0	11.6	-3.5	-12.9	4.8
Indonesia	88.0	0.1	3.7	4.3	-8.1
Malaysia	60.9	8.7	1.4	-5.8	-4.3
Mexico	66.5	6.1	0.0	0.4	-6.5
Morocco	75.0	6.1	-7.6	-6.5	8.0
Peru	87.4	2.7	22.5	-15.5	-9.7
Philippines (the)	76.3	-6.1	1.4	7.4	-2.7
Republic of Korea	62.2	15.5	-0.6	-6.1	-8.8
Russian Federation (the)	86.3	0.8	8.7	-6.4	-3.1
Saudi Arabia	96.4	-0.6	5.3	-0.3	-4.4
Singapore	59.5	-1.6	-0.1	-4.2	5.9
South Africa	79.3	7.5	8.3	-12.3	-3.5
Thailand	62.7	13.1	1.1	-5.1	-9.1
Tunisia	65.9	9.3	2.7	-1.5	-10.5
Turkey	78.2	12.9	-0.3	1.8	-14.4
Viet Nam	63.7	14.6	-5.8	2.1	-10.9
Hong-Kong, China	79.6	-1.1	-0.3	-14.3	15.7
Taiwan Province of China	56.9	12.5	-0.2	-9.6	-2.7
Rest of the World[b]	89.5	-2.8	12.1	-4.9	-4.5
Developing economies[b]	75.3	4.2	4.3	-3.5	-5.1
Developed economies[b]	75.8	7.2	1.7	-10.1	1.1

Source: UNCTAD secretariat calculations, based on TiVA database.
Note: All other developing countries in the database are listed, including the category "Rest of the world", which covers many medium and small developing countries. TiVA's 37 developed countries are not reported here.
a "Services" also includes electricity, water and gas supply, and construction.
b Data only available until 2011.

points to 75.8 per cent, while that in developing countries fell by 4 percentage points to 75.3 per cent. But this more muted decline in developing countries was due to only two factors: for China, spectacular manufacturing expansion that entailed an increase in domestic value added in gross exports, and the growing weight of extractive industries in the trade balance of other developing countries. Excluding both China and extractive industries, the share of domestic value added in other developing countries' exports declined by 11 percentage points, an even sharper decline than in developed countries. This highlights some of the challenges that countries face when their firms link to GVCs (section D).

Figure 2.8 disaggregates the total exports of developing countries by the technological intensity of products, using the TDR 2002 classification of labour skill levels and technology intensity. While some caution is warranted with this approach,[11] it also points to significant differences across countries in both structure and dynamics. On the one hand, the first-tier NIEs and China display clear trends towards technological upgrading, even though questions remain about the extent to which this has benefited workers employed at the assembly stage in manufacturing GVCs (see section D.1). By contrast, Africa and West Asia showed limited progress as their exports remain extremely concentrated in commodities, with hardly

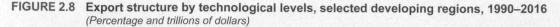

FIGURE 2.8   **Export structure by technological levels, selected developing regions, 1990–2016**
            (Percentage and trillions of dollars)

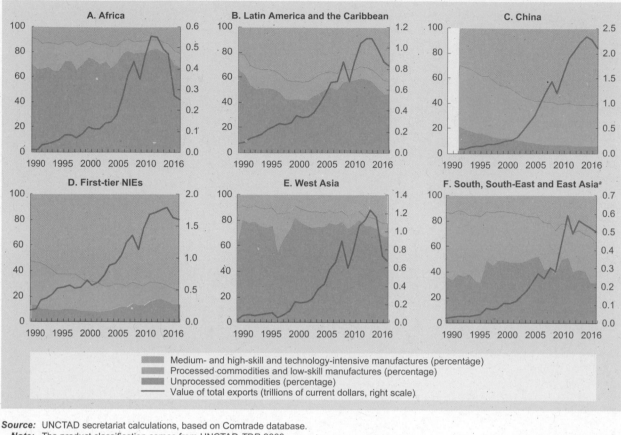

Source: UNCTAD secretariat calculations, based on Comtrade database.
  Note: The product classification comes from UNCTAD *TDR 2002*.
     a South, South-East and East Asia does not comprise China and NIEs (both tiers).

any increase in shares of technology-intensive manufactures, regardless of their labour skill levels. Latin America and the rest of South, South-East and East (SSEE) Asia fell between these two extremes. In Latin America, the 1990s were a period of some structural change with technological upgrading, but this pattern partly reversed during the commodity supercycle. As the commodity price boom receded, Latin America's trade structure returned to its position of the late 1990s. Although exports in current dollars more than doubled over this period, the data suggest that overall, technological upgrading did not really take place.

In the rest of SSEE Asia, tendencies towards relative technological upgrading appeared in export data only in the 2000s, with a shift towards high-skill labour and technology-intensive goods. However, there is still a long way to go to reach even the current structure of China and the first-tier NIEs. Indeed, the share of commodities and labour-intensive and resource-intensive manufactures, though declining, remained relatively high, at almost 30 per cent each.

Analysing exports by destinations sheds additional light on the underlying drivers. Figure 2.9.A–C show how export structures have changed in the developing regions of Africa, Latin America and SSEE Asia (except China and the NIEs), for the following destinations: (i) developed countries, (ii) intraregional, (iii) China, and (iv) developing countries other then China and the two tiers of Asian NIEs.

Figure 2.9.A illustrates that Africa's exports were highly concentrated in commodities. This was most evident for exports to China, and for exports to developed countries, and to a slightly lesser extent for other non-African trade partners. By contrast, intraregional trade was more in line with technological upgrading, with slightly larger shares of technology-intensive manufactures.

In Latin America, the export structure depended even more on its trade partners. In exports to developed economies, there was an increase in the share of technology- and medium-skill-intensive manufactures.

**FIGURE 2.9 Export structure by technological levels and selected partners,
selected developing regions, 1990–2016**
(Percentage and trillions of dollars)

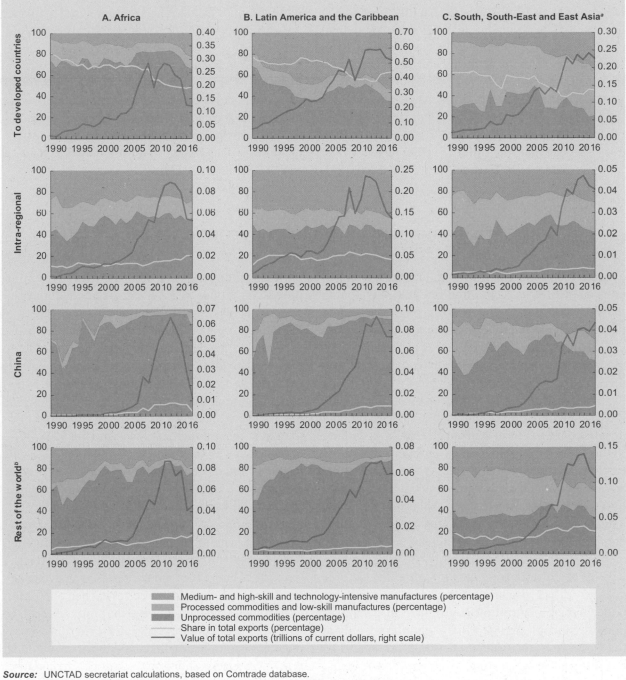

Source: UNCTAD secretariat calculations, based on Comtrade database.
 a   South, South-East and East Asia does not comprise China and NIEs (both tiers).
 b   Rest of the world excludes NIEs (both tiers).

However, this destination became relatively less important for Latin American exports. Meanwhile, intraregional trade consisted of more diversified goods, with technology-intensive manufactures accounting for about one half. Exports to China and other developing countries and transition economies remained highly concentrated in commodities, and

this pattern strengthened from the mid-2000s, to the extent that in 2016, 90 per cent of Latin America's exports to China consisted of commodities.

In SSEE Asian economies excluding China and the NIEs, overall exports experienced a process of upgrading. Exports to all destinations showed a relative decrease of commodities as well as of labour- and resource-intensive manufactures over the last decade. This pattern was less pronounced for the exports to China due to an increased share of labour- and resource-intensive manufactures, which suggest that the flying geese development paradigm (*TDR 1997*) remains at an early stage. Exports to all remaining developing countries and transition economies had the greatest share of technology-intensive goods, with high-skill labour-intensive manufactures representing the largest share.

This suggests that the rapid development of China (and more generally East and South-East Asia) has not triggered significant positive structural changes in the export structures of other developing regions; rather, it has intensified their role as providers of commodities. This need not be a negative outcome, if the revenues from such exports are used to finance domestic economic diversification and technological upgrading. But such a push typically requires systematic industrial policies in a context of rising domestic demand. In practice, such examples are not that common. By contrast, intraregional trade seems to have the greatest potential in terms of providing support to move up the ladder, confirming the validity of previous UNCTAD calls for strengthening regional trade (UNCTAD, 2013).

D. Trade and inequality under hyperglobalization

Trade under hyperglobalization, and the associated expansion of GVCs, is often pitched as widening the opportunities for inclusive growth and shared prosperity. The underlying assumption is that because GVCs allow developing countries to focus on individual links in the chain, their firms can integrate with the world economy "on a shoestring" without facing the large risks (and costs) incurred by investing in all the tasks required for producing the finished product or services (e.g. World Bank et al., 2017). According to this view, developing countries can thereby more easily reap the benefits of their major comparative advantage: abundant cheap labour. Following this logic, such integration in the global economy should lead to a reduction of inequality in the South as demand for unskilled labour increases.

Reality is, unfortunately, less obliging. Indeed, it is now increasingly acknowledged that trade patterns under hyperglobalization contributed to polarizing domestic income and wealth distribution not only in the North (e.g. Harrison et al., 2011; Temin, 2017), but also in the South (e.g. Goldberg and Pavcnik, 2007; Pavcnik, 2017), thus exacerbating domestic economic inequalities. Recently-released data that enable the disaggregation of the value added along GVCs support this view. They suggest that these outcomes are partly the result of the proliferation of GVCs and partly due to the behaviour of lead firms, mostly large TNCs that are today the most significant players in international trade.

This section examines this question. Section D.1 reports new evidence that GVCs and the spread of low-productivity assembly lines in export processing zones (EPZs) across the South have not just contributed to suppressing the wages of manufacturing workers in the North, but have also exacerbated the income gap between manufacturing workers and owners of capital in developing countries. Section D.2 analyses the rise of export market concentration under hyperglobalization, and the associated increase in the ability of large firms to extract rents. Much as was argued in *TDR 2017*, the evidence is that increased rents have largely resulted from newer and more intangible barriers to competition, reflected in heightened protection for IPR and abilities to exploit national rules and regulations for profit-shifting and tax-avoidance purposes. The consequent increase in returns from monopolies generated by IPR as well as a reduction in the relative tax costs of larger companies creates an uneven playing field. The empirical exercises carried out for this *Report* suggest that the surge in the profitability of top TNCs – a proxy for the very large firms dominating international trade and finance – together with their growing concentration, has acted as a major force pushing down the global labour income share, thus exacerbating personal income inequality.

Overall, these negative effects of international trade on inequality echo the concerns expressed by Raul Prebisch on the prevalence of oligopolistic enterprises in exports of manufactures and how export market structures can affect income distribution. However, as Milberg and Winkler (2013: 280–281) note, today this is less about the nature of the product exported and more about the governance of GVC where, "[m]any lead firms in global production networks maintain markups by operating in factor or input markets that are increasingly oligopolistic. Buying practices of lead firms can lead to shaving markups and cost cutting by suppliers that leave them unable to innovate and resistant to improvements in wages or labour standards". These processes also have wider macroeconomic repercussions, discussed in section E.

1. GVCs, jobs offshoring, processing trade and income polarization in manufacturing

Recently developed decomposition techniques shed new light on trends in income distribution following the global fragmentation of production. The World Input–Output Database (WIOD)[12] provides data suggesting that the reshaping of global manufacturing production and trade increased inequality in both developed and developing countries. Changes in factor income shares in global manufacturing GVCs between 1995 and 2008 mostly benefited the owners of capital, in the North as well as in the South. Globally, their share in income along all manufacturing GVCs increased by 6.5 percentage points to reach 47.4 per cent in 2008. High-skilled workers also benefited, although to a more limited extent. The share of low-skilled workers, who represent the demographic majority in the South, declined sharply by 6.3 per cent (Timmer et al., 2014). This challenges a key prediction of the Heckscher-Ohlin model that underpins the narrative of GVCs as vehicles for reducing inequality (e.g. Lopez Gonzalez et al., 2015).[13]

Examining how value added is distributed across capital and labour – split in two business functions (i.e. headquarter and fabrication)[14] performed along the "smile curve" – confirms this analysis (de Vries et al., 2018). At the global level, the share of capital income in manufacturing GVCs increased by 3 percentage points between 2000 and 2014 (table 2.2).

TABLE 2.2   Shares in exported value added in manufacturing GVCs, 2000–2014

Global level

	2000	2014	Difference
Capital	44.8	47.8	3.0
Labour	55.2	52.2	-3.0
Headquarter functions	31.7	30.4	-1.3
Fabrication	23.5	21.8	-1.7

Country groups

	High income			China			Other countries		
	2000	2014	Difference	2000	2014	Difference	2000	2014	Difference
Capital	40.3	42.3	2.0	57.0	49.6	-7.5	59.2	59.4	0.2
Labour	59.7	57.7	-2.0	43.0	50.4	7.5	40.8	40.6	-0.2
Headquarter functions	35.2	37.0	1.7	13.6	19.7	6.0	22.5	23.7	1.1
Fabrication	24.5	20.8	-3.7	29.3	30.8	1.4	18.3	16.9	-1.3

Selected countries

	Brazil			Indonesia			India		
	2000	2014	Difference	2000	2014	Difference	2000	2014	Difference
Capital	49.1	43.2	-5.9	59.9	59.0	-0.9	56.6	60.6	4.0
Labour	50.9	56.8	5.9	40.1	41.0	0.9	43.4	39.4	-4.0
Headquarter functions	22.3	30.3	8.0	25.6	27.6	2.0	29.7	28.9	-0.8
Fabrication	28.6	26.5	-2.1	14.5	13.3	-1.1	13.7	10.5	-3.2

	Mexico			Russian Federation			Turkey		
	2000	2014	Difference	2000	2014	Difference	2000	2014	Difference
Capital	68.3	76.7	8.4	51.3	47.4	-3.9	59.3	62.5	3.2
Labour	31.7	23.3	-8.4	48.7	52.6	3.9	40.7	37.5	-3.2
Headquarter functions	13.0	10.5	-2.4	22.4	30.5	8.1	17.0	15.3	-1.7
Fabrication	18.8	12.8	-6.0	26.3	22.1	-4.2	23.7	22.2	-1.5

Source: UNCTAD secretariat calculations, based on WIOD (2016).
Note: WIOD (2016 release) includes 43 countries plus one category for the "rest of the world", which is only included in the global aggregate figures. "High income" covers 34 countries, including the high-income developing economies of the Republic of Korea and Taiwan Province of China. "Other countries" includes two developed countries (Bulgaria and Romania) and six developing countries and transition economies (Brazil, India, Indonesia, Mexico, the Russian Federation and Turkey). All manufacturing sectors are included.

Meanwhile, the income share accruing to workers at the fabrication stage, who are good proxies for low- and medium-skilled labour, declined by 3.7 percentage points in high-income countries and 1.3 percentage points in most of G20 emerging economies but China (together with Bulgaria and Romania) which are regrouped under "other countries". Additional findings provided by Chen et al. (2017) and WIPO (2017) indicate that rising capital income was driven by growing returns to intangible assets, whose share in value added of global manufacturing trade is estimated to have risen from 27.8 per cent to 31.9 per cent between 2000 and 2007, representing almost twice the share of income accruing to tangible capital.

The only place where the share of labour income in fabrication increased is China, the "world factory", though only by 1.4 percentage points. By contrast, the income share of more skilled Chinese workers employed in pre- and post-fabrication stages, labelled under "headquarter functions", increased by 6.0 percentage points. Together with evidence of rising personal inequality in China (e.g. Galbraith, 2012), these findings support the hypothesis that the relative increase in the income share of less-skilled workers was driven by growing employment in manufacturing assembly lines (the quantity effect) rather than by an increase in the relative wage income of those workers compared to high-skilled workers and capitalists (the price effect).

In other developing countries, negative relative price effects combined with negligible or negative quantity effects depressed the income shares of low- and medium-skilled workers employed at the fabrication stage. Consequently, the share in value added accruing to fabrication declined in developing countries between 2000 and 2014, by 2.1 percentage points in Brazil, 1.1 in Indonesia, 3.2 in India, 6.0 in Mexico, 4.2 in the Russian Federation and 1.5 in Turkey (table 2.2). Though the labour income share in export manufacturing increased in Brazil, Indonesia and the Russian Federation, it benefited only a minority of more skilled workers performing headquarter functions. In India, Mexico and Turkey, the share of capital increased unambiguously to the detriment of all workers, by 4.0, 8.4 and 3.2 percentage points, respectively.

This increasing inequality reflected various forces. One important factor has been the increased bargaining power of corporations, in part due to growing market concentration under hyperglobalization, and the gradual dilution of their social and political accountability to national constituencies and labour in both developed and developing countries (Quentin and Campling, 2018; Bivens et al., 2018). The ability of TNCs to offshore plants and related low- and medium-skilled jobs (or simply to threaten to do so) and to shift their intangible assets almost at will decisively weakened the bargaining power of organized labour and public authorities. This further biased the distribution of productivity gains in favour of private capital owners. This polarizing dynamic unfolded most visibly in manufacturing GVCs, but it also affected jobs and working conditions in many service activities segmented into internationally traded tasks.[15] Another factor was the greater weight of finance in TNCs operations, which went hand in hand with greater emphasis on corporate strategies for maximizing shareholder value, repaying loans or embarking on share buy-back programmes (*TDR 2017*).

In developing countries, the negative impact of international trade on inequality was partly the result of the proliferation of special processing trade regimes and EPZs.[16] Many countries created regimes favouring exporters, with the objective of attracting or preserving investment, production and jobs on their shores.[17] The associated risk, however, is that such regimes merely subsidize labour-intensive assembly work or, more precisely, subsidize the organization of low-cost and low-productivity assembly work by large exporters or foreign TNCs in control of GVCs. Evidence accumulating in recent years, particularly from experiences in China, points to the limited benefits of such policies for the broader economy and their negative effects on income distribution. Interestingly, the export processing firms in China that expanded after 2001 were mostly foreign-owned,[18] and typically characterized by lower productivity, lower profitability, lower wages, lower capital and skills intensity and lower research and development expenditure, compared to non-processing exporters and non-exporters (Lu et al., 2010; Lu, 2010; Dai et al., 2016).[19] This meant that, while China could count on foreign TNCs to integrate its economy into GVCs, it could not rely on them to significantly upgrade the skills and the pay of its workforce or bolster its productive capacities.

The mixed outcomes of policies to promote processing trade often reflect the strategies of TNCs to capture value in GVCs that are designed on their own terms, with high-value added inputs and protected intellectual property content sold at high prices to processing exporters, with the actual production (fabrication) in developing countries accounting for only a tiny fraction of the value of exported final goods (e.g. Dedrick et al., 2010; Ali-Yrkkö et al., 2011; WIPO, 2017). This is consistent with evidence of the lower productivity of processing exporters in China as well as the decline in value added accruing to low- and medium-skilled workers at the fabrication stage in manufacturing GVCs, as shown in table 2.2.[20]

The ongoing success of China at bolstering its productive capacities – thus slowly breaking out of the trap of processing trade and moving up the value ladder – has crucially relied on its capacity to claim and use policy space to actively leverage trade through targeted industrial and other policies aiming at raising domestic value added in manufacturing exports (Poon, 2014, 2018). It has also relied on the ability of the Chinese authorities to develop independent financing mechanisms and acquire control over foreign assets, which are being perceived by developed countries as a threat to their own business interests (e.g. USTR, 2018).

The many specificities of China (institutional setting, size, diaspora, etc.) suggest that there is limited scope for imitating its development strategy by other differently placed developing countries. This raises questions about the benefits for workers in other Southern economies that have made strong bets on the spillovers expected from processing trade, such as Malaysia and Viet Nam in South-East Asia, but also Mexico and Kenya in other developing regions, where processing trade can represent up to more than 80 per cent of gross exports. Unless these countries manage to capture part of the surplus created by these GVCs and reinvest it in productive capacities and infrastructure, immediate gains in output and employment are unlikely to translate into a dynamic move up the development ladder (Meagher et al., 2016).

2. Concentration in export markets, intangible barriers to competition and corporate rents: A look at the top 2,000 TNCs

To an even larger extent than domestic markets, global exports today are dominated by very large companies, most of them TNCs.[21] Large firms have become the most relevant actors in international

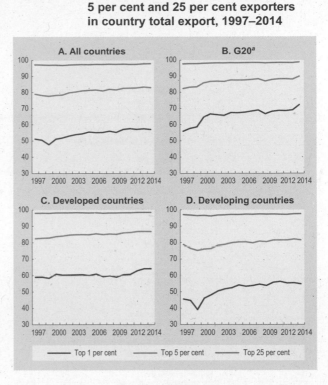

FIGURE 2.10 Average shares of top 1 per cent, 5 per cent and 25 per cent exporters in country total export, 1997–2014

A. All countries

B. G20[a]

C. Developed countries

D. Developing countries

Top 1 per cent — Top 5 per cent — Top 25 per cent

Source: UNCTAD secretariat calculations, based on the Exporter Dynamics Database described in Fernandes et al., 2016.
a The Exporter Dynamics Database contains only Brazil, Germany, Mexico, Turkey and South Africa of the G20 countries.

trade, although their dominance is hard to quantify precisely, because of data limitations and obstacles to combining country-level trade data with transnational firm-level data (see box 2.1).

Nevertheless, recent evidence from aggregated firm-level data on goods exports (excluding the oil sector, as well as services) shows that, within the very restricted circle of exporting firms, the top 1 per cent accounted for 57 per cent of country exports on average in 2014 (figure 2.10.A). Moreover, while the share of the top 5 per cent exceeded 80 per cent of country export revenues on average, the top 25 per cent accounted for virtually all country exports. The distribution of exports is thus highly skewed in favour of the largest firms, especially in G20 emerging economies and in developed countries. It is evident to a lesser extent in developing economies, though even in this group such concentration has been rising rapidly (figure 2.10.B, C and D).

The concentration is even more extreme at the top of the distribution. Freund and Pierola (2015) found that the 5 largest exporting firms account, on

FIGURE 2.11 Export market entrant survival rate in 2010
(Percentage)

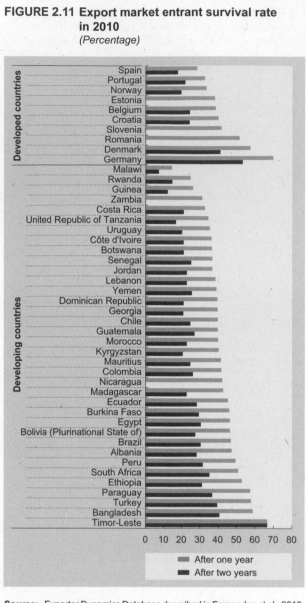

Source: Exporter Dynamics Database described in Fernandes et al., 2016.
Note: Data after two years are missing for Estonia, Nicaragua, Slovenia, Romania and Zambia.

average, for 30 per cent of a country's total exports. In 2012, the 10 largest exporting firms in each country accounted, on average, for 42 per cent of a country's total exports.[22] In the few G20 economies represented in the sample, the 10 largest firms (out of tens or hundreds of thousands of exporting firms)[23] provided 28 per cent of total exports (excluding oil) in Brazil, 23 per cent in Germany, 23 per cent in Mexico, 15 per cent in Turkey and 34 per cent in South Africa.

Not surprisingly, new entrants and relatively smaller exporters tend to have low survival rates: on average, 73 per cent of firms stopped exporting only two years after having started, with exporting firms in

developing countries faring slightly worse than those in developed countries (figure 2.11).[24] If all firms (large and small) were competing on a level playing field, the low survival rate among new exporting firms could be interpreted as a sign of strong competition, likely to be associated with low firm profitability and high consumer surplus. But the significantly higher profitability of the largest firms that dominate export markets casts doubt on such an interpretation. This is more likely to be a fallout of the "winner takes most" syndrome that partly results from the market structures and institutional and regulatory conditions that have nurtured new monopolistic practices and enabled TNCs to capture a growing share of the economic surplus (*TDR 2017*: chap. VI).[25] This obviously tends to further polarize income distribution.

The dominance of a small number of TNCs over trade was acknowledged long ago (e.g. Kindleberger, 1969, 1970), but took on a new significance as the legal framework and meaning of "trade" deepened after the 1990s (box 2.2). While mainstream trade theory did seek to integrate the presence of TNCs (e.g. Markusen, 1984; Markusen and Venables, 1998), their dominance in international trade was only incorporated into the set of core trade modelling assumptions much later, and that too under the neutral label of "heterogeneous" firms (Melitz, 2003). Similarly, the existence of monopolistic rents in international trade have been taken note of in mainstream theory, but the additional step of acknowledging the wider implications was rarely taken. As discussed in section E, these implications include both the polarizing effects of trade on income distribution resulting from concentration and monopolistic behaviour of large firms, as well as plausible negative macrofinancial externalities that harm the potential for inclusive development. This is because corporate rents (and thus higher profits) also arise out of strategies aimed at instrumentalizing other actors, by lobbying policymakers, buying out competitors, sharing markets, collusion, blocking new entrants, etc.[26]

Paradoxically, even as tangible barriers to trade imposed by governments, such as tariffs and quotas, have been declining over the last 30 years or so, intangible barriers to competition rooted in "free trade" treaties and erected by large firms themselves have surged, as they exploit the increased legal protection of intellectual property and the broadening scope for intangible intra-firm trade. According to some estimates, intangible assets may represent up to two thirds of the value of large firms (Menell and

FIGURE 2.12 Payments and receipts related to the use of foreign IPR, selected country groups, 1995–2015

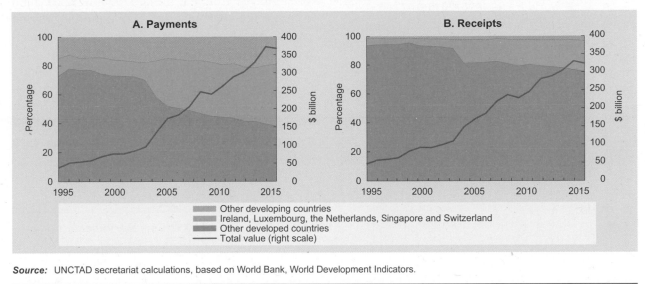

Other developing countries
Ireland, Luxembourg, the Netherlands, Singapore and Switzerland
Other developed countries
Total value (right scale)

Source: UNCTAD secretariat calculations, based on World Bank, World Development Indicators.

Scotchmer, 2007). This is obviously so for firms that are often positively coined as "knowledge-intensive", such as the digital firms considered in chapter III. Yet, knowledge can be valuable in diverse settings and for a variety of reasons: for its scarcity (e.g. a patent protecting a technological innovation) or precisely because it is widely shared and engrained in the minds of consumers (e.g. brand recognition). As the World Trade Organization (WTO, 2012) notes, "many products that used to be traded as low-technology goods or commodities now contain a higher proportion of invention and design in their value", that is, protected intellectual property content. In short, knowledge-intensive intangible assets are valuable because they ensure a certain degree of market power, not because they represent an inherent and benevolent force for innovation and technological progress.

Returns to knowledge-intensive intangible assets proxied by charges for the use of foreign IPR rose almost unabated throughout the GFC and its aftermath, even as returns to tangible assets declined. At the global level, charges (i.e. payments) for the use of foreign IPR rose from less than $50 billion in 1995 to $367 billion in 2015 (figure 2.12.A).[27] To the extent that charges for the use of foreign IPR reflect transactions taking place between unaffiliated firms, they genuinely indicate their market or "arm's length" value and the cost charged to final consumers. Yet, a growing share of these charges represent payments and receipts between affiliates of the same group, often merely intended to shift profit to low-tax jurisdictions.[28] Recent leaks from fiscal authorities,

banks, audit and consulting or legal firms' records, revealing corporate tax-avoidance scandals involving large TNCs, have made clear why major offshore financial centres (such as Ireland, Luxembourg, the Netherlands, Singapore or Switzerland) that account for a tiny fraction of global production, have become major players in terms of the use of foreign IPR (figure 2.12.A).

IPR charges are merely one of the many forms of more widespread profit shifting within companies or groups, that weigh negatively on public finances and collective wage bargaining in many countries.[29] Indeed, the largest recipient country (the United States) is simultaneously the victim of the most massive IPR-related corporate tax avoidance by TNCs "trading" intangibles.[30] Far from promoting innovation or competition, such schemes illustrate how corporate cost-saving strategies (especially in relation to wages and taxes) rely on international arbitrage and free-riding; and while they may be successful for creating monopolistic rents and crushing competition effectively they do so at the cost of public welfare (*TDR 2017*: chap. VI; Diez et al., 2018).

The rise of intangible barriers that further distort competition, increase corporate leverage and foster monopolistic rents has been partly supported by changes to domestic laws in many countries. But international treaties may have been even more significant, such as double non-taxation agreements and new generation trade agreements that include provisions strengthening the protection of IPR,

FIGURE 2.13 Top 2,000 TNCs revenues and world trade, 1995–2015
(Trillions of current dollars)

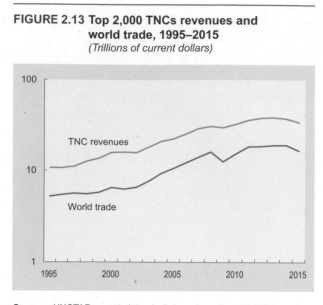

Source: UNCTAD secretariat calculations, based on UNCTADstat and UNCTAD database of consolidated financial statements, based on Thomson Reuters Worldscope.

Note: The logarithmic scale on the vertical axis is used to show the similar trajectories of the two variables.

foreign investment, etc. Moreover, unlike domestic rule-making in a democracy, international treaty negotiations tend to be much more secretive, providing more room for detrimental lobbying by large rent-seeking firms (Rodrik, 2018).

This is probably why very large firms, which account for the bulk of international trade, have experienced rising rents under hyperglobalization, leading to rising profits. This is confirmed by empirical analysis of the largest 2,000 TNCs.[31] While these firms represent a limited subset of the top 1 per cent of exporters discussed above, they cover listed firms involved in the oil and services trade, including financial services.[32] However, it is not possible from this database to distinguish firms' cross-border activities from their domestic activities, so the results described here relate to the aggregate size and activities of these top 2,000 firms.

In this context, it is no surprise that total revenues from top TNCs have been greater than world trade throughout the period 1995 to 2015 (figure 2.13). Yet, to the extent that the revenues of top TNCs have moved very much in tandem with global trade because they are responsible for the bulk of it, some selected indicators can reveal both the extent of concentration and the rents (here proxied by profits) captured by TNCs, including through cross-border trade.

The annual profits[33] of these top 2,000 companies rose from $0.7 trillion in the late 1990s to $2.6 trillion in recent years (table 2.3).[34] While profits grew on average by 8.5 per cent per year, the average annual growth rate of revenue was only 6.8 per cent. This disparity led the profit to revenue ratio to increase from 5.7 per cent in the late 1990s to 7.0 per cent in recent years, a 23 per cent increase. The five-year averages shown in table 2.3 smooth out profit volatility, but between 1996 and 2015 this ratio rose even more dramatically, by 58 per cent.

TABLE 2.3 Top 2,000 TNCs – key indicators, 1996–2015
(Trillions of dollars)

	1996–2000	2001–2005	2006–2010	2011–2015
Net sales or revenues	12.8	18.7	29.7	36.8
Net income or profits	0.7	1.0	2.0	2.6
Ratio of profit to revenue	**5.7%**	**5.4%**	**6.8%**	**7.0%**

Source: UNCTAD database of consolidated financial statements, based on Thomson Reuters Worldscope.

Note: Data relate to annual averages.

There were many sources of this rising profitability. Besides the growing market power noted above, deepening financialization certainly played a central role (see *TDR 2017*: chap. V). TNCs strengthened their ability to operate on a global scale through debt-financed mergers and acquisitions that expanded their control over potential competitors.[35] The greater weight of finance in their operations went hand in hand with greater emphasis on corporate strategies for maximizing shareholder value, including through share buy-back programmes.[36] Furthermore, as documented by Baud and Durand (2012) for the retail sector, a growing number of non-financial TNCs have relied on financial operations to generate profits,[37] and even in the supposedly most innovative and booming sectors, such as digital technologies, tech giants are exploiting financial activities to boost their profit (e.g. Platt et al., 2017).

This increase in profits of large firms has been a major driver of global functional inequality, associated with declines in the global labour income share during the last two decades. Market concentration increases as industries become progressively dominated by

FIGURE 2.14 Top 2,000 TNCs profit and the global labour income share, 1995–2015
(Percentage of world gross product)

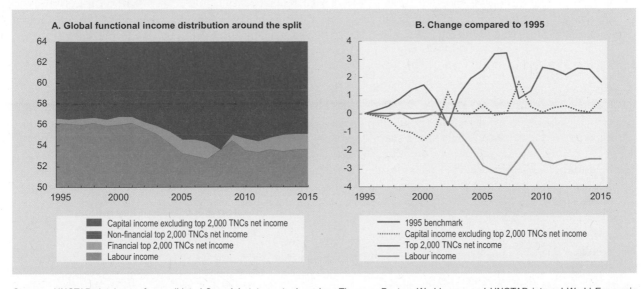

Source: UNCTAD database of consolidated financial statements, based on Thomson Reuters Worldscope and UNCTAD internal World Economic Database.

Note: In panel A, all three areas coloured red or pink add up to the share of capital income. Pink areas represent the net income or profit of top 2,000 TNCs (both financial and non-financial, measured in corporate accounts) as a share of global GDP (measured in national accounts). As an approximation, they were subtracted from the share of capital income (measured in national accounts only) even though methodologies differ in several regards across both sets of accounts.

"superstar" firms with high profits and low shares of labour in firm value added, and as the importance of superstar firms increases, the aggregate labour share tends to fall (Autor et al., 2017a). For example, in the United States and several other developed countries, industry sales became increasingly concentrated in a small number of firms; more intense industry concentration was associated with larger declines in industry labour income shares; and so the fall in the labour share was mostly driven by such declines in large firms (Autor et al., 2017b).

Obviously, a decline in the labour share necessarily involves a rise in the capital income share. But since measured value added accruing to capital is not net of depreciation, a rise in the capital income share can be caused by two different processes: by a rise in the cost of capital, which may be compatible with declining and even zero profit; or by a rise in corporate profit. Barkai (2016) found that the cost of capital in the United States declined even more rapidly than labour income between 1984 and 2014, as the share of corporate profits in value added increased by 12 points.

Kohler and Cripps (2018) showed that globally, the rising share of capital income since 1995 was driven by the accelerated expansion of the profits of top

TNCs. While the share of capital income other than profits accruing to the top TNCs increased slightly under hyperglobalization (red area in figure 2.14.A), the rapid growth of the profits of top TNCs (pink areas) was the major force pushing down the global labour income share (blue area). This dropped from 56.1 per cent in 1995 to 52.8 per cent in 2007, before rising slightly in the aftermath of the GFC to reach 53.6 per cent in 2015. As a result, the rise in the profits of top TNCs accounted for more than two thirds of the decline in the global labour income share between 1995 and 2015. Therefore, although the rising share of the profits of top TNCs has come at the expense of smaller enterprises, it has also been strongly correlated with the declining labour income share since the beginning of the new millennium (figure 2.14.B). This points to the key role of the largest 2,000 TNCs dominating international "trade" and finance in driving up global functional income inequality.

In sum, the evidence in this section describes a widening gap between a small number of big winners in GVCs and a large collection of participants, both smaller companies and workers, who are being squeezed. Rising export market concentration and intangible barriers to competition, both of which have increased the rents of top TNCs (the largest players in international trade and finance) have exacerbated

BOX 2.3   **"There's no place like home": The geographical location of headquarters of the top TNCs**

This chapter shows how the "rise of the South" other than China has been moderate at best. As noted in section B, the share of the South in global trade in 2011 was nearly 48 per cent in gross value terms and 44 per cent in value added terms; but excluding extractive industries, first-generation NIEs and China, the share was less than 23 per cent. This means that the claims of a "Great Convergence" (Baldwin, 2016) are still far-fetched. However, the picture of international inequality is even more dire in terms of the locations of the headquarters of TNCs.

Obviously, the geographical networks of TNCs activities and ownership structures are much more complex than can be deduced from a simple mapping of TNC headquarters. Nevertheless, the geographical location of the headquarters remains a key criterion for establishing from where effective control over a corporate entity is exerted. Unsurprisingly, the vast majority of top TNCs remain headquartered in developed countries. Accordingly, the distribution of the returns to transnational capital is much more skewed in favour of investors resident in developed countries than the distribution of (exported) value added more generally (Quentin and Campling, 2018). In short, if trade is nurturing growing concentration and corporate rents, these disproportionately benefit Northern investors. Through its impact on corporate rents, "trade" thus adds to international and functional inequality.

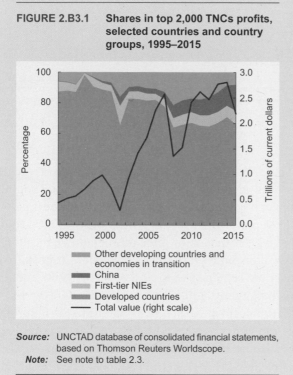

FIGURE 2.B3.1   Shares in top 2,000 TNCs profits, selected countries and country groups, 1995–2015

Source: UNCTAD database of consolidated financial statements, based on Thomson Reuters Worldscope.
Note: See note to table 2.3.

Reflecting the rise of China in global trade and finance, the number of Chinese top TNCs increased rapidly over the past two decades from zero to about 200. Although they are taking a growing share the profits of top TNCs (17 per cent in 2015), their expansion does not seem to threaten top TNCs headquartered in the United States (Starrs, 2014), which still account for 37 per cent of the profits of top TNCs, almost as much as in 1995 (figure 2.B3.1). Interestingly however, the share of Chinese financial TNCs in top TNCs profit expanded rapidly to more than 10 per cent to total top TNCs profits, exceeding those of United States financial top TNCs in 2015. Much like the top United States TNCs, those headquartered in NIEs seem to hold their ground as their big neighbour is rising. In relative terms, the expansion of Chinese top TNCs thus seems to have come about at the expense of other developed countries' TNCs, which could explain some of the ramped-up rhetoric in the incipient trade wars.

TNCs headquartered in other developing countries accounted for less than 10 per cent of top TNCs profits in 2015, much the same share as it was before the decade-long commodity boom. (Even within this, it should be borne in mind that an unknown fraction of the small profit share accruing to top Southern TNCs actually accrued to Northern investors owning shares in these companies.) Thus, the stake of the "Rest of the South" in the control over top TNCs, including global production decisions and transnational capital income, remains negligible. Their marginality is all the more striking given the important and growing demography of the "Rest of the South" (68.2 per cent of world population in 2015).

other impacts of trade on inequality. Furthermore, as large TNCs have increased their weight in rule-making at all levels, they have become ever less accountable from a social perspective (see e.g. Carroll, 2012; Carroll and Sapinski, 2016; Zingales, 2017) as well as with respect to environmental concerns.[38] This is one of the main reasons why trade liberalization under hyperglobalization did not

deliver the promised shared prosperity in the North or the South. Rather, it promoted debt-fuelled market concentration dominated by a relatively small number of top TNCs, deepened the financialization of the global economy and vastly increased the influence of transnational capital over national and international policy decisions that affect global production, employment and income distribution. Much as in

Prebisch's time, albeit for different types of activities, the dynamics (and the rules) of international trade still reflect the imbalances between, on the one hand, powerful exporting firms with monopolistic control whose rents are concentrated in the developed countries (see box 2.3) and, on the other hand, "peripheral" firms (and their employees), in both developed and developing countries, involved in providing goods and services with low barriers to entry. This kind of polarization compounds the more classical Prebisch-type outcome described in section C, which was related to the ways in which trade still contributes to the persistence of specialization in primary products in many developing regions.

E. Unequalizing trade: Macroeconomic risks and development policy challenges

The belief that international trade can be an "engine for development" and help establish an inclusive growth path, as recently affirmed in the 2030 Agenda for Sustainable Development, is neither new nor unreasonable. Yet, these objectives should not lead to simplistic advocacy of untrammelled free trade. When UNCTAD was convened for the first time in 1964, policymakers from the South were concerned that their countries were increasingly being marginalized by an international trading system that added to polarizing pressures in the global economy (UNCTAD, 1964). This was not seen as the ineluctable consequence of market or technological forces but the outcome of institutions, policies and rules, at the national and global levels, that always and everywhere animate and channel these forces in both creative and destructive directions, and could be changed if the balance was seen as unfair and undesirable. More than half a century later, and despite myriad changes in the volume, direction and governance of cross-border trade, such concerns have surfaced once again, in advanced economies as well as in developing economies.

It is evident that increased trade under hyperglobalization has created opportunities for structural change, but only in very limited parts of the Global South. Besides the first-tier NIEs and more recently China, only a few countries have managed to leverage trade as a means for mobilizing and reallocating productive factors away from primary commodities towards higher value added manufacturing and service activities, and even then in a sporadic manner. As global trade has decelerated since the GFC, underlying structural weaknesses have been revealed in many countries. In many cases, the growth spurts that occurred were on the back of unsustainable booms in extractive industries, which in turn

further entrenched patterns of hyperspecialization, when what was needed was to move towards more diversified structures. In developing countries that did increase manufactured exports via the offshoring of production, the underlying shift in corporate strategy to minimize costs and maximize the capture of rents has, in combination with the indiscriminate application of neoliberal policies, exacerbated the unequalizing impact of trade.

These outcomes pose several macroeconomic risks and development challenges, which are starkly evident today. The main concern is probably the negative impact that trade under hyperglobalization has had on aggregate demand (*TDR 2016*). As capital progressively acquired a larger share of world income at the expense of labour, within-country wage, income and wealth inequality rose in most countries in a self-reinforcing manner. Many economists have noted that rising inequality together with the higher propensity to save of the rich creates a bias towards underconsumption or, alternatively, has encouraged debt-led consumption enabled by financial deregulation; both of these processes tend to end badly. Before the GFC, this pattern, as discussed in previous *Report*s, was reflected in, and compounded by, global imbalances that were prolonged by premature external opening.

Global financial markets and major transnational financial institutions have, with some justification, become the principal villains in this story but it is now evident that non-financial corporations cannot remain immune from criticism. Facing weaker prospective sales in a context of weak aggregate demand and compounded by the post-crisis turn to austerity, large corporations have cut back on investment, further depressing aggregate demand and contributing to slower trade in recent years. The expansion of ICT and digital companies (discussed in chapter III) has not changed this trend; if anything it has, by introducing newer kinds of market control and rent-seeking behaviour, made the situation worse.

In such an environment, incentives are strong for seeking to boost profitability through means other than raising productivity, such as intensifying international competition between workers and between governments to reduce labour and tax costs, crushing or buying up competitors to build up market dominance and increase markups, etc. The unfortunate truth is that the attempts of individual TNCs to enhance their own market position through such strategies only makes the broader economic system more fragile and vulnerable, since together they lead to more inequality, underconsumption, debt and, consequently, macroeconomic vulnerability.

In an interdependent world characterized by financial instability and low growth, trade risks becoming a zero-sum game. Unilateral actions by governments to reinvigorate their own economy by trade protectionism, currency depreciation or wage restraint risk increasing tensions between countries and ending in a self-defeating spiral. But simple-minded calls for more trade liberalization are no substitute for development strategies either (e.g. *TDR 2016*). It is true that trade has been successfully leveraged for promoting structural change by some countries, most recently China. But without policy interventions to generate structural change, channel profits into productive investment and bring better quality employment, trade can nurture more economic, social and environmental damage, at odds with the Sustainable Development Goals.

While "best practice" is a poor guide for development policy (World Bank, 2017), the experiences of successful industrializers should be used as a source of policy experimentation for other developing countries to develop their own strategy based on their national specificities. In such context, governments should realize that relying on so-called "second-best" approaches is often preferable for their economies and populations (Chang, 2003).

The various pieces of evidence examined in this chapter call for a more evidence-based and pragmatic approach to managing trade as well as to designing trade agreements. Crucially, it is important to address trade with a narrative that departs from unrealistic assumptions, such as full employment,

perfect competition, savings-determined investment or constant income distribution, which underpin mainstream computable general equilibrium trade models and the associated policy discourse on trade policy. Instead, the insights of new trade theory that acknowledge the impact of trade on inequality need to be combined with an assessment of the causal relationship between rising inequality, corporate rent-seeking, falling investment and mounting indebtedness.

As the benefits of hyperglobalization are increasingly concentrated, the mood of populations in many countries is changing and new narratives are needed. As UNCTAD has argued consistently in the past few years (*TDRs 2011, 2014, 2017*), a new international compact is required – a Global New Deal – that would aim for international economic integration in more democratic, equitable and sustainable forms.

There are several elements of such a Global New Deal that have already been elaborated in previous *Report*s. Specifically, with reference to strategies for international trade and the architecture that sustains it, there is a strong case for revisiting the Havana Charter 1948,[39] which emerged, albeit ephemerally, from the original New Deal and still provides important insights for our contemporary concerns. First of all, the Charter (chap. II, art. 2.1) looked to nestle trade in the appropriate macroeconomic setting, noting that:

> the avoidance of unemployment or underemployment, through the achievement and maintenance in each country of useful employment opportunities for those able and willing to work and of a large and steadily growing volume of production and effective demand for goods and services, is not of domestic concern alone, but is also a necessary condition for the achievement of the general purpose … including the expansion of international trade, and thus for the well-being of all other countries.

This focus on employment has largely been lost in the period of hyperglobalization, and also finds little reflection in the "trade" and "economic cooperation" agreements that have dominated the landscape. Yet it must be revived if the widespread backlash against trade is not to gather more strength.

Second, the Charter recognized the links between labour-market conditions, inequality and trade, calling for improvements in wages and working conditions in line with productivity changes. It also sought to prevent "business practices affecting international trade which restrain competition, limit access to markets or foster monopolistic control" (chap. V, art. 46.1) and dedicated an entire chapter to dealing with the problem of restrictive business practices. Revisiting these goals in light of twenty-first-century challenges should be a priority.

Third, the Charter insisted that there were multiple development paths to marry local goals with integration into the global economy and that countries must have sufficient policy space to pursue pragmatic experimentation to ensure a harmonious marriage. This need for policy space also brings to the forefront the matter of negotiating trade agreements that have in recent decades privileged the requirements of capital and limited the possibilities for development in line with social priorities. ∎

Notes

1 In this context, Rodrik, 2018: 74, commented on the unanimous consensus among 38 polled economists that North American Free Trade Agreement (NAFTA) had on average made citizens of the United States better off as follows:

> The economists must have been aware that trade agreements, like free trade itself, create winners and losers. But how did they weight the gains and losses to reach a judgement that US citizens would be better off "on average"? Did it not matter who gained and lost, whether they were rich or poor to begin with, or whether the gains and losses would be diffuse or concentrated? What if the likely redistribution was large compared to the efficiency gains? What did they assume about the likely compensation for the losers, or did it not matter at all? And would their evaluation be any different if they knew that recent research suggests NAFTA produced minute net efficiency gains for the United States economy while severely depressing wages of those groups and communities most directly affected by Mexican competition?

2 For presenting compelling stylized facts doing justice to the complexity of the task at hand, this chapter exploits several databases. All of them suffer from limitations. Yet they shed light on distinct aspects of this global puzzle. In addition to gross merchandise trade from United Nations Comtrade (https://comtrade.un.org/), which proposes the broadest coverage in terms of time scale and number of countries, but excludes services and suffers from double counting, sections B and C also use data from the joint OECD–WTO Trade in Value-Added (TiVA) initiative (http://www.oecd.org/sti/ind/measuring-trade-in-value-added.htm). TiVA addresses double counting issues and includes trade in services, though without fixing deeper-running methodological issues (box 2.1). Unlike section B, which uses value added data from TiVA to map production and trade, section D.1 relies on value added data from the World Input–Output Database (WIOD) (http://www.wiod.org) to map trade and income distribution in manufacturing GVCs (de Vries, 2018; de Vries et al., 2018). More precisely, it examines whether trade is associated with a deepening "smile curve" and polarizing distributional effects across production factors and business functions, thus hurting lower-skilled workers. Then, section D.2 uses firm-level data from the Exporter Dynamic Database (Fernandes et al., 2016) (https://datacatalog.worldbank.org/dataset/exporter-dynamics-database) on exports from 70 countries, mostly developing countries, to assess the trend of market concentration in goods exports. The analysis of market concentration is complemented by UNCTAD data on the consolidated financial statements of the top 2,000 largest TNCs, based on Thomson Reuters Worldscope, which provide a more global perspective and further account for the growing role of services, especially financial services, in global production and trade. Data on charges for IPR is also exploited to highlight growing returns to intangible assets and the pervasive challenge of profit shifting, which biases the level playing field, bolstering rents and market concentration. As nation-based mappings of trade in times of rising cross-border ownership and (intra-firm) trade in intangible services are subject to growing distortions (box 2.1), box 2.3 again exploits Thomson Reuters EIKON data (https://customers.thomsonreuters.com/eikon/) to pin down the headquarter location of top TNCs as an imperfect proxy for the nationality of owners of transnational capital, and stresses how elusive the "rise of the South" remains in terms of its control over transnational capital. Finally, data from the Global Policy Model's World Database (https://www.un.org/development/desa/dpad/publication/united-nations-global-policy-model/) is crossed with the profits of top TNCs to illustrate the role of top TNCs in driving down the global labour income share, in accordance with the most recent academic research findings conducted at the country-level (Barkai, 2016; Autor et al., 2017a, 2017b).

3 The decline was similar even in terms of value-added trade.

4 TiVA data show that the share of manufactures exports in total trade has remained roughly constant at about 50 per cent between 1995 and 2011 (the latest year, for which TiVA provides data).

5   Considering the EU-27 as one single entity and its trade with the rest of the world (extra-European Union trade in goods), the export revenues in dollars from China overtook the ones from the EU-27 in 2014.

6   Brazil, the Russian Federation, India, China and South Africa.

7   The Russian Federation, India, Brazil and South Africa.

8   Or put it differently, East Asia's exports of manufactures to the world accounted for about 63 per cent of total developing-country exports of manufactures to the world, while East Asia's exports of manufactures to the developing and transition economies accounted for 67 per cent of total developing-country exports of manufactures to developing countries and transition economies.

9   These findings do not appear directly in table 2.1 but in its underlying data since in table 2.1 "agriculture" was merged with extractive industries into the same column, for presentation purposes.

10   This is confirmed by the analysis in chap. III.

11   Earlier UNCTAD research had already stressed that this type of analysis can be problematic as what could appear as a success (i.e. exporting a larger share of more sophisticated products) may not represent a truly positive structural change. This is because for many goods intensive in technology and high and medium skills it might well be that the exporting country is only engaged in assembly activities intensive in low-skilled labour within a GVC. Thus, the apparent technological "leapfrogging" that gross trade data can suggest might represent a statistical mirage (*TDR 2002*: 77–81). For this reason, this approach should be interpreted as a rather optimistic picture that might require further investigation. On the flip side, absent any progress (or even worse, a deterioration) using this biased approach suggests, at best, a non-upgrading situation or a plausible degradation (downgrading).

12   The 2016 version of the WIOD database covers 43 countries for 2014 and a model for the rest of the world for the period 2000–2014. Data for 56 sectors are classified according to the International Standard Industrial Classification revision 4.

13   The positive narrative on trade and GVCs does not only rely on the rather old-fashioned Heckscher-Ohlin model. It is also inspired by more recent developments of mainstream trade theory. Several shortcomings of (new) trade theory models are discussed in section D.2.

14   In this chapter, headquarter functions comprises the following professions defined by de Vries et al., 2018: (1) Management: general managers, financial managers, human resources and other support functions; (2) Research and development: engineers and related professionals, computing professionals; (3) Marketing: sales persons, client information clerks, customer services representatives. See chapter III and de Vries et al., 2018, for more details. This framework offers a preliminary attempt to track the distributional impact of GVCs.

15   Moreover, irrespective of GVCs, the polarizing impact of trade has long been particularly acute for extractive industries and commodity exports, because of their higher capital-intensity, which constrains the benefits in terms of employment and income for indigenous people, who still are on numerous occasions dispossessed of their land and livelihood. Gender segmentation also plays an important role in the polarizing role of trade, see *TDR 2017*, chap. IV.

16   Processing trade regimes dispense firms located in EPZs from any import or export duty, submitting them to much lighter regulations and sometimes even granting them tax rebates and other advantages; for a detailed discussion of EPZs and their record with respect to economic and social upgrading, see Milberg and Winkler, 2013: chap. 7.

17   As of 2006, the International Labour Organization (ILO) counted over 130 countries with laws providing for EPZs, compared to only 46 in 1986. During the same period, the number of EPZs worldwide increased from 176 to 3,500, harbouring at least 66 million jobs (ILO, 2014). In the United States, over 300 "foreign trade zones" account for 13 per cent of manufacturing output (Grant, 2018) and in the European Union inward processing regimes account for 10 per cent of total European Union exports (Cernat and Pajot, 2012). In China, processing trade still accounts for nearly half of its exports, exceeding gross exports of most countries, except Germany and the United States (Lu, 2010; Dai et al., 2016; Kee and Tang, 2016).

18   Part of those foreign firm may actually be owned by mainland Chinese investors, as part of inward-flowing foreign direct investment (FDI) is simply round tripping through Hong Kong (China).

19   Such observations challenge the popular claim that exporting firms (irrespective of the nationality of their owners and despite evidence of pervasive processing trade in many developing countries) are more competitive than non-exporting firms, because exporting firms are necessarily more productive (e.g. Melitz, 2003).

20   In addition to earning wages that are in relative decline, low-skilled assembly employees are regularly submitted to exploitative and sometimes even hazardous working conditions, in China (e.g. China Labor Watch, 2012; Merchant, 2017) and elsewhere (e.g. Richardson et al., 2017).

21   Most firms are not involved in exports. For instance, in the United States only 1 per cent of firms are involved in exports (Lederer, 2017). This share may be somewhat higher in small export-oriented economies, but given high export market concentration, the

number of exporting firms only represents a small fraction of the total number of domestic firms.

22 Additional data related to the Exporter Dynamics Database provided by Fernandes et al., 2016.

23 In Germany, for instances, more than 110,000 firms are involved in exports.

24 Similar findings appear across all sectors and are not driven by extraordinary levels of concentration or new export firm mortality in a particular industry.

25 At a minimum, available evidence challenges the claim that international trade in the era of GVCs offers growing opportunities for individual entrepreneurs, small and medium enterprises and the poor in developing countries.

26 The characteristics of corporate rent-seeking schemes can be sector-specific. See Havice and Campling, 2017, and references therein.

27 Developing countries remain net payers for the use of foreign IPR, and they have so far failed to increase their share of receipts, which is close to zero (figure 2.12.B).

28 Five high-income offshore financial centres accounted for 42 per cent of global payments in 2015. Also, note that reported payments are higher than reported receipts. Moreover, the number of reporting countries peaked around the GFC, with a maximum of 154 and 143 countries reporting foreign IPR-related payments and receipts, respectively, in 2008/2009. In 2015, these numbers had declined to 148 and 129, respectively. About one third of the low-tax jurisdictions classified as "non-cooperative" by the OECD in 2009 never reported these charges. Despite a decline in the number of reporting countries, IPR charges increased after the GFC.

29 The IPR regime in tandem with the "broken" international tax regime (IMF, 2013) provide a legal cover for large TNCs to transfer their IPR to affiliates in jurisdictions with low tax rates or offering special tax deals. For instance, a TNC headquartered in the United States can license its IPR to an affiliate in Ireland, thus maintaining its IPR under the stronger protection of the jurisdiction of the United States. The Irish affiliate will pay undervalued charges for this licence, but in exchange it will cash in much larger profits generated by those IPR and pay close to no taxes in Ireland. For a more detailed discussion of IPR-based profit shifting schemes and possible solutions, see Blair-Stanek, 2015. For a typology of the different forms of intellectual property trade and value capture, see Fu, 2018: table 1.

30 According to a widely cited reference focusing on the United States (Grubert, 2003), IPR profit shifting schemes may be the most effective ones, slightly ahead of creative loans. Congressional Research of the United States finds that IPR profit shifting schemes alone may deprive the authorities of the United States from between $57 billion and up to $90 billion every year (Keightley, 2013), i.e. between 25 and 40 per cent of corporate tax revenue collected by the authorities. Other developed countries are also affected by such schemes and developing countries may be those most affected in relative terms by profit shifting more generally (Crivelli et al., 2015). Such (tax) cost-saving schemes only available to larger firms have been acknowledged to bias competition and threaten the survival of competing small and medium enterprises unable or unwilling to engage into systematic tax avoidance.

31 Data were derived from Thomson Reuters Worldscope Database, from which UNCTAD has constructed a database of consolidated financial statements of publicly listed companies in 56 developed and developing countries, but headquartered in a total of 121 countries. After ranking them by asset value and selecting the 2,000 largest, it appears that the top 2,000 TNCs were headquartered in a total of only 63 countries. The choice regarding the number of TNCs comes from the Forbes Global 2,000 list, which designates, since 2003, the largest 2,000 TNCs. Rather than looking at a smaller set of TNCs, like the largest 100 TNCs as used for instance in the *World Investment Report*s by UNCTAD, it was decided to consider a larger number of TNCs to make sure that it has a broader coverage in terms of sectors and ultimately that these 2,000 firms span almost all the traded activities worldwide.

32 For this reason, some of these top TNCs are not part of the underlying firms that are considered in Exporter Dynamic Database discussed above.

33 Profit or net income represents income after all operating and non-operating income and expense, reserves, income taxes, minority interest and extraordinary items, converted to United States dollars using the fiscal year end exchange rate.

34 Far from being evenly distributed, rising returns to transnational capital mainly accrue to developed countries, where the large majority of top TNCs remain headquartered and, to a lesser though growing extent, to first-tier NIEs and China. For further discussion on this aspect, see box 2.3.

35 According to the Institute for Mergers, Acquisitions & Alliances (https://imaa-institute.org/mergers-and-acquisitions-statistics), the last two decades were characterized by a very high level of merger activity, which exceeded $2 trillion in value per year.

36 Recent evidence suggests that this process has further intensified in the very recent past. See Pearlstein, 2018.

37 For instance, in the retail sector, supermarkets can resort to tricks, such as charging slotting fees.

38 As an example of the environmental unaccountability of large players in international trade, the 2015 Paris Agreement does not set any emissions reduction targets for maritime transport and civil aviation, which represent key enablers for merchandise and services (notably tourism) trade, even

though they together account for 10 per cent of global emissions and their emissions are projected to grow by 250 per cent by 2050. Such an outcome was supported by developed countries governments (European Union Trade Policy Committee, 2015) stating that "the EU's overall objective is to have COP decisions without any explicit mention of trade

or IPR issues and to minimize discussion on trade-related issues. Any attempt to create any kind of provision/agenda item/work programme/mechanism on trade/IPR at the UNFCCC discussions cannot be accepted".

39   Available at: https://www.wto.org/english/docs_e/ legal_e/havana_e.pdf.

References

Ali-Yrkkö J, Rouvinen P, Seppälä T and Ylä-Anttila P (2011). Who captures value in global supply chains? Case Nokia N95 Smartphone. *Journal of Industry, Competition and Trade*. 11(3): 263–278.

Atalay E, Hortaçsu A and Syverson C (2014). Vertical integration and input flows. *American Economic Review*. 104(4): 1120–1148.

Autor D, Dorn D, Katz LF, Patterson C and Van Reenen J (2017a). Concentrating on the fall of the labor share. *American Economic Review*. 107(5): 180–185.

Autor D, Dorn D, Katz LF, Patterson C and Van Reenen J (2017b). The fall of the labor share and the rise of superstar firms. Working Paper No. 23396. National Bureau of Economic Research.

Baldwin RE (2016). *The Great Convergence: Information Technology and the New Globalization*. Harvard University Press. Cambridge, MA.

Barkai S (2016). Declining labor and capital shares. Mimeo. London Business School. Available at: http://facultyresearch.london.edu/docs/BarkaiDecliningLaborCapital.pdf.

Baud C and Durand C (2012). Financialization, globalization and the making of profits by leading retailers. *Socio-Economic Review*. 10(2): 241–266.

Bivens J, Mishel L and Schmitt J (2018). It's not just monopoly and monopsony: How market power has affected American wages. Report. Economic Policy Institute. Washington, D.C. Available at: https://www.epi.org/publication/its-not-just-monopoly-and-monopsony-how-market-power-has-affected-american-wages/.

Blair-Stanek A (2015). Intellectual property law solutions to tax avoidance. *UCLA Law Review*. 62(1): 4–73.

Carroll WK (2012). Global, transnational, regional, national: The need for nuance in theorizing global capitalism. *Critical Sociology*. 38(3): 365–371.

Carroll WK and Sapinski JP (2016). Neoliberalism and the transnational capitalist class. In: Springer S, Birch K and MacLeavy J, eds. *The Handbook of Neoliberalism*. Routledge. New York, NY: 39–49.

Cernat L and Pajot M (2012). "Assembled in Europe": The role of processing trade in EU export performance. Chief Economist Note. European Commission. Issue No. 3. Available at: http://trade.ec.europa.eu/doclib/docs/2012/october/tradoc_150006.pdf.

Chang HJ (2003). *Globalisation, Economic Development and the Role of the State*. Zed Books. London.

Chen W, Gouma R, Los B and Timmer MP (2017). Measuring the income to intangibles in goods production: A global value chain approach. Economic Research Working Paper No. 36. World Intellectual Property Organization.

China Labor Watch (2012). *Beyond Foxconn: Deplorable Working Conditions Characterize Apple's Entire Supply Chain*. China Labor Watch. New York, NY. Available at: http://www.chinalaborwatch.org/report/62.

Crivelli E, De Mooij R and Keen M (2015). Base erosion, profit shifting and developing countries. Working Paper No. 15/118. International Monetary Fund.

Dai M, Maitra M and Yu M (2016). Unexceptional exporter performance in China? The role of processing trade. *Journal of Development Economics*. 121: 177–189.

de Sousa J (2012). The currency union effect on trade is decreasing over time. *Economics Letters*. 117(3): 917–920.

de Vries GJ (2018). Global value chain and domestic value added export analysis using the World Input–Output Database: Methods and an illustration. Background material prepared for the *Trade and Development Report 2018*.

de Vries GJ, Miroudot S and Timmer M (2018). Functional specialization in international trade: An exploration based on occupations of workers. Mimeo. University of Groningen.

Dedrick J, Kraemer KL and Linden G (2010). Who profits from innovation in global value chains? A study of the iPod and notebook PCs. *Industrial and Corporate Change*. 19(1): 81–116.

Diez F, Leigh D and Tambunlertchai S (2018). Global market power and its macroeconomic implications. Working Paper No. 18/137. International Monetary Fund.

Driskill R (2012). Deconstructing the argument for free trade: A case study of the role of economists in policy debates. *Economics and Philosophy*. 28(1): 1–30.

Escaith H and Gaudin H (2014). Clustering value-added trade: Structural and policy dimensions. Staff

Working Paper ERSD-2014-08. World Trade Organization.

European Union Trade Policy Committee (2015). TPC – 20.11.2015: UNFCCC and Trade-related issues and intellectual property. Internal document leaked. Available at: https://corporateeurope.org/sites/default/files/attachments/trade_and_climate_-_trade_policy_committee.pdf.

Feenstra RC, Lipsey RE, Branstetter LG, Foley CF, Harrigan J, Jensen JB, Kletzer L, Mann C, Schott PK and Wright GC (2010). Report on the state of available data for the study of international trade and foreign direct investment. Working Paper No. 16254. National Bureau of Economic Research.

Fernandes AM, Freund C and Pierola MD (2016). Exporter behavior, country size and stage of development: Evidence from the exporter dynamics database. *Journal of Development Economics.* 119: 121–137.

Freund C and Pierola MD (2015). Export superstars. *The Review of Economics and Statistics.* 97(5): 1023–1032.

Fu X (2018). Trade in intangibles and a global value chain-based view of international trade and global imbalance. Working Paper Series No. 078. Technology and Management Centre for Development. University of Oxford.

Galbraith JK (2012). *Inequality and Instability: A Study of the World Economy Just Before the Great Crisis.* Oxford University Press. Oxford.

Gallagher KP and Zarsky L (2007). *The Enclave Economy: Foreign Investment and Sustainable Development in Mexico's Silicon Valley.* MIT Press. Cambridge, MA.

Goldberg PK and Pavcnik N (2007). Distributional effects of globalization in developing countries. *Journal of Economic Literature.* 45(1): 39–82.

Grant M (2018). Why special economic zones? Using trade policy to discriminate across importers. Mimeo. United States International Trade Commission. Available at: https://drive.google.com/file/d/0B_4Z5rmKH1P5VE0yV1QxZ0JaZTg/view.

Grubert H (2003). Intangible income, intercompany transactions, income shifting, and the choice of location. *National Tax Journal.* 56(1, part 2): 221–242.

Hanson GH (2012). The rise of middle kingdoms: Emerging economies in global trade. *Journal of Economic Perspectives.* 26(2): 41–64.

Harrison A, McLaren J and McMillan M (2011). Recent perspectives on trade and inequality. *Annual Review of Economics.* 3: 261–289.

Havice E and Campling L (2017). Where chain governance and environmental governance meet: Interfirm strategies in the canned tuna global value chain. *Economic Geography.* 93(3): 292–313.

Hofmann C, Osnago A and Ruta M (2017). Horizontal depth: A new database on the content of preferential trade agreements. Policy Research Working Paper No. 7981. World Bank.

Hummels D, Ishii J and Yi KM (2001). The nature and growth of vertical specialization in world trade. *Journal of International Economics.* 54(1): 75–96.

ILO (2014). *Trade Union Manual on Export Processing Zones.* International Labour Organization. Geneva.

IMF (2013). *Fiscal Monitor 2013: Taxing Times.* International Monetary Fund. Washington, D.C.

Johnson RC (2018, forthcoming). Measuring global value chains. *Annual Review of Economics.* August. Published online ahead of print. Available at: https://www.annualreviews.org/doi/10.1146/annurev-economics-080217-053600.

Kee HL and Tang H (2016). Domestic value added in exports: Theory and firm evidence from China. *American Economic Review.* 106(6): 1402–1436.

Keightley MP (2013). An analysis of where American companies report profits: Indications of profit shifting. CRS Report No. R42927, Congressional Research Service. Available at: https://digital.library.unt.edu/ark:/67531/metadc462866/.

Kindleberger CP (1969). *American Business Abroad: Six Lectures on Direct Investment.* Yale University Press. New Haven, CT.

Kindleberger CP, ed. (1970). *The International Corporation: A Symposium.* MIT Press. Cambridge, MA.

Kohler P and Cripps F (2018). Do trade and investment (agreements) foster development or inequality? New evidence on the impact of GVC-led fragmentation and top 2000 TNC-driven concentration. GDAE Working Papers. Tufts University.

Kohler P and Storm S (2016). CETA without blinders: How cutting "trade costs and more" will cause unemployment, inequality, and welfare losses. *International Journal of Political Economy.* 45(4): 257–293.

Koopman R, Wang Z and Wei S-J (2014). Tracing value-added and double counting in gross exports. *American Economic Review.* 104(2): 459–494.

Lederer EM (2017). SBA: Only 1 percent of America's small businesses export overseas. Associated Press. 12 May. Available at: https://www.inc.com/associated-press/linda-mcmahon-small-business-administration-exports-only-1-percent-small-business.html.

Lewis A (1979). The slowing down of the engine of growth. Lecture to the memory of Alfred Nobel. 8 December. Available at: https://www.nobelprize.org/nobel_prizes/economic-sciences/laureates/1979/lewis-lecture.html.

Lipsey RE (2009). Measuring international trade in services. In: Reinsdorf M and Slaughter MJ, eds. *International Trade in Services and Intangibles in the Era of Globalization.* University of Chicago Press. Chicago: 27–70.

Lopez Gonzalez J, Kowalski P and Achard P (2015). Trade, global value chains and wage-income inequality. Trade Policy Papers No. 182. Organisation for Economic Cooperation and Development.

Lu D (2010). Exceptional exporter performance? Evidence from Chinese manufacturing firms. Mimeo.

University of Chicago. Available at: http://crifes.psu.edu/papers/DanLuJMP.pdf.

Lu J, Lu Y and Tao Z (2010). Exporting behavior of foreign affiliates: Theory and evidence. *Journal of International Economics*. 81(2): 197–205.

Maddison A (2006). *The World Economy (Two-in-One Edition). Volume 1: A Millennial Perspective; Volume 2: Historical Statistics*. OECD Publishing. Paris.

Markusen JR (1984). Multinationals, multi-plant economies, and the gains from trade. *Journal of International Economics*. 16(3/4): 205–226.

Markusen JR (2004). *Multinational Firms and the Theory of International Trade*. MIT Press. Cambridge, MA.

Markusen JR and Venables AJ (1998). Multinational firms and the new trade theory. *Journal of International Economics*. 46(2): 183–203.

Meagher K, Mann L and Bolt M (2016). Introduction: Global economic inclusion and african workers. *The Journal of Development Studies*. 52(4): 471–482.

Melitz MJ (2003). The impact of trade on intra-industry reallocations and aggregate industry productivity. *Econometrica*. 71(6): 1695–1725.

Menell PS and Scotchmer S (2007). Intellectual property law. In: Polinsky AM and Shavell S, eds. *Handbook of Law and Economics, Volume 2*. North-Holland. Amsterdam: 1473–1570.

Merchant B (2017). *The One Device: The Secret History of the iPhone*. Bantam Press. London.

Milberg W and Winkler D (2013). *Outsourcing Economics: Global Value Chains in Capitalist Development*. Cambridge University Press. New York, NY.

Namur Declaration (2016). 5 December. Available at: http://declarationdenamur.eu/wp-content/uploads/2016/12/EN-D%C3%A9claration-de-Namur-EN-.pdf.

Paus E (2014). Industrial development strategies in Costa Rica: When structural change and domestic capability accumulation diverge. In: Salazar-Xirinachs JM, Nübler I and Kozul-Wright R, eds. *Transforming Economies: Making Industrial Policy Work for Growth, Jobs and Development*. International Labour Office. Geneva: 181–211.

Pavcnik N (2017). The impact of trade on inequality in developing countries. Working Paper No. 23878. National Bureau of Economic Research.

Pavlínek P (2016). Whose success? The state–foreign capital nexus and the development of the automotive industry in Slovakia. *European Urban and Regional Studies*. 23(4): 571–593.

Pavlínek P and Ženka J (2016). Value creation and value capture in the automotive industry: Empirical evidence from Czechia. *Environment and Planning A: Economy and Space*. 48(5): 937–959.

Pearlstein S (2018). Beware the "mother of all credit bubbles". *Washington Post*. 8 June.

Piketty T (2016). We must rethink globalization, or Trumpism will prevail. *The Guardian*. 16 November. Available at: https://www.theguardian.com/commentisfree/2016/nov/16/globalization-trump-inequality-thomas-piketty.

Plank L and Staritz C (2013). "Precarious upgrading" in electronics global production networks in Central and Eastern Europe: The cases of Hungary and Romania. Working Paper No. 31. Austrian Foundation for Development Research.

Platt E, Scaggs A and Bullock N (2017). How Apple and co became some of America's largest debt collectors. *Financial Times*. 15 September.

Poon D (2014). China's development trajectory: A strategic opening for industrial policy in the South. Discussion Paper No. 218. UNCTAD. Available at: http://unctad.org/en/PublicationsLibrary/osgdp20144_en.pdf.

Poon D (2018). China broke the rules of global trade – but for good reason. *South China Morning Post*. 21 June. Available at: https://www.scmp.com/comment/insight-opinion/united-states/article/2151688/china-broke-rules-global-trade-good-reason.

Quentin D and Campling L (2018). Global inequality chains: Integrating mechanisms of value distribution into analyses of global production. *Global Networks*. 18(1): 33–56.

Ramondo N, Rappoport V and Ruhl KJ (2016). Intrafirm trade and vertical fragmentation in U.S. multinational corporations. *Journal of International Economics*. 98: 51–59.

Richardson B, Harrison J and Campling L (2017). Labour rights in Export Processing Zones with a focus on GSP+ beneficiary countries. European Parliament Think Tank. Available at: http://www.europarl.europa.eu/thinktank/en/document.html?reference=EXPO_STU(2017)603839.

Rodrik D (2011). *The Globalization Paradox: Democracy and the Future of the World Economy*. WW Norton. New York, NY.

Rodrik D (2017). The fatal flaw of neoliberalism: It's bad economics. *The Guardian*. 14 November. Available at: https://www.theguardian.com/news/2017/nov/14/the-fatal-flaw-of-neoliberalism-its-bad-economics.

Rodrik D (2018). What do trade agreements really do? *Journal of Economic Perspectives*. 32(2): 73–90.

Rose AK (2004). Do we really know that the WTO increases trade? *American Economic Review*. 94(1): 98–114.

Setser BW and Frank C (2018). Figure: The scale of global tax arbitrage. In: Setser, BW. The impact of tax arbitrage on the U.S. balance of payments. Blog post. Council on Foreign Relations. 9 February. Available at: https://www.cfr.org/blog/impact-tax-arbitrage-us-balance-payments.

Starrs S (2014). The chimera of global convergence. *New Left Review*. 87(May/June): 81–96.

Temin P (2017). *The Vanishing Middle Class: Prejudice and Power in a Dual Economy*. MIT Press. Cambridge, MA.

Timmer MP, Erumban AA, Los B, Stehrer R and de Vries GJ (2014). Slicing up global value chains. *Journal of Economic Perspectives*. 28(2): 99–118.

UNCTAD (1964). *Proceedings of the United Nations Conference on Trade and Development. Geneva,*

23 March–16 June. Volume I. Final Act and Report (United Nations publication. Sales No. 64.II.B.11. New York and Geneva).

UNCTAD (2013). *Economic Development in Africa Report: Intra-African Trade – Unlocking Private Sector Dynamism* (United Nations publication. Sales No. E.13.II.D.2. New York and Geneva).

UNCTAD (2017a). *Review of Maritime Transport 2017* (United Nations publication. Sales No. E.17.II.D.10. New York and Geneva).

UNCTAD (2017b). *Report of the Intergovernmental Group of Experts on Financing for Development on Its First Session.* Trade and Development Board Intergovernmental Group of Experts on Financing for Development. First session. TD/B/EFD/1/3. Geneva, 8–10 November.

UNCTAD (*TDR 1995*). *Trade and Development Report, 1995* (United Nation publication. Sales No. E.95.II.D.16. New York and Geneva).

UNCTAD (*TDR 1996*). *Trade and Development Report, 1996* (United Nations publication. Sales No.E.96.II.D.6. New York and Geneva).

UNCTAD (*TDR 1997*). *Trade and Development Report, 1997: Globalization, Distribution and Growth* (United Nations publication. Sales No. E.97.II.D.8. New York and Geneva).

UNCTAD (*TDR 2002*). *Trade and Development Report, 2002: Developing Countries in World Trade* (United Nations publication. Sales No. E.02.II.D.2. New York and Geneva).

UNCTAD (*TDR 2003*). *Trade and Development Report, 2003: Capital Accumulation, Growth and Structural Change* (United Nations publication. Sales No. E.03.II.D.7. New York and Geneva).

UNCTAD (*TDR 2011*). *Trade and Development Report, 2011: Post-Crisis Policy Challenges in the World Economy* (United Nations publication. Sales No. E.11.II.D.3. New York and Geneva).

UNCTAD (*TDR 2014*). *Trade and Development Report, 2014: Global Governance and Policy Space for Development* (United Nations publication. E.14.II.D.4. New York and Geneva).

UNCTAD (*TDR 2016*). *Trade and Development Report, 2016: Structural Transformation for Inclusive and Sustained Growth* (United Nations publication. Sales No. E.16.II.D.5. New York and Geneva).

UNCTAD (*TDR 2017*). *Trade and Development Report, 2017: Beyond Austerity: Towards a Global New Deal* (United Nations publication. Sales No. E.17.II.D.5. New York and Geneva).

United Nations (2015). Resolution adopted by the General Assembly on 25 September. Transforming Our World: The 2030 Agenda for Sustainable Development (A/RES/70/1).

USTR (Office of the United States Trade Representative) (2018). Finding of the Investigation into China's Acts, Policies, and Practices Related to Technology Transfer, Intellectual Property, and Innovation under Section 301 of the Trade Act of 1974. Available at: https://ustr.gov/sites/default/files/Section%20301%20FINAL.PDF.

WIPO (2017). *World Intellectual Property Report 2017: Intangible Capital in Global Value Chains.* World Intellectual Property Organization. Geneva.

World Bank (2017). *World Development Report 2017: Governance and the Law.* World Bank. Washington, D.C.

World Bank, the Institute of Developing Economies, the Organisation for Economic Co-operation and Development, the Research Center of Global Value Chains and the World Trade Organization (2017). *Global Value Chain Development Report: Measuring and Analyzing the Impact of GVCs on Economic Development.* World Bank. Washington, D.C.

WTO (2012). Intellectual Property Issues. World Trade Organization. Available at: https://www.wto.org/english/news_e/infocenter_e/brief_ip_e.doc.

Zingales L (2017). Towards a political theory of the firm. *Journal of Economic Perspectives.* 31(3): 113–130.

ECONOMIC DEVELOPMENT IN A DIGITAL WORLD: PROSPECTS, PITFALLS AND POLICY OPTIONS

III

A. Introduction

Digital technologies have already transformed how people communicate, learn, work and shop. They are also changing the geography of economic activity through their impact on corporate strategy, investment behaviour and trade flows. From a development perspective, the promise of digitalization is that it will open new sectors, promote new markets, boost innovation and generate the productivity gains needed to lift living standards in developing countries. Fulfilling this promise of a new digital future will, for many developing countries, require an ambitious programme of infrastructure support and skills training. However, assessing the wider use and impact of these new technologies, particularly with respect to the 2030 Development Agenda, cannot be divorced from the economic environment in which they are nested.

As discussed in previous *Reports*, today's hyperglobalized world has become more unequal, unstable and insecure: rent extraction has become an acceptable feature of doing business at the top of the corporate food chain and unchecked competition has made for precarious working conditions for many at the bottom. As a result, the gains from technological progress and open economies have been captured by a small portion of society, while their costs have been carried by an increasingly frustrated majority. A key question therefore is whether, given this "winner-takes-most" environment, the spread of digital technologies risks further concentrating the benefits among a small number of first movers, both across and within countries, or whether it will operate to disrupt the status quo and promote greater inclusion.

If history is any guide, while skill development and infrastructure provision will be necessary for helping developing countries integrate into the digital economy, ensuring developmental benefits from digitalization will require a more comprehensive strategy and a much fuller range of policy measures. Among the most critical additional policy challenge is that of adopting competition and regulatory frameworks to address potential adverse effects on market structure, innovation and the distribution of gains from digitalization. The combination of network effects and rent-seeking behaviour associated with the digitization of data that transcend borders, must also be closely monitored and carefully managed. Accordingly, developing countries will need to preserve, and possibly expand, their available policy space to effectively manage integration into the global digital economy.

Another critical challenge will be harnessing new digital technologies to local development capacity so that developing countries can enjoy rising shares of value added in manufacturing and service activities. *TDR 2017* examined this challenge with specific reference to robot-based automation; this chapter examines how a broader set of digital technologies, from computer aided design to big-data analysis, could transform the entire manufacturing process. The chapter uses the value chain framework to explore the potential for, and the risks to, developing countries from using new digital technologies.[1] It argues that digitalization and the associated erosion of the boundary between industry and services may make value chains shorter, customized production possible and smaller production runs more profitable by allowing for the design, production and post-production segments of the manufacturing process to be more closely interwoven. This could either open new manufacturing possibilities for developing countries or reduce some that are currently available. Whether the high value added pre- and post-production segments move to developing countries will depend on the governance of these chains, the structure of markets, the bargaining power of local firms and policymakers and the policies employed to effect a more strategic pattern of integration into the digital economy.

The wider use of digital technologies is still unfolding, particularly in developing countries, and their precise impacts remain uncertain. A clear understanding of the channels through which these technologies may affect income generation in developing countries is crucial to monitoring and influencing these effects. Contributing to such an understanding and indicating associated policy options are the main objectives of this chapter.[2]

The chapter is structured as follows. The next section examines some of the channels through which digitalization may affect the various segments of the production process, the way it is organized through value chains and the possible distributional consequences. The key takeaway is that by making the various segments of the process more closely interwoven, digitalization alters the distribution of value added in value chains. This may provide developing countries with new opportunities for upgrading towards high value added segments of the manufacturing process, especially if they can leverage data on market demand for design and manufacturing decisions. However, control over both design and marketing processes is required for this, and this has been constrained by monopolies driven by intellectual property rights, as noted in *TDR 2017*. To date, the evidence suggests that both labour and local producers in developing countries are being squeezed, particularly in the production stages of these chains. Section C examines the policy options that might facilitate wide diffusion and adoption of new digital technologies while ensuring an equitable sharing of their benefits. It argues that efforts towards bridging digital divides and building digital capabilities need to be complemented by adapting innovation, industrial and regulatory policies to a digital world, including in an internationally coordinated way through South–South and broader multilateral cooperation. It also cautions against a premature commitment by developing countries to trade and investment rules driven by one-sided interests and with long-term impacts. South–South digital cooperation is suggested as a way forward for developing countries for building their digital capacities. This could be added to their on-going regional integration agendas. Section D summarizes the main findings and policy conclusions.

B. Digital technologies in value chains: Potential opportunities for income generation and upgrading

Digital technologies (table 3.1) are based on information that is recorded in binary code of combinations of the digits 0 and 1, also called "bits", which represent words and images (Negroponte, 1995). This enables very large amounts of information to be compressed on small storage devices that can be easily preserved and transported, and reduces the costs and accelerates the speed of data transmission.

The industrial use of these technologies is currently at different stages of readiness. Industrial robots have experienced rapidly growing deployment, especially since 2010, even though they have remained concentrated in developed and a few developing countries at more advanced stages of industrialization (*TDR 2017*). The use of additive manufacturing (or 3D printing), is at an even earlier stage but is also growing rapidly. But this growth depends on the expiry of some core patents; currently, the more accessible 3D systems use technology that is somewhat dated, whereas frontier 3D systems for professional industrial use remain expensive (Ernst and Young, 2016). Wider accessibility is expected for this technology over the coming decade (WEF, 2015; Basiliere, 2017) as well as for big data and cloud computing (Purdy and Daugherty, 2017) and for AI (WEF, 2015).

1. The distribution of value added and upgrading in traditional value chains

The international division of labour is increasingly structured around global value chains (GVCs) (*TDR 2002, 2014*; World Bank et al., 2017). Participation in these chains by developing countries is expected to attract more foreign direct investment, provide easier access to export markets, advanced technology and know-how, and generate rapid efficiency gains from specializing in specific tasks, appropriately guided by

TABLE 3.1   Digital technologies

Technology	Attributes	Examples
Robotics and Artificial Intelligence (AI)	Algorithmic techniques that make it possible for computers and machines embodying computers to mimic human actions.	Software that can make machines perform routine manual or clerical tasks; robots assisting in surgeries; digitally enabled robots with advanced functionality to collaborate with or replace humans.
Additive manufacturing (3D printing)	Building products from numerous cross-sectional layers that are each less than a millimetre thick. This shortens stages of manufacturing like design, prototyping and product layout (all of which are created digitally) and enables production to be tailored to individual design specifications.	Consumer production using plastics, casting moulds, prototype parts for production, machine components.
Industrial Internet of Things	Digitally charged manufactures that can embed themselves into the broader technological ecosystem in which they operate.	Sensors that are embedded into products to provide new features for consumers and to gather data about production and use for data analytics.
Blockchains	Internet-based peer-to-peer network based on a decentralized system of digital ledger-keeping that is transparent and efficient.	Originally created for the Bitcoin currency in 2008 to allow for the issuance and record-keeping of online currency transactions.

Source: UNCTAD secretariat.

the "lead firm" in the chain. Such participation is seen as particularly important for developing countries with small domestic markets whose firms confront a range of technological and organizational constraints stemming from the fact that the minimum effective scale of production often far exceeds that required to meet their prevailing level of domestic demand.

This has meant that policy objectives are usually focused on providing an attractive business climate for the lead firm (including adequate infrastructure and a sufficiently trained labour force) and avoiding any restrictions on the free flow of goods and finance that connect suppliers along the chain. However, in the absence of solid evidence on significant "spillovers" from participation in value chains (*TDR 2016*),[3] policymakers should also continue to look for ways to establish domestic forward and backward linkages that facilitate a rising share of domestically generated value added, encourage more widespread transfers of technology and diffusion of knowledge, and support economic diversification and upgrading towards higher value added activities that rely on more sophisticated technology and skill sets. The evidence indicates that only a small number of developing countries – mostly in East Asia – have been

able to build such linkages and achieve upgrading within GVCs (*TDR 2016*).

Divergence between expectations and outcomes from participation in GVCs is, in part, a reflection of the fact that the private interests of international firms do not necessarily coincide with the developmental interests of the host countries. This disconnect is, of course, familiar to many developing countries from their participation in commodity-based value chains, reflecting, in part, the asymmetric structure of markets and pricing power of firms from the North and South. It also highlights the importance of strategic policies, as countries look to shift towards a greater reliance on manufacturing (and service) activities and exports and is an important reminder that reductions in policy space can hamper industrialization and catching up in late developers (*TDR 2014*).

Since many developing countries have faced difficulties in achieving the policy objectives mentioned above, their place in GVCs has tended to be located on the lower portions of what is sometimes referred to as the "smile curve" (figure 3.1). The smile curve conceptualizes international production as a series of linked tasks and sees international trade organized

FIGURE 3.1 Stylized manufacturing value chain smile curve

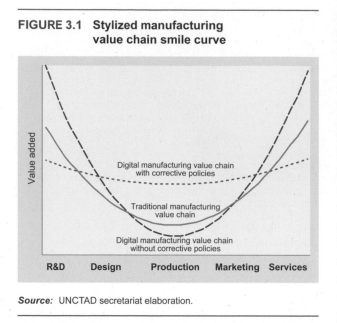

Source: UNCTAD secretariat elaboration.

within GVCs as involving trade in those tasks rather than trade in goods. The resulting fragmentation of production carries significant consequences for the spatial division of labour and the distribution of economic power and privilege. Most of the pre-production and post-production segments of the manufacturing process, with their higher return activities, are usually located in advanced economies, with developing countries often left with the lower value added activities of the production segment of the manufacturing process. As Stephen Hymer (1972: 101) recognized over 40 years ago, as international production fragments along these task lines, "output is produced cooperatively to a greater degree than ever before, but control remains uneven"; in particular, the lead firm tends to concentrate its own tasks at the two ends of the smile curve where "information and money" provide the main sources of control and where profit margins tend to be higher. These "headquarter" economies are still located predominantly in the North (now including parts of East Asia) while "factory" economies are, largely, in parts of the South (Baldwin and Lopez-Gonzalez, 2013). Indeed, as these chains have spread across more countries and sectors over the past three decades they have been accompanied by a more and more uneven distribution of those benefits.

In developed countries, the concern is that that low- and medium-skilled production jobs in traditional manufacturing communities have been "outsourced", first to lower-wage regions of the developed world and then "offshored" to developing countries, and wages have stagnated while new jobs created at the

ends of the chain have not only been insufficient in number to replace those being lost, but are often out of reach to those "left behind" both geographically and in terms of the skills required. The result is socio-economic polarization and a vanishing middle class (Temin, 2017). Developing countries worry about being stuck in low-value-added activities, unable to upgrade towards higher value added activities in R&D and design, marketing and management, and becoming trapped in "thin industrialization" or experiencing "premature deindustrialization"; here the problem is less one of a vanishing middle class and more one of a receding middle class, as a growing urban labour force (whose incomes may still be rising above the extreme poverty levels found in the rural and urban informal economies) experiences diminishing employment opportunities in higher productivity manufacturing and service sectors.

The critical question is whether and how the new digital technologies might aggravate or assuage these anxieties. In other words, new digital technologies could aggravate the inequalities already apparent across the value chain, as depicted in figure 3.1, or with different national and global policies they could be associated with a flatter curve and more inclusive outcomes. Some of the concerns are elaborated below, while some possibilities for deriving greater benefits for developing countries are noted in section D.

2. Digitalization: Potential impacts on the manufacturing process

Digitalization is often considered a game changer with respect to how the manufacturing process is undertaken and organized in value chains (e.g. De Backer and Flaig, 2017) even though the geographical location of these changes is as yet uncertain and will depend on a range of factors (Eurofound, 2018). This is because digitalization gives intangibles a more prominent role in income generation, including along value chains. Intangibles refer to R&D, design, blueprints, software, market research and branding, databases etc. (e.g. Haskel and Westlake, 2018: table 2.1).[4] The data that embody these intangibles and their codification drive the various new digital technologies which, as a consequence, are often more closely identified with service activities. This means that, in a digital world, services increasingly permeate the goods sector and that the traditional boundaries between goods and services in the manufacturing process become blurred. By the same token, various segments of the manufacturing process become more closely interwoven. An important part of the data revolution involves sales and other market-related information and the ability to customize production to the increasingly demanding and heterogenous tastes of consumers, including in growing markets in the South (Baldwin, 2016).[5] The increase in the share of intangibles in the production process can have other implications: as noted by Pérez and Marín (2015) these technologies allow materials to be redesigned to make them more closely specified to their use, thereby reducing material use per unit of output, as well as reduce energy consumption and pollutant emissions.[6] What may be most significant of all is that digital technologies enable more decentralized and flexible production and distribution, reducing some of the scale economies that dominated the era of mass production. This can result in a "hyper-segmentation of markets, activities and technologies" (Pérez, 2010: 139) whereby companies of varying sizes can respond to and accommodate multiple demand segments, and small producers can cater to niche markets that need not be in geographical proximity. The use of new digital technologies may, therefore, allow developing countries to add more value in their production stages, whether or not the final product is for export or domestic consumption. However, this depends crucially not only on available infrastructure but on access to data and a supportive ecosystem.

(a) Potential impacts on income generation

(i) The production segment

Much of the debate on digitalization has focused on the use of industrial robots in the production segment of the manufacturing process. As discussed in *TDR 2017*, the stock of robots remains concentrated in a few developed countries, and in relatively high-wage sectors, despite its recent rapid increase in some developing countries, especially China. The *Report* suggested that, for now at least, robot-based automation per se does not invalidate the traditional role of industrialization as a development strategy for lower-income countries moving into manufacturing activities (such as clothing and leather sectors) dominated by manual and routine tasks, although in countries already experiencing premature deindustrialization and low rates of investment, the danger of getting trapped in these low-value-added sectors is likely to increase. In the longer run, and even in

the absence of reshoring to advanced countries (ILO, 2018), as the cost of robots declines further (and their dexterity increases), their spread to lower-wage manufacturing sectors and eventually to lower-income countries could have significant consequences for employment creation.

The production segment may also be affected by additive manufacturing, combining computer-aided design and manufacturing (CAD/CAM), or any other 3D software that creates digital models, with 3D printers that build products by adding materials in layers. This can also be seen as an opportunity: the likely reduction in the number of assembly stages in the production process, the heightened opportunity to customize production and the increase in the modularity of value chains could ease the integration of remote (and smaller) firms in the world economy. Firms employing digitized processes typically gain in flexibility and so may be better able to cater to increasingly diverse and fragmented consumer preferences in both domestic and external markets.

To assess the extent of digitization of the manufacturing process, the share of telecommunications, computer programming and information service activities in total intermediate consumption in manufacturing may be a useful gauge.[7] Cross-country evidence for the period 2000–2014 (figure 3.2) indicates that this share remains low and accounts for less than 1 per cent for most countries. It also shows wide variation across countries. Sweden and Finland record the largest shares while a few developing countries show very low shares. However, there is no clear divide between developed and developing countries. Among developing countries, it is perhaps surprising that for 2014 the share of India ranks fourth, while that of China remains among the smallest of all countries and even declined by more than half between 2005 and 2014. For most countries, computer programming and information service activities as a share of total intermediate consumption is of significantly greater importance than telecommunications, even though there is no clear pattern either across countries or over time.

Several factors may explain the apparent low importance of ICT services in manufacturing.[8] The small shares across all economies could indicate that digitalization is little more than a media hype. But these small numbers could also be a result of the slack in global demand following the global financial crisis, which has been a key factor holding back productive

FIGURE 3.2 Selected ICT services as a share of total intermediate consumption in manufacturing, selected economies, 2000–2014

(Percentages)

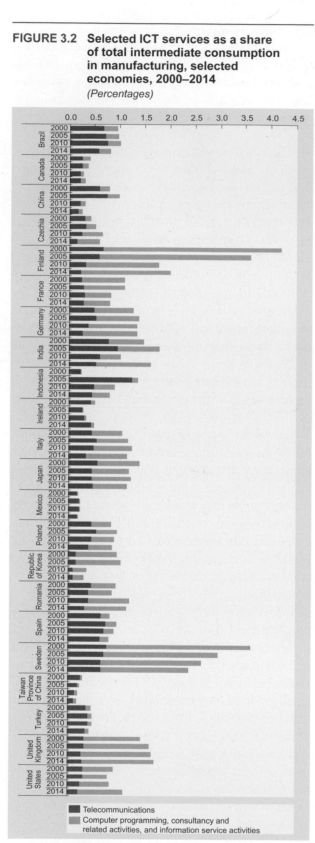

Telecommunications

Computer programming, consultancy and related activities, and information service activities

Source: UNCTAD secretariat calculations, based on World Input–Output Database (WIOD), University of Groningen, National Supply-Use Tables, 2016 release.
Note: ICT services refer to divisions J61–J63 of the International Standard Industrial Classification (ISIC) Revision 4 and distinguish telecommunications (J61) from computer programming, consultancy and related activities, and information service activities (J62 and J63). Manufacturing refers to ISIC Revision 4 divisions C5–C23. Shares calculated from weighted averages in national currency.

investment. The finding could, alternatively, point to another form of the Solow paradox – you can see the computer age everywhere but in the productivity statistics – in that digitization can be seen everywhere except in the national accounts statistics (Brynjolfsson et al., 2018). One reason for this could be that many digital services come free of charge in monetary terms (Turner, 2018). Accurate measurement of intangibles such as ICT services is difficult. But when estimated as a residual, their importance appears to be large and increasing, currently accounting for about one third of total production value (WIPO, 2017). Measurement issues could play an important role particularly in indicators based on input–output data, such as in figure 3.2, because firms may prefer producing most intangibles in-house, because of concerns regarding intellectual property protection. Intangibles sourced in-house are not reflected in input–output tables, which rely on purchased inputs. The surprisingly small shares for China in figure 3.2 could also reflect such measurement issues, as Chinese companies may have a particularly large degree of vertical integration.

(ii) The pre- and post-production segments

The new digital technologies and especially ICTs associated with the Internet of Things – such as cloud computing and big-data analysis – make the post-production segment of manufacturing more important, as this is where intangible assets are used intensively. Such ICTs tend to reduce coordination costs and increase the efficiency of production schedules, logistics, inventory management and equipment maintenance. Cloud computing and big-data analysis reduce the need for hard digital infrastructure. This makes it cheaper for firms, even in developing countries, to collect data and analyse them for their business purposes, reinforcing the customization and flexibilization possibilities mentioned above. This can occur for intermediate products, which would support functional upgrading and building more integrated industry structures; as well as final products, which would enable intersectoral upgrading and entering new product lines.

These mechanisms, which equally apply to foreign and domestic markets, sharply increase the number of interactions between firms and customers, even if these interactions are not always evident to customers. Firms that own the data from these interactions and possess the required analytical capabilities can identify the heterogeneity of demand patterns both between and across foreign and domestic markets and customize the characteristics of their products accordingly. This allows for more personalized advertising and distribution campaigns that go beyond traditional marketing, reducing marketing costs while reaching out to more potential customers, and increasing the effectiveness of advertising expenditure.

The economic benefits of owning data in terms of transforming it into a profitable asset increase with the volume of data. This gives an advantage to first movers. They are most easily able to scale up their initial investment in data intelligence and analytics, thereby increasing the value of their data and associated knowledge base. The ensuing increased productivity and profitability also provide additional finance to acquire complementary databases or software and exploit associated spillovers and synergies. Such acquisitions may include start-ups, whose activities may even have been deliberately targeted at being complementary, rather than at being genuinely innovative and providing a substitute for incumbent firms. Such cumulative processes aggravate already existing tendencies towards concentration and centralization. When this occurs, genuine technological progress and competitive pressure may be reduced. Equally significant, the high profitability of incumbent firms also allows for rent-seeking and spending on regulation and lobbying, such as for reduced tax bills or for "blocking" patents or copyrights that keep potential rivals out.[9]

Such first-mover advantages underline both the urgency with which developing countries need to act and the difficulties and associated policy challenges related to their engaging in activities in the post-production segment of digitized value chains.

The greater role of demand-related post-production variables in the manufacturing process may be further enhanced in the pre-production segment, as the new digital technologies tend to make design more flexible and reduce its cost. Digital design simulation reduces the number of work hours required to create new goods.[10] It may also reduce the expertise needed to design goods. The rise in flexibility and the decline in cost of pre-production activities may be further enhanced by additive manufacturing (e.g. Ubhaykar, 2015). It compresses the development cycle of products that may subsequently be mass-produced based on traditional technology and infrastructure (e.g. UNCTAD, 2017b), or be chosen for more customized production based on digital technologies.

Using digital technologies in the pre-production phase could at least partly help to compensate developing countries for the lack of skilled designers and an established machinery industry.

It is clear that some developing countries have already moved some way towards digitalization in production. This could provide a stepping stone for additional broader engagement also in the pre- and post-production segments of the manufacturing process where returns are traditionally higher. However, whether this happens depends on the way value chains are governed.

(b) Potential impact on governance and distributional outcomes

Corporate governance involves a mixture of coordination, contracts and control. In the context of value chains, it determines how and where lead firms organize production patterns across a dispersed set of suppliers and tasks, how transactions are made between these contracting parties, the marketing of the final good or service and how the value generated from the final sale of the product or service is distributed across the different actors operating within the chain.

Value chains have a long history, particularly in the exploitation of natural resources (Hopkins and Wallerstein, 1986). While commodity chains were often constructed on the back of the political power and authority of a colonizing state, the economic power of the lead firm in these chains traditionally reflected a combination of technological know-how, scale economies and restrictive business practices which enabled a degree of monopoly control over the extraction, processing and/or distribution of a specific commodity and monopsony control over suppliers of support services, allowing the lead firm to make above-normal profits; Standard Oil is the emblematic case (Lewis, 1881). As these commodity chains involved more and more developing countries, their income losses from rent extraction through monopoly pricing was often compounded by a movement in the terms of trade in favour of manufacturing exporters (Prebisch, 1949).

More recently, as value chains have entered (and reconfigured) manufacturing sectors and as developing countries have provided more links in these chains, the international division of labour has become more fragmented, employment relations more fractured and governance arrangements more complex. At the same time, large corporations have shifted their attention to "core competencies" and increasingly employed a range of financial instruments, such as share buy-backs and mergers and acquisitions, to increase their "value" while cost containment, through outsourcing, work intensification, segmented labour markets and insecure supplier contracts, has become the principal strategy in managing the production process. These pressures have contributed to, and been reinforced by, growing market concentration across many sectors of the economy which, together with a tighter control over key strategic assets such as intellectual property, has allowed for a rise in super profits through rent-seeking behaviour. These changes in corporate governance have been readily extended to the international level through the working of GVCs.

The interplay of these micro- and macro changes has, in turn, been associated with steadily declining labour shares in national income, albeit with variations across countries, sectors and firms. In this regard, the spread of GVCs over the last 30 years has reinforced an already established trend of weakening bargaining power for labour by augmenting the possibilities of lead firms outsourcing inputs to suppliers operating in highly competitive markets, while strengthening control over strategic assets in the pre- and post-production stages that allows them to capture rents (Milberg and Winkler, 2013).

Digitalization is likely to alter further the governance structure of value chains. On some assessments, digitalization may reduce the control by lead firms and shift relationships away from captive towards more relational and modular types of governance; as discussed earlier, increased possibilities for product customization could move the control of value chains towards customers whose specific desires regarding the functionality and features of products may guide design and production patterns. But reaping these benefits crucially depends on a supplier's digital capabilities. This is because digitalization also satisfies demands for more granular financial and managerial control and contributes to greater flexibility for lead firms in choosing among an increased number of suppliers. This could increase the risk for producers that lack digital capabilities to be marginalized or excluded.[11]

Examining the manufacturing process as a "pipeline" that creates value by coordinating a linear series of activities where inputs enter at one end of the chain and undergo a series of steps that transform them into more valuable products that exit as outputs at the other end of the chain assumes a benign view of the lead firm and downplays the hierarchical division of labour behind the smile curve as well as changes in corporate control more generally over the past three decades. As such, it does not give the full picture of the likely impact of digitization on manufacturing processes.

The lead firm in most GVCs is basically a cosmopolitan extension of a large national firm. As discussed in *TDR 2017*, corporate governance, beginning at the national level, has – over recent decades – been transformed through a combination of financialization, neo-liberal ideology and technological advances in ICTs. As a result, vertically integrated firms have focused on core competencies, outsourcing many tasks (particularly in the production stage) that were previously undertaken in-house. This has coincided with and further encouraged a very different approach to value creation and distribution focused on shareholder value and rent-seeking behaviour.

To assess changes in distribution, it may be useful to disaggregate total value added in manufactured output into the contributions by the four functions that characterize labour activities in the manufacturing process (management, marketing, R&D and fabrication), taking the capital share as a residual, and calculating the domestic shares of the contribution of each of these factors.[12] Doing so indicates that the domestic share of total value added declined in all countries shown in figure 3.3, except China. This reflects the well-known process of globalization during the period 2000–2014, as well as the reduction in the import-intensity of manufacturing in China during those years. Moreover, the domestic share of labour income in total value added declined in almost all the countries shown in the figure, while China experienced a sizeable increase in this share.

The evidence for the domestic part of the capital share is more mixed, but it increased sizably in the United States and to a lesser extent in Mexico, while it declined in Brazil and China.[13] It should be noted that evidence on the domestic part of the capital share is affected by transfer pricing and related practices, which cause returns on capital to show up in low-tax jurisdictions rather than the country where such returns originate. Regarding the four business functions, the domestic share of fabrication declined in all countries, except Canada and China, with the

FIGURE 3.3 Domestic value added shares in manufactured products finalized in an economy, selected economies, 2000 and 2014
(Percentages)

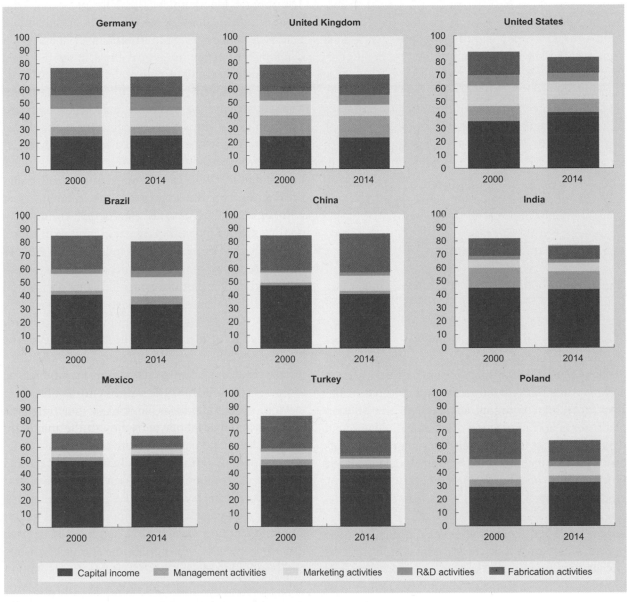

Source: UNCTAD secretariat calculations, based on de Vries, 2018.

latter country's share attaining almost 30 per cent of total value added in 2014. The evidence regarding changes for management and marketing activities is mixed, but the domestic share of R&D activities in total value added increased in most developed economies, and particularly in Japan. Developed economies also recorded the highest domestic shares of R&D activities in total value added. But there is also an increase in this share, although from relatively low levels, in a range of developing countries, notably Brazil, China, Indonesia, Mexico, Republic of Korea and Taiwan Province of China. This could be taken

to indicate a general increase in the importance of the pre-production segment of the manufacturing process across many countries in the world economy.

A second way in which digitization is impacting distribution is through the emergence of platform monopolies, in which the key strategic asset of the lead firm is control and use of digitized data to organize and mediate transactions between the various actors in the chain, combined with the capability of expanding the size of such ecosystems in a circular, feedback-driven process (e.g. Van Alstyne

FIGURE 3.4 Types of digital platforms

Types of digital platforms		
Category	Type	Examples
Transaction	Market places	Amazon, eBay, Alibaba, MercadoLibre, Google Play, Apple App Store, Airbnb, Uber, Ticketmaster, PayPal, PayU
	Social media and content	Facebook, Twitter, YouTube, Instagram
	Internet search services	Google, Yahoo, Bing, Baidu
	Digital advertising	AdWords, DoubleClick, Tradedoubler
	Funding	Kickstarter, Crowdcube, Startnext
	Talent management	LinkedIn, Monster, CareerBuilder
Innovation	Mobile ecosystems and apps	Android, iOS
	Industrial digital platforms	Google Cloud Platform, IBM Watson IoT, ThingWorx
	Participation and open services	Citadel, CitySDK, Busan Smart City Platform

Source: Adapted from United Nations and ECLAC, 2018.

et al., 2016). Digital platforms are technology-enabled operations that facilitate interaction and exchange between various groups, built on a shared and interoperable infrastructure and driven by data. They operate over a range of activities. Transaction platforms enable interaction between individuals who would otherwise not find each other; innovation platforms provide technological building blocks enabling innovators to develop complementary services or products. Figure 3.4 provides a typology of platforms.

Among marketplaces, there can be peer-to-peer platforms (mainly between private individuals); business-to-consumer platforms, where sellers are firms; and business-to-business platforms, where both buyers and sellers are firms. Marketplaces rely on varied business models. Some act as sellers or resellers of goods and services; some charge a commission for each transaction; some are financed by joining fees. As they collect large amounts of personal and non-personal data, they can increase their incomes by using big-data analytics, or sell these data to others. The largest and most powerful marketplaces are mostly based in the United States, with a few in China. E-commerce platforms have grown steadily and the largest ones have vast numbers of users, such as Alibaba Tmall (400 million but confined to China), Amazon (304 million users globally) and eBay (167 million users worldwide). Similarly, the main services marketplaces are based in the United States or Asia, and deal mainly in finance, housing

and accommodation, logistics and transport. Seven out of 11 of the largest payment platforms are based in the United States and the rest in the European Union. The top four marketplaces that have received the largest investor funding include three in the United States (Uber, Airbnb and Lyft) and one in China (DiDi Chuxing). The domination of the United States is also evident in social media and content platforms, with the top seven such firms all originating there. The only exception is China, which has been able to expand its own firms by preventing the global firms from entering its market. Similarly, Internet search platforms are dominated by United States firms, other than Baidu in China and Yandex from the Russian Federation. This is also true for mobile ecosystems, with three United States-based firms completely dominant: Android with 81.7 per cent market share, iOS with 17.9 per cent and Windows with 0.3 per cent of the global market. Internet of Things (IoT) or industrial digital platforms are similarly dominated by companies from the United States and Europe.

The structure of these emerging digital ecosystems is based on data ownership and management, including the reuse or sharing of data for more products or more functions within the manufacturing process. Data, like ideas and knowledge more generally, and unlike most physical private goods and services, are non-rivalrous and can be reproduced at no or minimal cost, although they are excludable and can thus be a source of monopoly. This means that a digital ecosystem's primary source of value is the size of the ecosystem itself. An expanding system could facilitate the entry of new participants. However, firms involved in the production of non-rivalrous goods will tend to seek ways to build fences around them in an attempt to artificially create a degree of scarcity and, in the process, generate rents from the assets they own.

Unlike a true public good, exclusion is possible in the digital ecosystem through a combination of strengthened property rights, scale effects, first-mover advantages, market power and other anticompetitive practices. Data intelligence, which is created by use of algorithms on big data, has helped lead firms to develop unique products and services, extend and coordinate complex supply chains and underpin the world of algorithmic decision-making. The "network effects" through which everyone gains by sharing the use of a service or resource have given rise to "demand-side economies of scale" which allows the largest firm in an industry to increase and lock-in its

FIGURE 3.5 Geographic location of big tech companies, selected companies

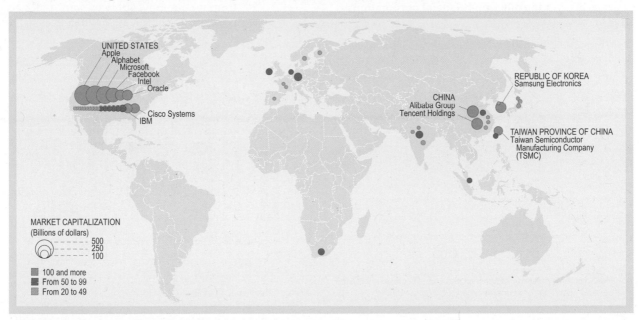

Source: UNCTAD database of consolidated financial statements, based on Thomson Reuters Worldscope.

attractiveness to consumers and gain market share. This makes it almost impossible for competitors with declining shares to remain attractive or competitive (Foster and McChesney, 2011).

The raising of legal and financial barriers as well as more informal mechanisms of control by large firms with monopolistic, or near monopolistic, powers has already opened up new avenues of profit-making in the digital economy. The resulting winner-takes-most environment allows lead firms to squeeze suppliers, capture rents created elsewhere in the economy, acquire competitors, and gouge the public purse even when it is reducing prices for consumers.

This environment imparts a strong spatial dimension to the distribution of rewards along the value chain. As Hymer, Prebisch and others warned in a pre-digital era, the rise of headquarter firms threatened a further concentration of economic power around heightened flows of information and capital which raised the danger, already visible from the asymmetries in trade and technology flows, of "the drainage of income through the transnational corporations, as they came to play a more and more active part in industrialization, often sheltering behind an exaggerated degree of protection" (Prebisch, 1986: 198). This danger seems likely to be compounded in the digital era and there is already some limited evidence that while markups have been rising significantly for larger

firms in advanced economies this is not the case for firms from developing countries.

A simple picture of a North–South digital divide is, however, complicated by polarization and informalization pressures within the advanced countries themselves. These are, as noted earlier, creating dual economic structures, by the increasing dominance of United States corporations over European and Japanese rivals, as well as by the emergence of global companies from developing Asia (figure 3.5).

Still, the drive for scale in the digital world is ubiquitous; "big tech" companies are not only bigger than ever but also increasingly bigger than most "traditional" TNCs, assuming a growing presence in the top 100 global companies in the world. Figure 3.6 shows how the shares of large ICT companies in assets, sales, profits and market capitalization, which fell (albeit slightly) after the bursting of the dot-com bubble in 2000, have been rising after the global financial crisis.[14] By 2015, the 17 ICT companies that were in the top 100 TNCs globally accounted for a quarter of the total market capitalization of these top companies and 18 per cent of their profits, even though their sales revenues amounted to less than 10 per cent of the total.

In addition, there has been significant increase in concentration within the ICT industry, as evident

FIGURE 3.6 Share of "big tech companies" in top 100 non-financial corporations
(Percentages)

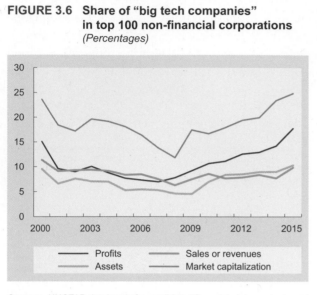

Source: UNCTAD database of consolidated financial statements, based on Thomson Reuters Worldscope.

FIGURE 3.7 Shares of top 1 per cent companies from technology, software and IT-services sector, 1996–2015
(Percentages)

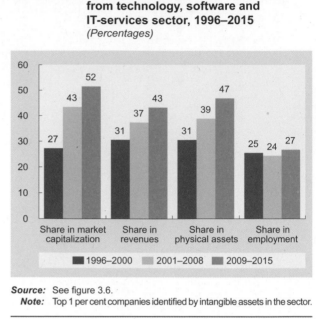

Source: See figure 3.6.
Note: Top 1 per cent companies identified by intangible assets in the sector.

from figure 3.7. Within all the ICT companies in the database, the top 1 per cent accounted for increasing and dominant shares of physical assets, revenues and market capitalization – but nearly stagnant shares of employment.

The emergence of some big ICT companies from the Global South, primarily in East Asia (including, most recently, China), indicates that successful late industrialization experiences, can give rise to large firms able to exploit new opportunities in the digital economy. These newcomers not only have access to data but the capability to translate them into economically meaningful knowledge and can target potentially overlapping customer bases with distinctive new offerings, such as links to local innovators, designers or producers that may provide better

customized products and create effective competition to an established ecosystem.

Whether such competition becomes a more general feature depends on legal and policy frameworks that determine the extent to which lead firms in digital ecosystems must share some of their data or the value that accrues from data ownership. More generally, the capacity of the different stakeholders along a value chain to appropriate the income generated is also circumscribed by rules and regulations from actors external to the chain, mainly national governments and supranational institutions. Such rules and regulations can mediate value sharing between customers and platforms that own data, on the one hand, and incumbent platforms and competitor platforms, on the other hand, as further discussed in the next section.

C. Adapting economic policies to a digital world

While new digital technologies may provide additional impetus to income generation in developing countries, they also pose challenges because of the potential for greater monopoly control in some areas and the distributional implications of corporate rent-seeking. Experiencing the benefits of moving towards a digital world is obviously contingent upon the appropriate physical and digital infrastructure as well as digital capabilities, but additional policy

frameworks and regulations are also necessary to ensure fair and equitable sharing of these benefits. While the precise policy strategy will be distinct for each country and reflect its specific conditions, there are some broad principles that can provide a framework. International cooperation, including in the form of South–South cooperation, is particularly relevant for overcoming digital divides and addressing fiscal and regulatory issues.

1. Facilitating integration into a digital economy and ensuring an equitable sharing of its benefits

(a) Digital infrastructure and digital capabilities: Basic conditions for integrating into a digital world

A digital economy is built on digital infrastructure and digital capabilities. Three broad interrelated components of digital infrastructure which can be identified are networks, software and data; and digital capabilities are needed to use them effectively. Over the past two decades, countries have been steadily building their digital networks (i.e. ICT and broadband infrastructure) as the principal tool for collecting and transmitting information flows. This ICT infrastructure forms the base of the digital infrastructure as it provides Internet access to the population, while broadband infrastructure helps in delivering large amounts of data at a much faster speed. Much of the initial work behind ICT infrastructure tends to be undertaken with public funding and through various forms of public and private collaboration to improve network connectivity, affordability and accessibility. Subsequently, Internet access and connectivity through broadband have become dominated by private Internet service providers. However, by the late 2000s it became clear that wired broadband connectivity especially to remote areas was not adequately served by private companies. Since the universality of broadband infrastructure is a prerequisite for a more equitable digital economy, this points to the need for enhanced public investment in broadband infrastructure in most developing countries.

The second interrelated component of digital infrastructure is software and its use across a full range of economic activities, with increasing emphasis on access through a cloud computing infrastructure. Cloud computing provides computing services remotely as a general utility to Internet users. It can be just sterile infrastructure like storage, means for processing, networking and servers (infrastructure as a service, or IaaS), or also provide operating software and platforms for building custom applications (platform as a service, or PaaS) or consist of remote provision and management of the whole range of computing needs right up to fully functional applications and data-based processes (software as a service or SaaS). Cloud computing therefore combines software power with network power allowing quick, wide and deep global spread of relatively inexpensive cutting-edge technologies. However, cloud applications provide its owners immense power, as dependencies increase from IaaS through PaaS to SaaS models: for example, global cloud applications have provided Google, Facebook, Uber, etc. the power to become the virtual control panels for reorganizing entire sectors. This creates a policy challenge for developing countries whose national antitrust legislation may not be adequate to address the cross-sectoral market power increasingly held by such multinational companies.

The third interrelated component of digital infrastructure is data, which provide platforms with the raw material they need to operate. This is, arguably, the most important component of the digital infrastructure, providing the basis for generating huge profit streams and potentially changing the relative positions of countries in terms of their shares in global production, consumption, investment and international trade. Many observers have termed "data" the "new oil", not only because they have to be extracted and processed from an initially unrefined state, but because processed data can also give monopolistic powers to its owners. Indeed, because (unlike oil) data are not a finite resource, the ability to exclude competitors from access can generate even more monopoly power and rent-seeking behaviour.

The challenges faced by developing countries in ensuring such digital infrastructure are evident from the still large gaps in most developing countries. Fixed broadband subscriptions in developing countries are still less than one quarter of the number in developed countries in per capita terms, while in least developed countries (LDCs) the number has barely increased and the penetration rate is less than 1 per cent. Mobile-broadband subscriptions were around 78 per 100 population in the United States and Europe in 2016, but only 20 per cent in Africa. Two thirds of the population of developing countries – around 4 billion people – remained offline in 2015/16.[15] Mobile-broadband subscriptions have grown more rapidly in the developing world recently, but figure 3.8 shows that they are still only around half of the per capita levels in the developed world. One reason for this is the high price: figure 3.9 indicates that despite recent declines, broadband prices in the developing world are on average over eight times those in developed countries (and over 20 times in LDCs) when seen in relation to per capita income. While Internet access has increased everywhere, the coverage in Europe is nearly four times that of Africa (figure 3.10).

FIGURE 3.8 Active mobile-broadband subscriptions, 2007–2017
(Per 100 inhabitants)

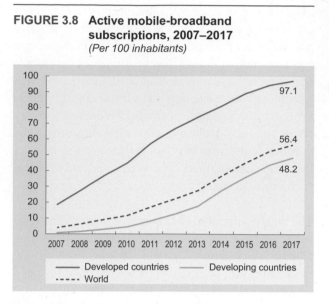

Source: ITU, ICT Facts & Figures, The world in 2017. Available at: https://www.itu.int/en/ITU-D/Statistics/Documents/facts/ICTFactsFigures2017.pdf.

FIGURE 3.10 Individuals using the Internet, 2005–2017
(Individuals per 100 inhabitants)

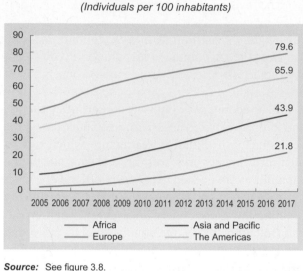

Source: See figure 3.8.

FIGURE 3.9 Mobile-broadband prices, 2013 and 2016
(Percentages of gross national income per capita)

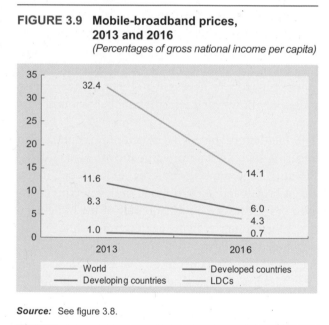

Source: See figure 3.8.

Broadband speed is a crucial determinant of the potential for digitalization and related business, and it remains relatively much slower in most developing countries. Reducing these large infrastructure deficits is a huge task that will require large investments.

In addition to digital infrastructure, building a digital economy obviously requires the presence of supportive physical infrastructure and institutions, of which continuous power connections and access to banking and financial institutions are obviously crucial. While these are taken for granted as necessary preconditions for other digital policies in advanced economies, they are still significantly underprovided in much of the developing world, and not addressing these issues would further add to digital divides. Similarly, the digital capabilities discussed below also require minimum levels of education across the society. In their absence, much of the talk of digital "leapfrogging" is highly exaggerated.

Digital capabilities are also referred to as digital skills or digital competence. They cover information management, collaboration, communication and sharing, creation of content and knowledge, ethics and responsibility, evaluation and problem solving, and technical operations (Ferrari, 2012). ILO-ITU (2017) describe four kinds of such skills: (1) basic digital skills, related to the effective use of technology, including web research, online communications, etc.; (2) soft skills necessary to ensure collaborative work among professionals; (3) advanced digital skills related to technology development such as coding, software and app development, etc.; and (4) digital entrepreneurship which includes digital skills required by entrepreneurs for strategic planning, market research, business analysis, etc. Due to rapid advancement of digital technologies there is a growing "digital skill gap" which is being felt by both developed and developing countries. To develop digital skills, efforts have to be made by the developing countries at various levels: introducing digital education in schools and universities, upskilling the digital skills of the existing workforce, running special basic and advanced skill development programmes for the youth and older persons, including digital skill training programmes in existing professional development programmes, and providing financial support to develop digital entrepreneurship. All these should ideally be part of an overall national strategy of building digital skills for the twenty-first century.

(b) Industrial policy

Successive *Trade and Development Report*s have consistently argued for proactive industrial policies to manage structural transformation; *TDR 2016* concluded that an "active" industrial policy is key to building the backward and forward linkages that can sustain productivity growth and rising living standards through a process of structural transformation. Two elements of the changing dynamics of the world economy may be crucial for the effectiveness of industrial policies: (1) the move towards a digital economy and its associated increased systemic interactions between innovation, education, production and services activities; and (2) the increased weight of developing countries in the global economy, which may allow for a rebalancing of external and domestic markets as destinations of developing countries' production activities.

The previous discussion of the infrastructural needs of the digital economy has already specified the supply-side interventions that are necessary parts of contemporary industrial policies, to ensure bandwidth and connectivity, as well as universalizing Internet access and other measures. Similarly, the development of digital capabilities also requires public investment and government support, for example in digital education and training, ensuring access to banking systems and credit, and so on (Vijayabaskar and Suresh Babu, 2014). In addition, demand-driven policy instruments can be key determinants for the creation of demand for domestic innovation and the potential creation of entirely new sectors (Saviotti and Pyka, 2013; Salazar-Xirinachs et al., 2014; Santiago and Weiss, 2018). A government can do this in several ways: (1) as a direct consumer and investor, it can act through government procurement; (2) as a regulator, it can affect competition, and hence the level of demand enjoyed by individual firms, by determining the number of licences for certain activities or by imposing certain industry standards; (3) it can steer the direction of innovation by taking the lead in undertaking innovation activities or incentivize

firms and other players to form research consortia; (4) it can promote private demand, such as through tax incentives and subsidies, to stimulate investment and innovations by domestic firms; (5) as a knowledge broker, it can link innovators, producers and consumers (for more detailed discussion, see Elder, 2013; and Chang and Andreoni, 2016).

Industrial policies for digitalization must seek to exploit the potential of using new technologies for transformational purposes to create and shape new products and new markets, as well as to compensate for the job destruction that the application of such technologies may cause. The strong synergies between supply-side and demand-side pressures in establishing a "digital virtuous circle" (of emerging digital sectors and firms, rising investment and innovation, accelerating productivity growth and rising incomes, leading to expanding markets) speaks to the need for moving towards a mission-oriented industrial policy in a digital world.

This involves using more dynamic metrics in policy evaluation to assess the degree to which public investment can open and transform sectoral and technological landscapes. Moreover, governments could engage in more than just helping to fund new technology. They could become investors of first resort regarding digital innovation by investing directly in corporate equity (Mazzucato, 2017). One way of doing so would be for governments to acquire stakes in the commercialization of successful new technologies by establishing professionally managed public funds, which would take equity stakes in new technologies, financed through bond issues in financial markets, and which would share its profits with citizens in the form of a social innovation dividend (Rodrik, 2015). In this way, the fruits of high productivity growth from technological change could spread more widely and fuel aggregate demand also for output from lower productivity sectors, thereby increasing employment and average productivity at the same time. Empirical evidence suggests that companies with large shareholders, such as publicly held companies and sovereign wealth funds, tend to invest more in innovation than companies with dispersed equity ownership (Edmans, 2014). This is because such shareholders typically base buying and selling decisions on the company's long-term prospects, including those built on intangible capital. Such investment could ensure long-term thinking across the digital ecosystem and enable benefits from the spillovers and synergies that intangible assets may generate across companies (Haskel and Westlake, 2018).

A digital strategy must also adapt to the changed structure of finance for investment in the digital economy. Contrary to tangible assets – such as buildings, machines or particular plots of land – intangible assets, such as data, software, market analysis, organizational design, patents, copyrights and the like, tend to be unique or most valuable within narrowly defined specific contexts. Therefore, they are difficult to sell or value as collateral. This makes it cumbersome to finance investment in intangibles from traditional sources, such as bank loans and marketable bonds, and, in addition to private equity finance, increases the role of retained profits as a source of finance for investment. However, the profit–investment nexus has seriously weakened over the past two decades, especially through the increased emphasis that corporate managers have given to norms, metrics and incentives from the financial sector, increasing the distribution of dividends, buy-backs of stocks and other speculative financial operations in the process. As a result, supporting investment in intangibles may well imply an increased role for development banks as sources of finance or of specialized financing vehicles – such as the guidance funds attached to the new industrial strategy of the Government of China (Kozul-Wright and Poon, 2017) – as well as policy measures designed to strengthen the profit–investment nexus, such as changing financial reporting requirements or imposing restrictions on share buy-backs and dividend payments when investment is low, or preferential fiscal treatment of reinvested profits (e.g. *TDR 2008* and *TDR 2016*).

In addition, regulatory measures (discussed in more detail below) such as data localization requirements, Internet filtering and technology transfer requirements (i.e. disclosure of source code) can serve as important industrial policy tools to promote domestic digital firms and allow them to catch up with the leading multinational firms.

(c) Innovation policy

The acquisition and adoption of technology, as well as its adaptation to local circumstances, is a costly process. To speed up and support this process, developing countries were advised to ensure appropriate absorptive capacity, including in terms of the skill level of the labour force and institutional structures to facilitate technology development and transfer

(see also section B.1 above). Recently, proactive innovation policy has also found a prominent place on the agenda of developing country policymakers.[16] One reason for this is the improvement in some developing countries' technological capabilities and technology-related institutions, reflected in higher educational attainments and enhanced R&D expenditure and patent filings. The World Intellectual Property Organization's global innovation index shows that a few developing countries have caught up on certain innovation variables, even though significant divides remain (Cornell University et al., 2017; UNCTAD, 2018a). An additional element of the changed environment that is of particular importance in the context of digitalization regards the increased spending power and emerging middle classes in some developing countries, particularly in Asia, which is creating new markets and thereby generating new potential for innovation to meet this growing demand. As a result, developing countries are being seen not merely as recipients but also as sources of innovation, particularly innovations aimed at developing customized goods and services catering to specific markets at relatively low cost.[17]

Such customization of new digital technologies can be related to the idea of frugal innovations, which are those that provide "new functionality at lower cost" (Leliveld and Knorringa, 2018: 1; see also Zeschky et al., 2014).[18] These rely on developing country residents both as consumers and producers, by focusing on the specific opportunities for innovation, production and consumption in a particular geographical location. Unconstrained by developed country demands, developing country firms can benefit from local cost advantages, better local sourcing conditions and better knowledge about local circumstances, preferences and needs. They can use these elements to design goods and services with new functionalities and features that are customized for local firms and for local low-income or middle-class consumers. Such local innovations also help to reduce foreign exchange outflows by shifting domestic demand towards domestically produced customized goods. Digitalization may provide specific opportunities for frugal innovation by developing country firms because they tend to reduce the cost of innovation.

Similarly, the digital economy may also open up new possibilities for more reverse innovation, which refers to ideas, technologies and products that may be generated in developing countries but are subsequently used by firms from developed countries

(Immelt et al., 2009; Zeschky et al., 2014). These do not have to be "frugal" but can include sophisticated and expensive products and processes. Reverse innovation may be done by affiliates of developed country firms that face sluggish overall demand in their head firm's home markets and, as a reflection of growing distributional inequality, a shift in the composition of this demand towards simpler and cheaper products. It may also be part of the internationalization strategy of local firms in some large developing countries that initially respond to growing domestic demand, but later attempt to tap into lower-income segments of developed country markets. Such reverse innovation tends to achieve economies of both scope and scale by enabling customized production for smaller domestic and larger foreign markets.

Such innovations, however, increasingly rely on big-data analytics and other digital technologies. Greater interaction between innovators, producers and consumers is important from the supply side for design and production decisions, while product-specific marketing and distribution based on digital media could help customers in their spending decisions. In developing countries, using these digital devices could allow reducing or even removing the long chains of intermediation that often characterize user–producer interactions (e.g. Foster and Heeks, 2014), thereby making them both more flexible and more cost-effective. Obviously, this is only possible if firms and innovators within developing countries have access to such data that are typically collected by multinational platform companies. Therefore, policies designed to prevent monopolistic control and to ensure that small and medium producers and potential innovators have affordable access to such data, are obviously important.

While intellectual property rights (IPR) rules do constrain technology transfer, the more so as these have been tightened in the context of free trade agreements, some recent success stories suggest that it is still possible to overcome the obstacles that they pose.[19] Cross-industry surveys have led some observers to conclude that design-related IPR are considered relatively ineffective, as also illustrated by firms' often significant additional investment in brand image and other reputational assets intended to increase value capture from their designs (Filitz et al., 2015).[20] Given that digitalization may bring about entirely new products, as well as enable new functionalities and ways of use, it would appear that existing IPR protection still leaves some scope for active design-oriented innovation policy in developing countries. Nevertheless, maintaining this scope will also require containing practices such as interlocking patents and patent trolls, which have become important features of competition mainly in the smartphone and pharmaceutical industries (see also *TDR 2017* and section C.1.d below).

Moving towards a digital world may also broaden the scope for developing country firms to engage in cross-licensing arrangements with developed country firms. At least some of these firms may privilege protecting their designs through trade secrets but others could still be interested in licensing, and thereby disclosing, their designs to developing countries. They could wish to do so in exchange for innovative design features regarding functionality and ease of use that firms in developing countries have developed for their domestic customers, which could also appeal to the lower-income groups in developed countries. IPR owners may also wish to create new revenue streams by commercializing template CAD files or software that purchasers can subsequently customize.

To boost digital skills and capabilities, many developing countries are encouraging digital start-ups. Digital start-ups differ from IT start-ups that provide core technical services in the form of SaaS, in that the former aim at digitally transforming specific sectoral services like education, health, transport, etc. (Singh, 2017). These digital start-ups represent a new wave of entrepreneurship, which, if appropriately harnessed, could usher in some highly efficient digital solutions as well as boost digital capacities, becoming a primary source of digital innovation in a country. However, instead of being used for expanding digital technology frontiers in a country, these innovations are increasingly being bought and used by big tech companies to expand their operations. For example, AI start-up acquisitions increased by 155 per cent in the period 2015–2017, rising from 45 to 115. The digital start-ups therefore need to be supported by national policies and regulatory measures in order to nurture and advance national digitization efforts.

In addition to a sizeable increase in R&D spending and the size of in-house design departments, enhanced skilled labour migration in the form of both intellectual returnees and skilled expatriates from developed countries could provide substantial support to developing countries' more active innovation policy. While returnees appear to have played a crucial role for example in the development of the photovoltaic industry in China (Luo et al., 2017), expatiates have been instrumental in creating the designs for automobile production in developing countries such as Brazil, India and Morocco, as well as in Romania. There, designers have focused on the functionalities and price ranges that would appeal to customers in developing countries, as well as to relatively low-income customers in developed countries (Midler et al., 2017).

(d) Regulatory policies

The digital economy creates significant new regulatory policy challenges because the network effects and economies of scale associated with digitalization can cause rising inequality and generate barriers to market entry. As noted above, first-mover advantages in the form of benefits from controlling and scaling large volumes of data tend to create a few highly profitable large firms and "winner-takes-most" concerns. Such advantages can also become self-reinforcing, as data gleaned from one market can facilitate entering new markets or even new business lines. The resulting increases in market concentration may sizeably augment the financial power of a few leading firms and cause increased rent-seeking, anticompetitive practices and attempts to block actual or potential competitors. This means that established competition and antitrust policies may be unsuited to the digital economy.[21]

The overwhelming control over digital platforms by a few firms, mostly based in the United States, the United Kingdom and some other European countries, points to the need for active consideration of policies to prevent anticompetitive behaviour by such firms, as well as potential misuse of data that are collected in the process. It also provides an inkling of the difficulties associated with developing countries wishing to break into these areas. Even when innovators based in developing countries come up with new products and processes, they may be unable to reap the benefits in an oligopolistic environment, or may be taken over by the dominant firms. There are other ways in which such digital platform companies can slip through regulatory cracks. The concerns about lack of labour standards associated with supposedly peer-to-peer platforms that are effectively business-to-consumer platforms (such as Uber) are now well known. But for developing countries an additional concern could be the concentration of profits generated in such platforms by the companies that are largely based in the North. Such super-platforms

(companies that dominate the digital landscape like Google, Apple and Amazon) are increasingly using algorithms based on big data to drive away competition. According to Ezrachi and Stucke (2016) algorithms can foster tacit collusions when each firm programs its algorithm with a strategy to maximize profits. The algorithms monitor the price changes and swiftly react to competitor's price reduction, similarly it also follows price increases when sustainable, such as when others follow in a timely manner, so that all competitors raise prices and profit together leading to an outcome not much different from that arrived by collusion. But unlike humans, the computers do not fear detection! Further, these computers have no specific commands that may trigger collusion. This makes it extremely difficult to hold the super-platforms liable for the pricing decisions of their self-learning algorithms, which may transfer wealth from consumers to sellers.

Although the super-platforms compete, they can also become "frenemies" to maximize joint profits and drive away competition.[22] This interdependence of super-platforms can severely hinder innovations as companies know that they cannot effectively reach consumers unless admitted by super-platforms. On the other hand, platforms need an ecosystem to flourish and contest other platforms. A platform will therefore attract independent application developers to build solutions to attract users. More users in turn will attract more application developers and this feedback loop makes the platform grow bigger, with the subsequent economies of scale further increasing its market power. The bigger the super-platform, the greater will be the network effects and more difficult it will become for competitive forces to displace it.

These growing collusions and anticompetitive practices of the super-platforms pose new challenges for competition and antitrust policies. AI determines independently the means to optimize profits and leads to an anticompetitive outcome, with no evidence of any anticompetitive agreement or intent. Further, the new market dynamism injected by technological advances leads to a transfer of wealth from consumers to super-platforms with consumers being unaware of the underlying mechanisms; it eradicates competition from small firms through acquisitions or exclusionary practices; and it promotes network effects to grow and assimilate further market power.

Competition agencies need to understand the changing contours of competition and the underlying market mechanisms that help the "big" get "bigger", and to prepare themselves for regulating these super-platforms. This will require new tools and regulations as the existing language of antitrust laws may not allow the regulators to fully address the growing challenges. This is better understood in the developed countries, where the enforcers are intervening in some scenarios to regulate the activities of super-platforms.[23] However, most developing countries are yet to understand and adapt their regulations to address the anticompetitive practices of the super-platforms.

While anticompetitive practices have traditionally been addressed by antitrust and competition policies, the goal of these policies has increasingly shifted from a concern with market structure and market behaviour to an emphasis on maximizing consumer welfare.[24] Moreover, the remit of these policies has generally been confined to national boundaries. Recent concerns regarding regulation of the digital economy have also focused on consumer welfare, particularly regarding the preservation of data privacy[25] and Internet security, as well as avoidance of undesirable changes in how societies function. By contrast, the extraction of economic rent has received insufficient attention from policymakers despite its central role in the functioning of hyperglobalization.

One form of rent extraction is aggressive tax optimization by locating a firm's tax base in low-tax jurisdictions.[26] According to estimates by Tørsløv et al. (2018: 2), "close to 40% of multinational profits are artificially shifted to tax havens in 2015". The digital economy may exacerbate tax-base erosion because a multinational enterprise (MNE) whose main assets are intellectual property or data can easily offshore such assets. While the OECD's Base Erosion and Profit Shifting (BEPS) initiative has taken some useful steps towards safeguarding fiscal revenues, critics have called for wider and more inclusive discussion and argue that the reform proposals "have failed to ensure that profits are taxed where activities take place …, in favour of where the companies that receive income are based", mainly because "the revisions to transfer pricing rules continue to cling to the underlying fiction that a MNE consists of separate independent entities transacting with each other at arm's length" (ICRICT, 2018: 5).[27]

Taxing where activities are done rather than where firms declare as being headquartered redistributes rents and can help build the tax bases of developing countries. But it does not tackle the anticompetitive features that give rise to rents. Price-based measures of competition may well prove inadequate in a digital world where control and use of data is of paramount importance, where competition strategies and pricing decisions may be determined by the algorithms of machine learning, and where consumers often receive services in exchange for data, at zero nominal prices.[28] Established competition policy assumes that actors pursue a strategy focused on profit maximization whereby unjustifiably high prices are judged as harming consumer welfare. In a digital economy, by contrast, actors tend to privilege scale and market-share strategies. This may involve slashing prices, even to the extent of being willing to sustain losses, and/or increasing spending to expand capacity, including by acquiring firms and expanding into multiple business lines.

In the case of digital platforms, scale and market-share strategies may involve cross-subsidization, which implies that while one side of the platform benefits from a lower cost of service or free access, the other side pays higher costs for access. For example, Facebook services may be provided free of cost to the users, but the advertisers pay higher costs to access the users. Increasingly platforms start to organize the markets. These digital platforms have natural monopolistic tendencies which emerge from large economies of scale, large network effects and control over sectors' data which leads to the creation of private digital intelligence leading in turn to technological and institutional barriers to new entry. This results in very high asymmetry of information between the platform owner and all other actors in a sector which is then used to extract profit both from the sellers and the buyers (e.g. Singh, 2017).

Although the growing monopolistic powers of the digital platforms are being increasingly recognized, there have been few efforts by developing countries to design antitrust policies to combat their anticompetitive practices. Many challenges are faced in designing antitrust policies to regulate the data-based platforms comprising multiple customer groups with interdependent demand that offer products and services in many countries. These include the difficulty associated with defining the "market" involved and the power of companies within that market. The market is defined for a product or service; however, for platforms the data act as an intermediary product, are not sold or traded and have no identifiable demand and supply (e.g. Graef, 2015). This would imply that it is not possible to assess the market power of the platform in terms of raising the prices above the competitive levels for one side of the market and below competitive levels for the other side.

However, since the existing digital platforms are changing the competitive landscape, there is a need to regulate the digital platforms in order to provide developing countries' firms/platforms with an opportunity to compete with the existing platforms and avail themselves of new opportunities in the digital world. Some developed countries are using policy instruments to check the growing market powers of the digital platforms. For example, in 2013, the Dutch Data Protection Authority and the Canadian Privacy Commissioner's Office found that WhatsApp "did not delete non-users' mobile numbers once a user's phone contacts were transmitted to WhatsApp, which violated Dutch data protection law"[29] and therefore forced WhatsApp to make relevant changes for better protection of data and privacy. In 2017, the European Commission (EC) fined Google €2.42 billion for breaching European Union antitrust rules. According to EC, "Google abused its market dominance as a search engine by promoting its own comparison shopping service in its search results, and demoting those of competitors … It denied other companies the chance to compete on the merits and to innovate. And most importantly, it denied European consumers a genuine choice of services and the full benefits of innovation".[30]

One way of addressing rent-seeking strategies in a digital world would be through tighter regulation of restricted business practices, with strong monitoring and administration at the international level.[31] Another approach would be to break up the large firms responsible for market concentration (Foroohar, 2017). This takes literally the often-made comparison between oil in the analogue and data in the digital economy, in that Standard Oil was broken up in 1911 and required by law to split into multiple pieces. Forcing firms into joint ventures with certain majority rules could avoid market concentration arising and might be a feasible option for economies with nascent digitalization, including many developing countries. Closer monitoring of vertical integration, including by adding the scope and scale of data at stake as criteria for merger control, would be another policy strengthening competition.

An alternative would be accepting a digital world's tendency towards market concentration but regulate these tendencies with a view to limiting a firm's ability to exploit its dominance (Warren, 2017). Given that a country's data may have public utility features, one option could be regulating large firms as a public utility with direct public provision of the digitized service. This means that the digital economy would be considered similarly to traditional essential network industries, such as water and energy. The dominance of neo-liberal ideology has meant that public policy discussion has tended to have a negative approach to more state regulation, but increasing concerns with growing concentration in the digital economy, and potential misuse of personal data, are encouraging greater social acceptance of the need for regulations in this regard.[32]

For developing countries, as noted above, the regulatory concerns may be even greater if they are not to miss out on the benefits of the fourth industrial revolution. For example, it has been noted that disclosure of the source code of a software program may be necessary not only for security reasons, but also for developing software coding skills, as it would allow new software to be created, customized to suit local preferences and sensitivities, and even adapted to be used in local languages. It is obviously important to support developing countries' producers wishing to enter e-commerce activities at domestic, regional and international levels. Similarly, the localization of servers can be required for regulatory purposes, and such regulation can also operate to assist in the promotion of domestic providers of a range of goods and services.

In addition to scaling data and chasing market share, patent trolls and interlocking patents are widely used forms that can favour rent-seeking and act as barriers to market entry (e.g. *TDR 2017*). Moving towards a digital economy requires the right balance between stimulating innovation and ensuring technology diffusion. This in turn implies weakening, rather than strengthening, the rules governing IPR (see also Haskel and Westlake, 2018), including bolstering technology diffusion to developing countries.

Internet sovereignty is another key issue that requires much more international discussion and negotiation, since it is now clear that a supposedly "free and open Internet" is one that can be subject to hidden regulation by powerful states as well as manipulation by large private players like some multinational platform companies. Developing country governments need to be aware of these concerns before signing on to agreements that could effectively reduce their national sovereignty and policy space in the digital world.

(e) Control and use of data

All companies, and not just digital platforms, need to be able to collect and analyse data for innovation and efficiency gains.[33] However, access to and control of data can be, indeed has long been, a source of market power and can create barriers to entry for new players. Policymakers have had to strike a balance between these conflicting pressures. Perhaps the single biggest difference with firms and platforms in the digital economy is that controlling data is the business model. For countries to be able to build their data infrastructures and use their data to provide efficient public goods and services to their citizens, it is important for the countries to control their data and be able to use/share their data and regulate its flow. Doing so help them design policies for developing data processing skills in the pre-production and post-production stages as well as encourage customized production.

Data is not a homogeneous product and there is a need, from the outset, to have a clear distinction between personal and non-personal data. The former relates more specifically to data on the consumers' behavioural patterns or education data, transport data or health data of a country. Of course, there are also balancing acts required with respect to concerns about privacy of personal data and fears of monitoring and surveillance through the combination of corporate and state control over data, all of which need to be addressed in country-specific contexts. Although non-personal data needs to be allowed to flow freely within the country, ensuring protection of personal data is extremely important, especially in building trust within the country. The laws regarding personal data depends largely on personally identifiable information (PII), which is used to link data to individuals. However, it is argued that there is no uniform definition of PII and in many cases using advanced software non-PII can be linked to individual's data, which can be re-identified (Schwartz and Solove, 2011).

To build digital capacities and particularly big-data analytics capabilities, many countries have initiated policies for dealing with data. For example, Rwanda has designed a "Data Revolution Policy"[34] which is based on the principle of national data sovereignty, whereby Rwanda retains exclusive sovereign rights and power on its national data (see box 3.1).

Developing countries need to retain their data sovereignty to build their digital skills and avoid rules which restrict their ability to monitor the flow of their national data. Classification of data into personal and non-personal data and designing respective data policies are important steps towards building digital infrastructure. There is a need to ensure protection of personal data, and the recent European Data Protection Regulation offers some interesting guidance on how to achieve that. Aside from personal data, there are many other forms of data depending on the way they are collected, and the skills invested into deciphering them – data can be analysed (analytics), it can be inferred (codified), it can be converted into databases of the kind that derive information. Protecting data effectively will call for more serious consideration by policymakers, especially in the developing world.

To encourage domestic linkages of foreign investments and to develop domestic digital capacities and digital infrastructure to upgrade in value chains, many governments are using localization measures, akin to what they used when they designed their FDI policies. Localization policies are not entirely new, having been in use in developed and developing countries since the start of the Internet. In the context of the digital economy, localization measures include requirements such as locating servers and/or computing facilities within the national boundaries which can encourage foreign firms to invest in domestic digital infrastructure and allow local authorities to enforce national laws and regulations. For example, the Decree on Information Technology Services 2013 in Viet Nam required every digital service or website to locate at least one server in Viet Nam. In Indonesia, strict local content rules are being phased in on new smartphones, laptops, etc. (USTR, 2016). In the Philippines, a draft administrative order in 2014 required government agencies to buy cloud services from the Philippine Government's cloud. In some cases, data processing and/or storage must conform to unique national standards, or data transfers must be routed largely or solely within a national or regional space when possible. Such policies can be adopted to promote local digital capabilities; infant industry protection; avoiding long-term dependency on foreign-owned and located digital infrastructure; and/or to protect privacy of the citizens, their legal jurisdictions and national cybersovereignty (e.g. Hill, 2017).

BOX 3.1   The Data Revolution Policy of Rwanda

With a vision to build an innovation-data-enabled industry to harness rapid social economic development, Rwanda has launched a Data Revolution Policy (DRP) which will be executed in a span of five years from 2017 to 2022. With the objective of building big data and analytics capabilities, the DRP focuses on establishing standards and principles for data management; establishing a framework to develop human capital in data science; defining the framework for data creation–anonymization–release; conducting big data analytics and business intelligence; fostering data-enabled technology innovations; establishing an institutional governance framework for data; addressing concerns of security/privacy and data sovereignty; defining the role of the private sector and partnerships; and establishing a data portal warehouse. The National Institute of Statistics is responsible for implementing the DRP alongside other development partners.

To implement DRP, Rwanda has already enacted legal, policy and regulatory regimes guiding access to information in general and personal data protection, privacy and confidentiality matters. The organic law on statistics No. 45 of June 2013 stipulates mechanisms for coordination of statistical articles in regard to production, access and dissemination of data while the Penal Code (arts 286 and 287), and Law No. 18/2010 of 12 May 2010 relating to Electronic Messages, Electronic Signatures and Electronic Transactions, specifies data confidentiality matters. Regarding hosting, a Ministerial order No. 001/MINICT/2012 of 12 March 2012 law provides that all critical information data within Government should be hosted in one central national data centre.

The DRP embraces the principle of national data sovereignty whereby Rwanda retains exclusive sovereign rights on her national data with control and power over her own data. In conformity with this principle, Rwanda, however, remains open under agreed terms and governed by Rwandan laws, to host her sovereign data in a cloud or a collocated environment in data centres within or outside of Rwanda. Further, the DRP recognizes the importance of building a strong collaborative framework between Government and private sector players at local, regional and international levels.

Source: http://statistics.gov.rw/publication/rwanda-national-data-revolution-and-big-data.

2. Trade and investment rules in the digital era

In order to design targeted economic and industrial policies, as discussed in the preceding section, countries require policy space in their trade and investment agreements, especially those that seek deep integration. This was emphasized in *TDR 2014* where policy space was referred to as "the freedom and ability of governments to identify and pursue the most appropriate mix of economic and policies to achieve equitable and sustainable development in their own national contexts, but as constituent parts of an interdependent global economy" (vii). Contemporary trade agreements which seek deep integration among nations by going much beyond trade restrictions at the border and increasingly focusing on domestic rules and regulations, not only reduce policy space but are also likely to produce welfare-reducing outcomes (Storm and Kohler, 2016). The rules negotiated under these agreements are shaped to a significant extent by rent-seeking, self-interested behaviour on the export side and empower politically well-connected firms

(Rodrik, 2018). This section highlights some of the binding trade and investment rules in contemporary trade agreements which could severely impinge on countries' policy space to design the required policies needed in the digital world.

Localization rules, as discussed in the previous section, have been extensively used by the developed countries in the earlier phase of digitalization and are still being used (Bauer et al., 2016, identify 22 data localization measures still being used by European Union countries); some of the rules in existing trade agreements, as well as those under negotiation, restrict the flexibilities of the signatory governments to adopt these localization measures for encouraging upgrading in the production value chains. Under some agreements like the Trade in Services Agreement (TiSA), which is being negotiated, there is a proposal that for transferring data outside the national boundaries the operator simply needs to establish a need to transfer data offshore "in connection with the conduct of its business".[35] Other agreements, like the Trans-Pacific Partnership (TPP), include binding rules on governments' ability to restrict use or location of computing facilities inside the national boundaries (art. 14.13). Some of the proposals on e-commerce in the WTO include binding rules on cross-border data transfers and localization restrictions.[36] Such rules, being put forward as part of progressively expanding e-commerce chapters in free trade agreements (FTAs), may limit the ability of the governments to gain from FDI to build their national digital technological capacity and skills (Gehl Sampath, 2018).

To keep up in the ongoing technological revolution, developing countries are in urgent need of international technology transfers (ITT) from the developed countries and other developing countries which have been able to develop advanced digital technologies. The new digital technologies using AI, robots and IoT can potentially help developing countries to upgrade in value chains by increasing the digital content in the production stages. However, technology transfers from foreign firms by hosting FDI has rarely happened automatically and developing countries have always used targeted policies to encourage technology spillovers, through joint ventures, technology licensing, technology transfer clauses in their investment agreements, training arrangements, etc. These have been successful in generating ITTs (e.g. Newman et al., 2015). However, ITT have become much more complicated in the digital economy where technology and data analytics are being equated to trade secrets (e.g. Kowalski et al., 2017). These inputs, which are increasingly being protected in trade and investment agreements, further restrict governments from using the traditional FDI policies for encouraging technology transfers. One such binding rule applies to source-code sharing. Source code is a collection of computer instructions which are processed and executed, and whose human-readable version (called source code) is usually protected by copyright and often kept confidential to protect proprietary information. Recently negotiated trade and investment agreements place binding rules, namely the non-disclosure rule, which prohibits governments from designing policies requiring source-code sharing except for national security reasons (e.g. TPP, art. 14.17). For digital technology transfers in developing countries, policies around source-code sharing can play an important role in encouraging ITT and developing national digital skills.

A concept closely related to technology transfers in the digital world is technology neutrality which broadly means that the same regulatory principles should apply regardless of the technology used. It has also been interpreted as a restriction on governments in terms of favouring local technologies. With the ever-evolving technologies in the digital world, technology neutrality can have far-reaching implications. This would imply that if a country commits to allowing the supply of a service then the service provider can apply any technology to supply that service, including future technologies like driverless vehicles or drone deliveries. Many countries have taken commitments on the cross-border supply of services under The General Agreement on Trade in Services (GATS), which with technology neutrality commitment can limit their choice of technology in the future as well as their ability to restrict or regulate new means of delivering a service. Some of the FTAs, like Japan–European Union FTA (chap. 8, sect. F, art. 1.3) and e-commerce proposals at the WTO (e.g. US, JOB/GC/94) include technology neutrality as a core principle. Whether technology neutrality applies to the GATS commitment of the countries in the WTO is debatable (e.g. Wunsch-Vincent, 2006). Binding rules on adopting technology neutrality can reduce the regulatory flexibility of the countries in the digital world given the rapidly evolving digital technologies.

While technology transfers need to be encouraged, developing countries should be proactive in increasing the digital content in their production processes, by supporting more domestically produced digital services like ICT services and telecommunication services in their manufacturing or by using digital technologies to digitalize their production. Digitalized products refer to those products which were earlier exported physically but are now being electronically transmitted, for example, films, printed matter, sound and media, software and video games. While there is a lack of clarity on the scope of electronic transmissions defined in the WTO (e.g. whether it includes CAD files used for 3D printing or not), rules are being negotiated on electronic transmissions (ET). The WTO has a moratorium on custom duties on ET since 1998, which has been renewed for two years at every Ministerial Conference since then, including at the eleventh Ministerial Conference in 2017. However, as more products are being digitalized and exported electronically and as 3D printed products pose new challenges as these products can be exported as software and CAD files and printed in the host countries, zero custom duties on all such ET would imply a significant loss of tariff revenue, especially for the small island countries and least developed countries. UNCTAD (2017c) reports that in 2015, 101 developing countries were net importers of these digitalized products and a permanent moratorium can further increase their imports.

While many developing countries are striving to develop their national e-commerce policies/strategies for linking their domestic producers and consumers to e-commerce platforms, there is a need to recognize the associated risks, especially if these platforms are international. Not only do the countries expose their consumers to new products and producers and risk reducing domestic market shares of their domestic producers but also in the process lose out on valuable data that is generated by the transactions of consumers and producers. The "network effects" of these platforms allow them to gather huge data of the connected economies, which can then be used by these international platforms to predict market trends, flood the consumers with products associated to their tastes and preferences based on their personal data analytics, and effectively reorganize national production and sales. Many of the proposals in the WTO if accepted, will not allow the governments to restrict the outflow of the data of their producers and consumers in the future.

Gains from e-commerce for developing countries can become a reality only if they protect their "national e-commerce platforms" with the objective of improving the domestic and international market access of their producers. Public–private partnerships could be encouraged to form national e-commerce platforms to boost domestic as well as cross-border e-commerce and use the data analytics of the engaged customers to forecast future demand, and changing tastes and preferences. Linking domestic producers to the national e-commerce platforms should be a part of national trade promotion schemes. Chinese e-commerce platform policies can provide rich learnings to developing countries. For example, a Chinese e-commerce platform called KiKUU operates in six African countries, selling only Chinese goods.[37]

The bottom line is that the potential for development provided by digital technologies can be easily eclipsed if developing countries are not given the flexibility and policy space to design their economic and industrial policies and national regulatory frameworks to promote digital infrastructure and digital capacities.

3. South–South and triangular cooperation for a digital world

As discussed, a precondition for developing countries to be able to grasp the rising opportunities in the digital world is the building of their digital infrastructure as well as digital capabilities. However, given the speedy digitization of manufacturing production and exports in the developed world, the rise of monopolistic practices by lead firms and digital platforms across GVCs and the growing digital divide, it may be extremely difficult for developing countries, especially LDCs, to leapfrog into digital industrialization on their own. The previous section has suggested the need to rethink trade and investment agreements as one necessary step but South–South digital cooperation at the regional level can also play an important role. Digital cooperation at the regional level can be added to the ongoing regional integration initiatives in the South, including in Africa.

UNCTAD (2018b) has suggested a ten-point South–South digital cooperation agenda which includes:

- building a data economy
- building cloud computing infrastructure
- strengthening broadband infrastructure
- promoting e-commerce in the region
- promoting regional digital payments
- progressing on single digital market in the region
- sharing experiences on e-government
- forging partnerships for building smart cities
- promoting digital innovations and technologies
- building statistics for measuring digitization.

An important step towards digital cooperation is to build a regional data economy among neighbouring countries. This can help each country as they can use the big data of the region to develop AI for manufacturing customized digital products. However, to build a regional data economy, countries first need to "own" their data. Ownership of data at the national level by governments will allow the countries to decide with whom to share their data. Sharing data at the regional level will allow the pooling of regional data and digital capacities, and the use of existing digital infrastructure within the region to process the regional data. Similar national rules and regulations on ownership of data in countries within the region can also help in faster flow of data within that region. Further, free flow of non-personal data within the region can strengthen the regional integration process.

Regional strategies in data cooperation need to be discussed along with the ways to classify data and decisions need to be taken on what data can be shared regionally. A regional strategy around the ownership and sharing of data can provide substantial support to national digital industrial policies.

Along with building the data economy, South–South digital cooperation is needed for maximizing the benefits of cloud computing. Cost savings from cloud computing can only be realized through significant pooling of configurable computing resources which will lead to economies of scale and can drastically reduce the cost of using IT infrastructure (Alford and Morton, 2009). Cloud computing infrastructure at the regional level can provide significant benefits to the public as well as the private sector in the region in terms of cost, flexibility, efficiency and scalability. Such infrastructure should be accompanied by initiatives to build trust in local cloud service providers and a Cloud Code of Conduct that specifies the terms of data usage through the cloud. This needs to be supported by regional action for cybersecurity.

For all countries in a region to have a level playing field in terms of access to opportunities arising from cloud computing, it is important that all countries within a regional bloc have a similar broadband ecosystem. Broadband networks can be regarded as an interconnected multilayered ecosystem of high capacity communication networks, services, applications and users and are the foundation of digital economies. Bigger developing countries in a region can provide key support to other developing countries through investing in the development of their broadband infrastructure. Countries within regional blocs can undertake similar reforms in telecom rules to attract investments in broadband infrastructure in the region. Regional cooperation arrangements and the sharing of regulatory experiences and practices can help in developing this key infrastructure in the regions.

Further, regional markets can be served more effectively using digital technologies like e-commerce. However, for e-commerce to expand the market access of manufactured products within a region it is important that there are uniform cross-border e-commerce rules and regulations in that region. Uniform rules are needed for governing consumer protection,

intellectual property, competition, taxation and information security. Uniform rules are also required for tackling unjustified geo-blocking. A regional e-commerce strategy needs to be developed which supports the national e-commerce strategy.

Regional e-commerce needs to be supported by protected digital payment infrastructure capacities within the region. Obviously, this depends on sufficient physical infrastructure and connectivity being available, which is an important prerequisite. Digital payments are more transparent and traceable and are essential for e-commerce. But success in widespread use of digital payments requires a strong regulatory framework to supervise commercial banks, financial institutions and other e-money institutions and rules around consumer data protection and competition issues as well as legal provisions around payment clearing and settlement systems. Developing countries need to be extremely careful in their trade negotiations as well as investment treaties for preserving their policy space for regulating their digital payment platforms. This makes regional cooperation in digital payments challenging, but there exist some examples in the South. Southern Africa Development Community (SADC) members have developed an Integrated Regional Electronic Settlement System (SIRESS) at the regional level to facilitate financial transactions and cross-border payments. National and regional clearing houses have been set up to facilitate payments between financial institutions.

In the digital world, regional markets can be truly integrated only if they progress towards a single digital market in the region. A regional single digital market (RSDM) could move towards seamless access to online activities by all consumers and producers in the region, irrespective of their nationality and country of residence. This is an extremely difficult goal for the South, given the existing limited digital infrastructure and capacities, but should be the ultimate objective.

South–South (and triangular) cooperation is also needed for assisting countries to build smart cities in the South. Although the financial resources needed to create smart cities are huge from the perspective of small economies, moves in this direction can also help to generate financial resources in the future by increasing the returns to investments. Triangular partnerships and collaborations can be forged with advanced countries to strengthen broadband infrastructure and develop smart cities in the South, which rely heavily on digitization.

Another area of regional digital cooperation is digital innovations and technology. Many developing countries are in a process of incentivizing digital start-ups to encourage innovations. Small and medium enterprises are the main beneficiaries of these low-cost high-returns innovations. However, it is a challenge to retain successful digital innovations for furthering national digitalization efforts because of a high rate of acquisitions of these start-ups by the big tech firms, who pick out the most successful innovations. This is an area where South–South cooperation can greatly contribute. Development banks like the New Development Bank, the Asian Development Bank and the African Development Bank can play an important role in financially supporting these start-ups and encourage them to develop software and

digital technologies for use at the regional level. A regional strategy can be designed that encourages start-ups that cater to providing innovative digital solutions at the regional level. Intraregional investments in digital technologies can foster technology transfers and innovations if they allow source-code sharing and encourage tailoring of the digital technologies from open source codes to their needs and requirements. There can also be enormous learning opportunities for the South in its collaboration with the North for designing tools and statistics to benchmark digitization and trace its progress.

While South–South digital cooperation should adopt an ambitious agenda, realities on the ground mean that sequencing and prioritizing elements of that agenda will be important and need to be adapted according to the level and pace of digital development of the countries within the region.

D. The way forward for developing countries

Moving towards a digital economy holds both more and less potential for income and employment creation in developing countries than often thought. This is because many existing studies overestimate the potential adverse employment and income effects of some digital technologies, such as robots, as argued in *TDR 2017*. At the same time, there is an equally exaggerated tendency, bordering on digital utopianism, that attributes boundless opportunities for developing countries, through further rounds of liberalization, to leapfrog in to high value added and job-creating activities in all segments of the manufacturing process as well as services (IMF, 2018). But whatever position one takes, the rapid pace of digitalization is leaving many policymakers unprepared. Depending on a country's level of development, unpreparedness can take several forms – from skills and infrastructure deficits to inexistent or fragmented policy adjustment – and can have numerous adverse consequences, including falling further behind the technological frontier, stalled economic catch-up or even marginalization from the global economy. The tendency for market concentration and the emergence of a vicious Medici circle of reinforcing economic and political power in the digital world compounds that threat.

The simple truth for the governments of developing counties is that realizing the potential benefits from a digital world will be difficult, and that ensuring those benefits have a wide social reach will be more difficult still. It requires ambitious policies in a wide range of areas that must be employed in a coherent way. Engaging in digital trade is a promising first step, and will spur the provision of hard and soft digital infrastructure, which is a basic requirement for people and enterprises to engage successfully in the digital economy. Digital preparedness in many developing countries will require international support and cooperation; UNCTAD's eTrade For All initiative provides one possible model for such partnerships (UNCTAD, 2017d).

Digital trade is not an end itself. Narratives of the benefits of digital trade often take a consumer perspective, coached in dollar terms. But digitized exchanges are generally paid for in data: goods and services are delivered, often free of charge in dollar terms, in exchange of the customers' data. Looked at from a development perspective, merely increasing connectivity might empower larger and already more productive firms and sharpen the exclusion of other firms. Moreover, providing customer data to international platforms tends to result in a concentration of corporate power that may make it difficult for developing countries to get access to, own and use data regarding their economies and their citizens for their own economic development. Polarization is just as much, perhaps more, a threat in a digital world as an analogue world.

This means that policy changes in a wide range of areas should accompany increased digital connectivity. Policies that govern the access to and use of data are crucial, and should focus on making access to non-personal data as open as possible. Access to, ownership of and capabilities to analyse and transform data into economically meaningful knowledge will be central to reaping the benefits from a digital world. While ensuring that data governance frameworks appropriately address privacy and digital security considerations, policies should also encourage investment in data that have synergies both within and across industries.

Regarding competition and antitrust measures, policies on standards, public participation in long-term finance, public procurement, etc. may be necessary to increase the benefits to developing countries in the digital economy. Also required are bold demand-side policies, as developing countries can reap such benefits only if their consumers have the income required to turn their preferences into effective demand without recurring to debt. It must be understood that digitalization will not deliver against a backdrop of fiscal retrenchment and austerity.

In this sense, establishing a virtuous circle between the new digital technologies' greater emphasis on customized demand on the one hand, and greater involvement of developing countries in manufacturing processes that satisfy such demand on the other will require the adoption of more expansionary macroeconomic policies and reconnecting wage and productivity growth.

Some of the key policies that can help developing countries face the challenges posed by the digital revolution and increase their developmental gains from GVCs are briefly noted here.

1. Building digital infrastructure

ICT infrastructure, is a necessary condition for progressing in a digitalized world. But this in turn presupposes the availability of the necessary physical infrastructure, such as, most obviously, power connections. In addition to supportive physical infrastructure, it is important to develop strong banking and financial institutions providing substantially enlarged access to the entire population; this is still hugely underprovided in many developing and least developed countries. When laying the ground for the digital infrastructure, existing internal imbalances, such as rural–urban differences, should be addressed so that rural areas do not suffer a widening digital divide and can benefit from enhanced connectivity.

2. Devising national data regulatory policies

To the extent that data is the fuel of the digital age, its control, much like with oil in the Fordist era, opens huge profit opportunities to its owners (Tarnoff, 2018). It therefore becomes critical for countries to devise national data policies to ensure equitable distribution of gains arising from data which is generated within the national boundaries. Currently, such a policy does not exist in most of the developing countries and, de facto, data are owned by the one who gathers and stores data, mainly digital super-firms, who then have full, exclusive and unlimited usage property rights on it. National data policy should be designed to address four core issues: who can own data; how it can be collected; who can use it; and under what terms. It should also address the issue of data sovereignty which relates to what data can leave the country and are thereby not governed under domestic laws. The Data Revolution Policy of Rwanda can provide a good learning opportunity for developing countries.

But data, unless processed, may be of little value. Big-data analytics using algorithms have revolutionized production as well as distribution services. The limited ability of the developing world to transform data into economically meaningful knowledge has fuelled the growth of highly profitable digital platforms, which through "network effects" have been able to glean more data and use it to facilitate entry into new markets and new business lines. The rising rents of these super-platforms and their ability to kill competition from national platforms remains unchecked because of a lack of regulatory policies. This has not only restricted development of national platforms but has also closed a window of opportunity for the developing countries to develop their data analytics and upgrade to post-production higher value added activities.

3. *Regulating digital platforms and developing national marketing platforms*

Regulation is essential for developing countries to gain from e-commerce, else linking into existing platforms will only provide the super-platforms with more data, strengthening them further and facilitating their greater access to domestic markets. Tighter regulation of restricted business practices; break-up of large firms responsible for market concentration; regulating digital platforms as a public utility with direct public provision of the digitized service; and strong monitoring and administration at the international level are some of the options to regulate super-platforms.

4. *Taxing the super-firms*

Taxing these firms where their activities are based rather than where they declare their headquarters will help in redistributing their rents and increase government revenues.

5. *Drawing up digital industrial policies*

Once policies around data ownership and regulations for checking anticompetitive practices of super-platforms are in place, developing countries will be able to prepare themselves for the digital world. Digital industrial policies are needed to enhance the use of digital technologies and digital services in production as well as to build digital competencies in all sectors.

6. *Harnessing digital start-ups*

Innovations are key to digital industrial development. While many developing countries are encouraging digital start-ups as the primary source of digital innovations, there is a need for a more comprehensive policy with respect to digital start-ups, which prevents the gains of innovations flowing out of the country. Direct investment by governments in corporate equities can sustain digital innovations, enhance use of advanced technology and promote reverse innovations.

7. *Developing digital competencies*

Developing digital competencies to fill the digital gap will require efforts at various levels including introducing digital education in schools and universities, upskilling the digital skills of the existing workforce, running special basic and advanced skill development programmes and funding digital entrepreneurship.

Developing countries will not be able to digitally leapfrog on their own. They will need support both at the regional as well as international level. Regional integration agendas need to include regional support for building a data economy; building cloud computing infrastructure; strengthening broadband infrastructure; promoting e-commerce in the region; promoting regional digital payments; progressing on a single digital market in the region; sharing experiences on e-government; forging partnerships for building smart cities; promoting digital innovations and technologies; and building statistics for measuring digitization.

Given that large-scale use of digital technologies is still unfolding and that related impacts are still not fully understood, international cooperation to fill data gaps and develop comparable metrics needs to accompany policy efforts at the national level. The international community is just beginning a dialogue on what rules and regulations can harness the productivity and developmental potential of the digital economy. Agreement needs to be reached on what part of the issues around the digital economy are in the realm of the WTO and what part in that of other international organizations. A premature commitment to rules with long-term impacts in this fast-moving area where influential actors might be driven by narrow business interests should be avoided. It is perhaps worthwhile, here, recalling the conclusion of the respected Canadian development economist, Gerald Helleiner (2000: 12) in his Raúl Prebisch Lecture at UNCTAD just five years after the establishment of the WTO:

> I doubt whether there is any longer much dispute over the fact that many developing countries signed the Marrakesh Agreement without sufficient appreciation of its implications and/or in the expectation of considerably more change in industrial country protectionist practice than has so far materialized. Nor, I suspect, is there much disagreement that industrial countries vastly overestimated developing countries capacities (and, as it turns out, willingness) to implement all of its elements within the agreed timetables.

To avoid any such repetition, it is important to retain freedom and space to design digital policies which help in increasing developmental gains from trade and foreign investments, like policies around localization, restrictions on free flow of data, technology transfers and custom duties on electronic transmissions. Developing countries will need appropriately inclusive and comprehensive venues, such as UNCTAD's intergovernmental expert group on e-commerce and the digital economy, to discuss the complex issues involved and to help shape coherent development-oriented policies. ◼

Notes

1　Parts of UNCTAD (2017a) also addressed the digitalization of value chains but focused on implications for foreign direct investment and related policymaking, which complements the discussion in this chapter. The broad perspective of UNCTAD (2018a) regarding links between a wide range of frontier technologies and sustainable development further complements the focus on digital technologies and the manufacturing process in this chapter.

2　Beyond the questions examined in this chapter, the new digital technologies also raise macroeconomic issues. Digitalization and the associated greater importance of intangibles may well lead to a decline in the demand for physical capital goods. This raises issues of measuring output and inflation. It might also contribute to an ongoing decline in the price of physical capital goods and the long-term decline of fixed capital formation as a share of GDP, which has traditionally been considered the major driver of economic and productivity growth. The growing importance of intangibles also raises distributional issues. These issues are beyond the scope of this chapter, but distributional effects from robot-based automation and from drivers of market power and concentration were discussed in *TDR 2017*.

3　Fu et al. (2011: 1204) also conclude that "[s]tudies largely fail to provide convincing evidence indicating significant positive technology transfer and spillover effects of FDI on the local firms". De Marchi et al. (2018), provide similar evidence for the more recent period.

4　For discussion and further empirical evidence regarding the greater role of intangibles in economic activities, see e.g. WIPO, 2017.

5　While this aspect has been a mainstay in development economics and structural change analyses following Chenery and Syrquin (1975), in trade theory, Markusen (2013) revived attention to heterogeneous demand patterns.

6　The ratio of material use (measured in tonnes of raw ore or crops) to GDP has fallen in almost all regions of the world in the last three decades, most of all in Europe and the United States, and to a lesser extent in Africa, Oceania and Latin America (SERI/WU Global Material Flows Database).

7　This measure most likely underestimates the inputs from the digital sector to manufacturing. Some parts of the digital sector are probably classified in other categories than in ISIC Revision 4 divisions J61–J63. Only data referring to these divisions are used here because available data do not allow for disaggregation of data in divisions that may cover more than digital services that affect manufacturing.

8　According to IMF, 2018: 1, 7: "Available evidence suggests that the digital sector is still less than 10 percent of most economies if measured by value added, income or employment", even though "Estimates of the size of the digital sector can be sensitive to the choice of definition". Bukht and Heeks, 2017, estimate the digital economy to make up around 5 per cent of global output and 3 per cent of global employment. It should also be noted that the database used here is the only one available for assessing the role of digital services in manufacturing but that its country sample covers only 43 individual economies with the remainder comprising a rest-of-the-world aggregate.

9　Bessen, 2016, provides evidence for such rent-seeking strategies of firms in the United States. For further discussion, see also *TDR 2017*.

10　Such cost reductions may even apply to entire factories in that digital design simulation of factories can anticipate and resolve operational problems even before the facility exists physically.

11　For case-study evidence suggesting that digitization of value chains may hurt small African producers, see Foster et al. (2018). For more general discussion see e.g. Foster and Graham (2017).

12　Capital income represents the remainder when wages are subtracted from value added in exports. It is not further analysed as it cannot be allocated to business functions in the same way as labour income. For the rationale of defining business functions in this way and related measurement issues, see de Vries et al., 2018.

13　Data for some other developed and developing countries are provided in the online Appendix.

14　"Big tech companies" are defined here as companies of the "digital economy" (defined as sectors of "Technology Equipment" + "Software and IT services" of the Thomson Reuters Business Classification) that reached the top 100 of non-financial corporations by market capitalization.

15   Source: ITU, ICT Facts & Figures, The world in 2017. Available at https://www.itu.int/en/ITU-D/Statistics/Documents/facts/ICTFactsFigures2017.pdf.

16   One reflection of this is the string of Science, Technology and Innovation Policy (STIP) Reviews that UNCTAD has undertaken for developing countries and economies in transition. See http://unctad.org/en/pages/publications/Science,-Technology-and-Innovation-Policy-Reviews-(STIP-Reviews).aspx.

17   This contrasts with the traditional view, based on the product life-cycle theory (Vernon, 1966). As noted by von Zedtwitz et al. (2015: 12), who also discuss other departures from Vernon's initial notion, "[a]ccording to this traditional view, new products and technologies are first developed and launched in advanced countries, and only later introduced and commercialized in less developed countries when they have become increasingly mature, out-of-date, and obsolete. The flow of innovation, from a market point of view as much as from a technological perspective, is thus from advanced to developing countries".

18   For examples of frugal innovation see, for example, Laperche and Lefebvre, 2012. For additional discussion, see also UNCTAD, 2018a: chap. IV.

19   For example, the Chinese company Huawei developed its smartphone business by outcompeting main incumbent firms not simply through low-cost advantage but by relying on recent scientific knowledge and the integration of ensuing new technologies in its innovation strategies (Joo et al., 2016). Starting by producing low-end phones for the domestic market, its continued focus on local R&D and reverse engineering of foreign technology allowed it to become a global leader in telecommunications networks by 2012 (Kang, 2015).

20   For a succinct discussion of how intellectual property law affects 3D-printing see, for example, Malaty and Rostama (2017). For more detailed discussion see, for example, Osborn (2016: 270) who concludes: "perhaps the innovations most impacted by 3D printing should be removed from certain IP protections altogether. This argument is perhaps strongest in patent law, where the utilitarian nature of the inventions urges their introduction into the public domain".

21   For detailed discussion, see the literature on "two-sided markets". There is no accepted definition of "two-sided markets", but digital platform businesses are generally considered a crucial element that makes a market two-sided (see, e.g. Rysman, 2009; Gürkaynak et al., 2017), as these platforms have two distinct user groups that offer each other network benefits.

22   For example, iPad and Amazon's Kindle although competitors, collaborated and Amazon developed a Kindle Reader app for iPads, which Apple approved. Consumers can now read e-books they purchase on Amazon on either a Kindle Reader or iPad, which eliminates any competition from small application developers and drives them out of the ecosystem.

23   For example, in 2016 the European Union announced the antitrust case against Alphabet for imposing licensing conditions for the Android OS that favoured Google's products and apps for its rivals, making it difficult for other operators to develop alternative operating systems.

24   See *TDR 2017*. Lynn, 2017, provides an account of this shift in the United States, with a divergent view in Atkinson and Lind, 2018. For more general discussion see, e.g. Khan, 2017; and Vezzoso, 2016.

25   See, for example, the Human Rights Council HRC Resolution 34/7 adopted on 23 March 2017, http://ap.ohchr.org/documents/alldocs.aspx?doc_id=28120; and the European Union's General Data Protection Regulation (https://www.eugdpr.org/), which entered into force on 25 May 2018, requiring firms to give customers more control over their online information, and may be an important first step towards a better understanding of how companies themselves value data.

26   Davies et al., 2018, provide an account of the economic size of tax avoidance through tax havens.

27   For further discussion, see also *TDR 2017*: chap. VI.

28   One policy problem that this business model poses is difficulty in identifying when a market price is below cost, i.e. a criterion required to establish a case of predatory pricing on which established competition policy could act.

29   See https://autoriteitpersoonsgegevens.nl/en/news/canadian-and-dutch-data-privacy-guardians-release-findings-investigation-popular-mobile-app.

30   European Commission: Statement by Commissioner Vestager on Commission decision to fine Google €2.42 billion for abusing dominance as search engine by giving illegal advantage to its own comparison shopping service (see http://europa.eu/rapid/press-release_STATEMENT-17-1806_en.htm).

31   As further discussed in *TDR 2017*, a starting point for any such policies might be the Set of Multilaterally Agreed Equitable Principles and Rules for the Control of Restrictive Business Practices adopted by the United Nations General Assembly in 1980. Available at: http://unctad.org/en/docs/tdrbpconf10r2.en.pdf.

32   The European Union's new data protection laws provide a case in point.

33   See UNCTAD, 2018b, for detailed discussion on importance of data in the digital economy.

34   Available at: http://statistics.gov.rw/publication/rwanda-national-data-revolution-and-big-data.

35   Proposal in TiSA, art. 2.2, Annex on Electronic Commerce, undated (November 2016). See Kelsey, 2018.

36   United States and European Union proposals – US, JOB/GC/94; and para. 20, JOB/GC/97.

37   https://www.prnewswire.com/news-releases/kikuu-quietly-positioning-itself-to-become-africas-first-mobile-commerce-unicorn-300358163.html.

References

Alford T and Morton G (2009). The economics of cloud computing analyzed: Addressing the benefits of infrastructure in the cloud. Available at: http://tedalford.sys-con.com/node/1147473.

Atkinson RD and Lind M (2018). Commentary: Who wins after U.S. antitrust regulators attack? China. Available at: http://fortune.com/2018/03/29/commentary-who-wins-after-u-s-antitrust-regulators-attack-china/.

Baldwin R (2016). *The Great Convergence: Information Technology and the New Globalization*. Harvard University Press. Cambridge, MA.

Baldwin R and Lopez-Gonzalez J (2013). Supply-chain trade: A portrait of global patterns and several testable hypotheses. Working Paper No. 18957. National Bureau of Economic Research.

Basiliere P (2017). Gartner predicts 2018: 3D Printing changes business models. Available at: https://blogs.gartner.com/pete-basiliere/2017/12/12/gartner-predicts-2018–3d-printing-changes-business-models/.

Bauer M, Ferracane MF and van der Marel E (2016). Tracing the economic impact of regulations on the free flow of data and data localization. Global Commission on Internet Governance Paper Series No. 30. Available at: https://www.cigionline.org/publications/tracing-economic-impact-regulations-free-flow-data-and-data-localization.

Bessen JE (2016). Accounting for rising corporate profits: Intangibles or regulatory rents? Law and Economics Working Paper No. 16–18. Boston University School of Law. Available at: https://www.bu.edu/law/files/2016/11/Accounting-for-Rising-Corporate-Profits.pdf.

Brynjolfsson E, Eggers F and Gannamaneni A (2018). Using massive online choice experiments to measure changes in well-being. Working Paper No. 24514. National Bureau of Economic Research.

Bukht R and Heeks R (2017). Defining, conceptualising and measuring the digital economy. Development Informatics Working Paper No. 68. Global Development Institute. University of Manchester.

Chang H-J and Andreoni A (2016). Industrial policy in a changing world: Basic principles, neglected issues and new challenges. Cambridge Journal of Economics 40Years Conference. Available at: http://www.cpes.org.uk/dev/wp-content/uploads/2016/06/Chang_Andreoni_2016_Industrial-Policy.pdf.

Chenery H and Syrquin M (1975). *Patterns of Development 1950–70*. Oxford University Press. Oxford.

Cornell University, INSEAD and WIPO (2017). *The Global Innovation Index 2017: Innovation Feeding the World*. Ithaca, Fontainebleau and Geneva.

Davies RB, Martin J, Parenti M and Toubal F (2018). Knocking on tax haven's door: Multinational firms and transfer pricing. *The Review of Economics and Statistics*. 100(1): 120–134.

De Backer K and Flaig D (2017). The future of global value chains: Business as usual or "a new normal"? Science, Technology and Innovation Policy Papers No. 41. Organisation for Economic Co-operation and Development. Available at: http://dx.doi.org/10.1787/d8da8760-en.

De Marchi V, Giuliani E and Rabellotti R (2018). Do global value chains offer developing countries learning and innovation opportunities? *The European Journal of Development Research*. 30(3): 389–407.

de Vries GJ (2018). Global value chain and domestic value added export analysis using the World Input-Output Database: Methods and an illustration. Background material prepared for the *Trade and Development Report 2018*.

de Vries GJ, Miroudot S and Timmer MP (2018). Functional specialization in international trade: An exploration based on occupations of workers. Mimeo. University of Groningen.

Edmans A (2014). Blockholders and corporate governance. *Annual Review of Financial Economies*. 6(1): 23–50.

Elder J (2013). Review of policy measures to stimulate private demand for innovation: Concepts and effects. National Endowment for Science, Technology and the Arts Working Paper No. 13/13. Manchester Institute of Innovation Research. Available at: https://www.nesta.org.uk/report/review-of-policy-measures-to-stimulate-private-demand-for-innovation-concepts-and-effects/.

Ernst and Young (2016). How will 3D printing make your company the strongest link in the value chain? EY's global 3D printing report 2016. Available at:http://www.ey.com/Publication/vwLUAssets/EY-3d-druck-studie-executive-summary/$FILE/ey-how-will-3d-printing-make-your-company-the-strongest-link-in-the-value-chain.pdf.

Eurofound (2018). *Game Changing Technologies: Exploring the Impact on Production Processes and Work*. Publications Office of the European Union. Luxembourg.

Ezrachi A and Stucke ME (2016). *Virtual Competition: The Promise and Perils of the Algorithm-Driven Economy*. Harvard University Press. Cambridge, MA.

Ferrari A (2012). *Digital Competence in Practice: An Analysis of Frameworks*. European Commission. Joint Research Centre. Institute for Prospective Technological Studies. Seville. Available at: http://dx.doi.org/10.2791/82116.

Filitz R, Henkel J and Tether BS (2015). Protecting aesthetic innovations? An exploration of the use of registered community designs. *Research Policy*. 44(6): 1192–1206.

Foroohar R (2017). Release big tech's grip on power. *Financial Times*. 18 June.

Foster C and Graham M (2017). Reconsidering the role of the digital in global production networks. *Global Networks*. 17(1): 68–88.

Foster C and Heeks R (2014). Nurturing user-producer interaction: Inclusive innovation flows in a low-income mobile phone market. *Innovation and Development*. 4(2): 221–237.

Foster C, Graham M, Mann L, Waema T and Friederici N (2018). Digital control in value chains: Challenges of connectivity for East African firms. *Economic Geography*. 94(1): 68–86.

Foster JB and McChesney RW (2011). The Internet's unholy marriage to capitalism. *Monthly Review*. March. Available at: https://monthlyreview.org/2011/03/01/the-internets-unholy-marriage-to-capitalism/.

Fu X, Pietrobelli C and Soete L (2011). The role of foreign technology and indigenous innovation in the emerging economies: Technological change and catching-up. *World Development*. 39(7): 1204–1212.

Gehl Sampath P (2018). Regulating the digital economy: Are we moving towards a 'win-win' or a 'lose-lose'? Working Paper No. 5. United Nations University. Maastricht Economic and social Research institute on Innovation and Technology.

Graef I (2015). Market definition and market power in data: The case of online platforms. *World Competition*. 38(4): 473–505.

Gürkaynak G, İnanılır Ö, Diniz S and Yaşar AG (2017). Multisided markets and the challenge of incorporating multisided considerations into competition law analysis. *Journal of Antitrust Enforcement*. 5(1): 100–129.

Haskel J and Westlake S (2018). *Capitalism without Capital: The Rise of the Intangible Economy*. Princeton University Press. Princeton, NJ.

Helleiner G (2000). Markets, politics and globalization: Can the global economy be civilized? Tenth Raúl Prebisch Lecture. 11 December. UNCTAD. Geneva. Available at http://unctad.org/en/Docs/prebisch10th.en.pdf Hill R (2017). Second contribution to the June–September 2017 Open Consultation of the ITU CWG-Internet: Why should data flow freely?. Available at: www.apig.ch/CWG-Internet%202017-2bis.pdf.

Hopkins TK and Wallerstein I (1986). Commodity chains in the world economy prior to 1800. *Review (Fernand Braudel Center)*. 10(1): 157–170.

Hymer S (1972). The internationalization of capital. *Journal of Economic Issues*. 6(1): 91–111.

ICRICT (Independent Commission for the Reform of International Corporate Taxation) (2018). A roadmap to improve rules for taxing multinationals: A fairer future for global taxation. February. Available at: https://www.world-psi.org/sites/default/files/attachment/news/icrictunitarytaxationengfeb2018.pdf.

ILO (2018, forthcoming). *Robotics and Reshoring*. International Labour Organization. Geneva.

ILO-ITU (2017). Digital skills for decent jobs for youth campaign to train 5 million youth with job-ready digital skills. International Labour Organization and International Telecommunication Union. Available at: https://www.itu.int/en/ITU-D/Digital-Inclusion/Youth-and-Children/Pages/Digital-Skills.aspx

IMF (2018). Measuring the digital economy. International Monetary Fund. Washington, D.C. Available at: http://www.imf.org/en/Publications/Policy-Papers/Issues/2018/04/03/022818-measuring-the-digital-economy.

Immelt JR, Govindarajan V and Trimble C (2009). How GE is disrupting itself. *Harvard Business Review*. October: 56–65.

Joo SH, Oh C and Lee K (2016). Catch-up strategy of an emerging firm in an emerging country: Analysing the case of Huawei vs. Ericsson with patent data. *International Journal of Technology Management*. 72(1/2/3): 19–42.

Kang B (2015). The innovation process of Huawei and ZTE: Patent data analysis. *China Economic Review*. 36: 378–393.

Kelsey J (2018). How a TPP-style E-commerce outcome in the WTO would endanger the development dimension of the GATS acquis (and potentially the WTO). *Journal of International Economic Law*. 21(2): 273–295.

Khan LM (2017). Amazon's antitrust paradox. *Yale Law Journal*. 126(3): 710–805.

Kowalski P, Rabaioli D and Vallejo S (2017). International technology transfer measures in an interconnected world: Lessons and policy implications. OECD Trade Policy Papers No. 206. OECD Publishing. Paris. Available at: https://www.oecd-ilibrary.org/trade/international-technology-transfer-measures-in-an-interconnected-world_ada51ec0-en.

Kozul-Wright R and Poon D (2017). Learning from China's industrial strategy. *Project Syndicate*. 28 April. Available at: https://www.project-syndicate.org/commentary/china-industrial-strategy-lessons-by-richard-kozul-wright-and-daniel-poon-2017-04?barrier=accesspaylog.

Laperche B and Lefebvre G (2012). The globalization of Research & Development in industrial corporations: Towards "reverse innovation"? The cases of General Electric and Renault. *Journal of Innovation Economics & Management*. 10(2): 53–79.

Leliveld A and Knorringa P (2018). Frugal innovation and development research. *The European Journal of Development Research*. 30(1): 1–16.

Lewis HD (1881). The story of a great monopoly. *The Atlantic*. March. Available at: https://www.theatlantic.com/magazine/archive/1881/03/the-story-of-a-great-monopoly/306019/.

Luo S, Lovely ME and Popp D (2017). Intellectual returnees as drivers of indigenous innovation: Evidence from the Chinese photovoltaic industry. *The World Economy*. 40(11): 2424–2454.

Lynn BC (2017). The consumer welfare standard in antitrust: Outdated or a harbor in a sea of doubt? Testimony before the Senate Committee on the Judiciary: Subcommittee on Antitrust, Competition, and Consumer Rights. Available at: https://www.judiciary.senate.gov/imo/media/doc/12-13-17%20Lynn%20Testimony.pdf.

Malaty E and Rostama G (2017). 3D printing and IP law. *WIPO Magazine*. February. Available at: http://www.wipo.int/wipo_magazine/en/2017/01/article_0006.html.

Markusen JR (2013). Putting per-capita income back into trade theory. *Journal of International Economics*. 90(2): 255–265.

Mazzucato M (2017). Mission-oriented innovation policy: Challenges and opportunities. Institute for Innovation and Public Purpose. University College London. Available at: https://www.thersa.org/globalassets/pdfs/reports/mission-oriented-policy-innovation-report.pdf.

Midler C, Jullien B and Lung Y (2017). *Rethinking Innovation and Design for Emerging Markets: Inside the Renault Kwid Project*. CRC Press. Boca Raton, FL.

Milberg W and Winkler D (2013). *Outsourcing Economics: Global Value Chains in Capitalist Development*. Cambridge University Press. Cambridge.

Negroponte, N (1995). *Being Digital*. Vintage Books. New York, NY.

Newman C, Rand J, Talbot T and Tarp F (2015). Technology transfers, foreign investment and productivity spillovers. *European Economic Review*. 76:168–187.

Osborn L (2016). 3D printing and intellectual property. In: Olleros FX and Zhegu M, eds. *Research Handbook on Digital Transformations*. Edward Elgar Publishing. Cheltenham: 254–271.

Pérez C (2010). Technological dynamism and social inclusion in Latin America: A resource-based production development strategy. *CEPAL Review*. 100: 121–141.

Pérez C and Marín A (2015). Technological change and sustainable development in a world of opportunities for the region. Available at: http://www19.iadb.org/intal/icom/en/notas/39-6/.

Prebisch R (1949). Introduction: The economic development of Latin America and its principal problems. *Economic Survey of Latin America 1948*. ECLA. Santiago: xvii–xx.

Prebisch R (1986). Address delivered at the twenty-first session of ECLAC, Mexico City, 24 April. *CEPAL Review*. 29: 13–16.

Purdy M and Daugherty P (2017). How AI boosts industry profits and innovation. *Accenture*. Available at: https://www.accenture.com/t20171005T065812Z__w__/us-en/_acnmedia/Accenture/next-gen-5/insight-ai-industry-growth/pdf/Accenture-AI-Industry-Growth-Full-Report.pdfla=en?la=en.

Rodrik D (2015). From welfare state to innovation state. *Project Syndicate*. Available at: https://www.project-syndicate.org/commentary/labor-saving-technology-by-dani-rodrik-2015-01.

Rodrik D (2018). What do trade agreements really do? *Journal of Economic Perspectives*. 32(2): 73–90.

Rysman M (2009). The economics of two-sided markets. *Journal of Economic Perspectives*. 23(3): 125–143.

Salazar-Xirinachs JM, Nübler I and Kozul-Wright R (2014). Introduction. In: Salazar-Xirinachs JM, Nübler I and Kozul-Wright R, eds. *Transforming Economies: Making Industrial Policy Work for Growth, Jobs and Development*. International Labour Office. Geneva: 1–38.

Santiago F and Weiss M (2018). Demand-driven policy interventions to foster sustainable and inclusive industrial development in developing countries. Inclusive and Sustainable Industrial Development Working Paper No. 17. United Nations Industrial Development Organization.

Saviotti PP and Pyka A (2013). The co-evolution of innovation, demand and growth. *Economics of Innovation and New Technology*. 22(5): 461–482.

Schwartz PM and Solove DJ (2011). The PII problem: Privacy and a new concept of personally identifiable information. *New York University Law Review*. 86(6):1814–1894. Available at: https://scholarship.law.berkeley.edu/facpubs/1638/.

Singh PJ (2017). Digital industrialisation in developing countries: A review of the business and policy landscape. Available at: http://www.itforchange.net/sites/default/files/1468/digital_industrialisation_in_developing_countries.pdf.

Storm S and Kohler P (2016). CETA without blinders: How cutting "trade costs and more" will cause unemployment, inequality and welfare losses. Global Development and Environment Institute Working Paper No. 16-03. Tufts University. Medford, MA.

Tarnoff B (2018). Big data for the people: It's time to take it back from our tech overlords. *The Guardian*. 14 March. Available at: https://www.theguardian.com/technology/2018/mar/14/tech-big-data-capitalism-give-wealth-back-to-people.

Temin P (2017). *The Vanishing Middle Class: Prejudice and Power in a Dual Economy*. MIT Press. Cambridge, MA.

Tørsløv TR, Wier LS and Zucman G (2018). The missing profits of nations. Working Paper No. 24701. National Bureau of Economic Research.

Turner A (2018). Capitalism in the age of robots: Work, income and wealth in the 21st-century. Lecture at School of Advanced International Studies. 10 April. Johns Hopkins University. Washington, D.C. Available at: https://www.ineteconomics.org/research/research-papers/capitalism-in-the-age-of-robots-work-income-and-wealth-in-the-21st-century.

Ubhaykar R (2015). The emerging world of 3D printing. *Outlook Business*. 6 March. Available at: https://www.outlookbusiness.com/the-big-story/lead-story/the-emerging-world-of-3d-printing-590.

UNCTAD (2017a). *World Investment Report 2017: Investment and the Digital Economy* (United Nations publication. Sales No. E.17.II.D.3. New York and Geneva).

UNCTAD (2017b). The "new" digital economy and development. UNCTAD Technical Notes on Information and Communications Technology for Development No. 8. Available at: http://unctad.org/en/PublicationsLibrary/tn_unctad_ict4d08_en.pdf.

UNCTAD (2017c). *Rising Product Digitalisation and Losing Trade Competitiveness*. UNCTAD/GDS/ECIDC/2017/3. New York and Geneva.

UNCTAD (2017d). *Information Economy Report, 2017: Digitalization, Trade and Development* (United Nations publication. Sales No.E.17.II.D.8. New York and Geneva).

UNCTAD (2018a). *Technology and Innovation Report: Harnessing Frontier Technologies for Sustainable Development* (United Nations publication. Sales No. E.18.II.D.3. New York and Geneva).

UNCTAD (2018b). *South–South Digital Cooperation: A Regional Integration Agenda*. UNCTAD/GDS/ECIDC/2018/1. New York and Geneva.

UNCTAD (*TDR 2002*). *Trade and Development Report, 2002: Global Trends and Prospects, Developing Countries in World Trade* (United Nations publication. Sales No. E.02.II.D.2. New York and Geneva).

UNCTAD (*TDR 2008*). *Trade and Development Report, 2008: Commodity Prices, Capital Flows and the Financing of Investment* (United Nations publication. Sales No. E.08.II.D.21. New York and Geneva).

UNCTAD (*TDR 2014*). *Trade and Development Report, 2014: Global Governance and Policy Space for Development* (United Nations publication. Sales No. E.14.II.D.4. New York and Geneva).

UNCTAD (*TDR 2016*). *Trade and Development Report, 2016: Structural Transformation for Inclusive and Sustained Growth* (United Nations publication. Sales No. E.16.II.D.5. New York and Geneva).

UNCTAD (*TDR 2017*). *Trade and Development Report, 2017: Beyond Austerity: Towards a Global New Deal* (United Nations publication. Sales No. E.17.II.D.5. New York and Geneva).

United Nations and ECLAC (2018). *Data, Algorithms and Policies: Redefining the Digital World*. Economic Commission for Latin America and the Caribbean. Santiago (LC/CMSI.6/4).

USTR (Office of the United States Trade Representative) (2016). Request for public comments to compile the National Trade Estimate Report (NTE) on foreign trade barriers. Federal Register. 19 July. Available at: https://www.federalregister.gov/documents/2016/07/19/2016-16985/request-for-public-comments-to-compile-the-national-trade-estimate-report-on-foreign-trade-barriers.

Van Alstyne MW, Parker GG and Choudary SP (2016). Pipelines, platforms, and the new rules of strategy. *Harvard Business Review*. 94(4): 54–60.

Vernon R (1966). International investment and international trade in the product cycle. *Quarterly Journal of Economics*. 80(2): 190–207.

Vezzoso S (2016). Competition policy in a world of big data. In: Olleros FX and Zhegu M, eds. *Research Handbook on Digital Transformations*. Edward Elgar Publishing. Cheltenham: 400–420.

Vijayabaskar M and Suresh Babu M (2014). Building capabilities in the software service industry in India: Skill formation and learning of domestic enterprises in value chains. In: Salazar-Xirinachs JM, Nübler I and Kozul-Wright R, eds. *Transforming Economies.: Making Industrial Policy Work for Growth, Jobs and Development*. International Labour Office. Geneva: 239–266.

von Zedtwitz M, Corsi S, Søberg PV and Frega R (2015). A typology of reverse innovation. *Journal of Product Innovation Management*. 32(1): 12–28.

Warren E (2017). America's monopoly moment: Work, innovation, and control in an age of concentrated power. Speech, 6 December. Open Market Institute. Washington, D.C. Available at: https://openmarketsinstitute.org/events/americas-monopoly-moment-work-innovation-and-control-in-an-age-of-concentrated-power/.

WEF (2015). *Deep Shift: Technology Tipping Points and Societal Impact*. World Economic Forum. Available at: http://www3.weforum.org/docs/WEF_GAC15_Technological_Tipping_Points_report_2015.pdf.

WIPO (2017). *World Intellectual Property Report 2017: Intangible Capital in Global Value Chains*. World Intellectual Property Organization. Geneva.

World Bank, IDE-JETRO (Institute of Developing Economies, Japan External Trade Organization), OECD (Organisation for Economic Co-operation and Development), UIBE (University of International Business and Economics) and WTO (World Trade Organization) (2017). *Global Value Chain Development Report 2017: Measuring and Analyzing the Impact of GVCs on Economic Development*. World Bank. Washington, D.C.

Wunsch-Vincent S (2006). The Internet, cross-border trade in services, and the GATS: Lessons from *US–Gambling*. *World Trade Review*. 5(3): 319–355.

Zeschky MB, Winterhalter S and Gassmann O (2014). From cost to frugal and reverse innovation: Mapping the field and implications for global competitiveness. *Research-Technology Management*. 57(4): 20–27.

BRIDGING GAPS OR WIDENING DIVIDES: INFRASTRUCTURE DEVELOPMENT AND STRUCTURAL TRANSFORMATION

IV

A. Introduction

The last chapter recognized that building a digital infrastructure has to be a key part of any strategy to help developing countries grasp the benefits of emerging digital technologies. It also suggested that the strong scale and network effects exhibited by that infrastructure can give rise to economic rents and warned that leaving its provision to corporate interests rather than giving a lead role to public policy would probably skew outcomes in ways that would be neither inclusive nor sustainable, particularly in developing countries.

This concern reflects an older and wider discussion on the link between infrastructure and development. There is consensus among economists and economic historians that infrastructure has often been at the centre of the transformative shifts in the economy over the last 250 years, beginning with the canal network in Britain as its industrial revolution got under way. There is also broad agreement that many of these capital-intensive infrastructure projects – highways, airports, harbours, utility distribution systems, railways, water and sewer systems, telecommunication systems, etc. – have exhibited scale and network effects that engage both the public and private sectors in a variety of complicated financial, economic and political interactions. What is less clear is the best way to manage those interactions, the precise channels through which large infrastructure projects can help generate sustained development, whether the benefits derived match the costs incurred and, perhaps most difficult, whether those benefits and costs are shared in ways that generate inclusive outcomes.

In the face of such uncertainty, it is not surprising that numerous growth accounting exercises have failed to generate conclusive econometric results from the introduction of infrastructure variables, while myriad case studies have pointed to a disconnect between the microeconomic performance of infrastructure projects and their macroeconomic promise (see box 4.1). Nor is it surprising to find that many successful infrastructure programmes were as much the product of political ambition – "bold endeavours" as Felix Rohatyn (2009) put it – as careful public accounting and cold statistical calculation. Indeed, Albert Hirschman, in his seminal study titled *The Strategy of Economic Development* published exactly 60 years ago, was right in describing large-scale infrastructure planning as "a matter of faith in the development potential of a country or region" (1985: 84).

On that metric, the Washington Consensus, which has shaped much development policy thinking over the last 40 years, has shown little faith in the potential of developing countries. Infrastructure lending by the World Bank, which was its original rationale, dropped precipitously beginning in the 1970s, as its focus shifted to other forms of lending that concentrated on economic adjustment measures, good governance and social safety nets, rather than building infrastructure. However, this trend has been reversed in recent years (see figure 4.1).

The revival of interest in infrastructure reflects, in part, a growing acceptance in many advanced economies, since the 2008 financial crisis, given that such spending can have positive short- and long-term impacts on growth and, therefore, an important role in tackling secular stagnation (Summers, 2016). It is also a recognition of the central role that large infrastructure projects have played in the remarkable growth and poverty-reduction story that has unfolded in China. Indeed, the high ranking of China (relative to its income level) in the McKinsey Connectedness Index seems to indicate the faith placed by its leadership on infrastructure-led growth, including building a strategic advantage in the emerging digital economy

BOX 4.1   What do empirical studies tell us?

Aschauer's influential work (1989) found evidence for the widely accepted wisdom that "roads lead to prosperity" (see also Deng, 2013). Looking at the economy of the United States from 1948 to 1985, he concluded that infrastructure investments led to productivity increases, finding that a 10 per cent rise in infrastructure stock over time was associated with a 4 per cent increase in productivity. The study even showed that the converse also held: declining infrastructure investment from 1970 to 1985 was responsible for declining output per capita over the same period in the United States. These findings triggered a spurt of empirical research examining the contribution of infrastructure to growth. One strand has looked at the effects of aggregate infrastructure stocks and service flows on per capita GDP. This includes a majority of the macroeconomic studies, which look at expansion paths of per capita sectoral stocks with per capita GDP, thereby identifying countries that are outliers in terms of infrastructure investments in middle- and low-income regions (Ingram and Fay, 2008). Another strand has examined the effects of specific kinds of infrastructure interventions on growth and poverty reduction, usually focusing on particular geographical areas, enterprises or sectors (Straub, 2008).

However, there is still a lot of ambiguity on both conceptual and empirical fronts (see Estache, 2006; Estache and Garsous, 2012; Bom and Ligthart, 2014). The theoretical framework linking infrastructure and growth remains weak; and as Straub (2008) notes, a majority of the studies lack a clear hypothesis to be tested. As a result, although several studies after Aschauer (1989, 1990) focused on questioning the cause–effect relationship between infrastructure stocks and growth (see Gramlich, 1994), and the question of spurious correlations due to non-stationarity of data or missing variables (Holtz-Eakin, 1994), there is still a great deal of controversy on the direction and magnitude of the growth-enhancing effects of infrastructure (see Lakshmanan, 2011; Deng, 2013).

Empirically, the first critical issue is the measurement of infrastructure itself, as there continues to be no unified definition of the term (Cassis et al., 2016). Many studies measure infrastructure in terms of an investment flow or stock (public capital), or a single physical asset (Calderón and Servén, 2010; Lakshmanan, 2011; Deng, 2013), and consider the impact of one or the other kinds of infrastructure on growth (water, electricity, transport, or a combination thereof). But given that infrastructure investments are relatively heterogeneous in nature, and some forms of infrastructure (roads and telecommunications) have a greater impact on productivity than others (such as airlines), the scope of the study becomes an important issue in assessing findings and their relevance to the wider debate (Bröcker and Rietveld, 2009; Melo et al., 2013). Furthermore, macro- and microstudies often result in contradictory findings. This is because the most direct impacts of infrastructure on growth are obtained at the province or state level where network effects of infrastructure investments and indirect benefits are most evident, whereas in some cases, at the macro level expansion of infrastructure has been found to be associated with lower growth, for reasons that are not well explored.

A second issue that affects empirical comparisons relates to inadequacies in the data on infrastructure (Elburz et al., 2017). Infrastructure is a result of both public and private investment, with private investment ranging between 25 per cent to 70 per cent of total infrastructure investment in different countries. But since data on infrastructure are scant and typically do not provide a comprehensive total of private and public investments, public infrastructure is used as a proxy in a large number of studies, thereby potentially leading to undercounting of total infrastructure stocks of countries in existing empirical analyses. This problem is exacerbated by the fact that many countries have not maintained reliable public infrastructure investment figures until recently, which creates issues around comparability.

Third, infrastructure stock figures might not really convey the level of services offered, because there can be large differences between the quality and quantity of infrastructure services offered (Straub, 2008), especially in developing countries. Hence, existing estimates do not capture the efficiency of infrastructure and service quality, which is a very important determinant of growth.

In a widely accepted study, Calderón et al. (2011) estimated that a 10 per cent rise in infrastructure assets can directly account for an increase in GDP per capita of between 0.7 per cent and 1 per cent. But in general, the variability in the data used and its relevance to the central question of infrastructure's impact on growth, the model specification, the econometric methodology and the treatment of non-stationarity and causation, are all causes for inconclusive results. These data difficulties also make it hard to arrive at methodologies to compare and contrast the experiences of countries in promoting growth through increases in stock in infrastructure. Straub (2008: 22) reviewed 64 empirical studies linking infrastructure to growth to find that very few of them actually addressed the question directly and systematically.

FIGURE 4.1 Multilateral development banks: Finance for infrastructure as proportion of total banks' finance
(Percentage)

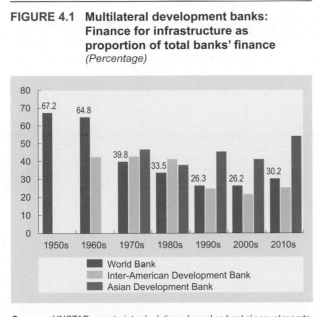

Source: UNCTAD secretariat calculations, based on banks' annual reports.
Note: Infrastructure includes energy, transportation and telecommunications. Values are averages for each decade, based on banks' annual commitments from both concessional and non-concessional windows. World Bank: includes International Bank for Reconstruction and Development and International Development Association only. Inter-American Development Bank: the 1960s are the average over 1967–1969. Asian Development Bank: based on figures available from 1971.

(Woetzel et al., 2017). Many other developing countries are keen to understand how China managed this process and to replicate its success.

Multilateral financial institutions, including new institutions from the South such as the Asian Infrastructure Investment Bank and the New Development Bank, have begun scaling up support for infrastructure investment in developing countries. There are also several international initiatives – such as the Belt and Road Initiative in China and the (much smaller) infrastructure plan for Africa from Germany – that have put infrastructure investments at their centre. Meanwhile, international institutional investors, ever on the lookout to strengthen their financial portfolios, seem keen on infrastructure as an asset class, since it offers a steady return on investment profile. All this chimes well with the 2030 Development Agenda, constructed around a series of ambitious goals and targets, which together add up to a massive infrastructure programme on a global scale; the Addis Ababa Action Agenda agreed at the Third United Nations Conference on Financing for Development in 2015, has reinforced this ambition.

But even as more resources have been made available for infrastructure projects, the scale of the financing challenge has, if anything, become more daunting. The World Bank has acknowledged this in its call to scale up efforts "from billions to trillions" to meet the 2030 Agenda and proffered a new framework to meet this challenge involving an enhanced role for the private sector through public–private partnerships, blending and de-risking techniques. This has focused the infrastructure debate on the "bankability" of projects (discussed in section D). While this focus has, no doubt, helped to raise awareness of the infrastructure challenge, it misses or, worse, sidelines, some key questions from a developing-country perspective beginning with how infrastructure can actually become a real force for structural transformation, raising productivity across sectors and activities, and creating a more virtuous development circle. Posing that question leads naturally to a series of related questions that policymakers from developing countries have begun to ask:

- How should they seek to channel new financing possibilities in the most effective and sustainable ways?

- How should they approach new initiatives coming from specific lead countries (such as the Belt and Road Initiative in China) and from regional arrangements?

- What are the important considerations to bear in mind when entering into specific financing deals for new infrastructure?

- What are the possible threats and how can they be avoided?

This chapter addresses the role of infrastructure in the process of structural transformation as its central question. It draws, in part, on the framework provided by Hirschman to make planning and programming activities more effective, in the face of the uncertainties, constraints and tensions inherent in the development process. Recognizing that development planning is a "risky business", Hirschman stressed the importance of sequencing and experimentation to establish the right balance between what was then commonly called "social overhead capital" (public infrastructure) and directly productive activities (private investment) (Hirschman, 1958: 83). Beginning from his description of development strategy as "diversified investment in the general growth of the economy rather than growth of one specific activity" (Hirschman, 1958: 85), the chapter proposes that crowding in private investment as part of an unbalanced growth strategy offers a useful framework within which to consider infrastructure investments in many of today's developing countries (Hirschman, 1958: 93). It seeks to show how public infrastructure investments can help to break the "interlocking vicious circles" (Hirschman, 1958: 5) that impede development and to help generate the kind of linkages that are key to structural transformation.

Building such linkages is neither an automatic nor a linear process. The growth effects of infrastructure depend on where infrastructure investments take place, and how these investments are planned, executed and sequenced. The links between infrastructure and transformation are best forged when infrastructure projects are clearly designed and placed as part of a wider development strategy that recognizes and actively fosters the positive feedback loops between infrastructure, productivity and growth. Indeed, throughout history from the development of Western Europe and the United States up until the recent cases of successful industrializers of East Asia, infrastructure development has been firmly tied to broader strategic objectives and institutional changes. These experiences provide an effective counter to the bankability approach, since they show that development strategies are not best pursued through emphasis on individual projects determined solely by criteria of financial viability. The alternative requires a more holistic approach, that includes projects based on developmental criteria, and which may not be financially viable in the short run.

The chapter is organized as follows. Section B situates the discussion on infrastructure and development by tracing it historically, providing a taxonomy of different types of infrastructure and how they can contribute to a virtuous development circle in the context of unbalanced growth. Section C maps recent estimates of infrastructure needs and raises some concerns about meeting those needs primarily as a question of the bankability of projects. Section D offers some elements for planning infrastructure investments, which it sees as key to growth promotion. Section E concludes.

B. Infrastructure matters: Conceptual issues and historical lessons

Physical and social infrastructure has always been at the centre of discussions in developing countries, beginning with the crude colonial imperative of extracting and exporting natural resources at minimum cost, in the commodity-based value chains that developed during the nineteenth century. Programmes to achieve minimum standards of nutrition, health and education made a brief appearance in the interwar period as a philosophy of "colonial trusteeship" sought to deflect growing social discontent (Arndt, 1987: 27–29). But it was only during the Second World War and the subsequent struggle for political independence and local control over natural resources that a more serious discussion on infrastructure and development was launched. Given the ideological currents of the time, that discussion was strongly shaped by an emerging development narrative focused on overcoming "market failures", seen as endemic in infrastructure provision, and requiring government involvement through public utilities (power, telecommunications, water, etc.), public works (highways, dams, irrigation, etc.) and public transport systems (railways, ports, airports, etc.). Infrastructure was again the focus of attention, but from an opposing perspective, in the 1980s, as talk of "government failures" accompanied the sharp neoliberal policy turn. At that time, privatization became the instrument of choice to boost efficiency, along with measures to enhance private participation in infrastructure provision by making it more profitable. This included – in a sense coming full circle – tying infrastructure to the right business environment to enable participation in global value chains. The 2030 Agenda has once again broadened the debate with a more ambitious infrastructure agenda.

Underpinning all these twists and turns is the abiding question of whether, and if so how, infrastructure programmes can help to trigger and sustain a virtuous circle of growth and structural transormation. Answering this requires unpacking the term "infrastructure" to consider the requirements, implications and consequences of different types of infrastructure creation.

1. Types of infrastructure

Infrastructure encompasses a broad category of goods and services that involve investments in both the social and physical stock of capital. Definitions of the term by development economists have been less than precise (Ingram and Fay, 2008: 301). Hirschman, for example, employing the umbrella term "social overhead capital", defined infrastructure as those "basic services without which primary, secondary and tertiary productive activities cannot function" (1958: 83), and provided or heavily regulated by public agencies. He further distinguished a "hard core" of transportation and power (characterized by technical indivisibilities and a high capital–output ratio), from a softer group of more traditional public goods such as health and education.

The tendency to identify infrastructure with "public goods" is somewhat misleading (as the defining characteristics of non-excludable and non-rival often do not apply)[1] but does serve as a reminder of the tendency to underinvest in their provision, since the strong presence of externalities can give rise to free-riding behaviour and drive a wedge between their social and private returns. This tendency, as Hirschman recognized, is particularly acute in developing countries. While individual projects associated with softer infrastructure are often smaller compared to harder projects such as in energy or transport, the difficulties of excluding some users and their non-rival nature means they are likely to be provided at less than full cost to users. Therefore, they have usually relied on significant and continuous public sector financing. Moreover, while recognizing the potential long-term benefits of these types of infrastructure spending in terms of productivity, innovation and employment creation, it can be difficult to measure these benefits in the short term, making them vulnerable to political expediencies and budgetary pressures. This is the case with health and education services, particularly in those areas heavily dependent on intangible investments (such as in R&D and skills), which may not require large sunk costs but do require ongoing investments to maintain and improve the services provided.

In many cases, however, infrastructure services, particularly those of the harder variety, are both rivalrous in consumption and excludable in access and cannot, therefore, be considered as public goods in the strict sense. However, externalities persist, and other market failures complicate their delivery. In particular, significant scale economies, large sunk costs and long gestation periods make for both natural monopolies and strong complementarities, whereby the effectiveness of investment in one sector depends on investments in others. This is particularly the case where infrastructure provision is closely linked to networks. These characteristics are found mainly in the energy, water, public transport and telecommunications sectors, although variations exist within sectors, across countries and over time.[2] These are, moreover, the sectors that have traditionally been seen as having a more direct impact on economic growth and structural transformation.

Networked infrastructure services can be delivered through hybrid systems with varying degrees of state ownership and regulatory oversight. This makes their provision a matter of policy choice and contestation. In addition, technological changes have an impact on the provision of such infrastructure, including through a shift to less capital-intensive techniques and increased competition (Markard, 2011; Torrisi, 2009; Kasper, 2015).

This is certainly the case with the power system, comprising energy generation, transmission and distribution. Electricity generation has historically relied on conventional fossil fuels and involved large centralized power stations. Transmission and distribution are responsible for moving electricity from power stations to users. Promoting such a system, from generation to delivery to the end users, requires long-term investment in large-scale projects; it also involves risks and uncertainty and therefore requires detailed planning (Markard, 2011). But its provision dramatically increases both economic productivity and quality of life. In rural areas, access to affordable energy can boost farm productivity because of its uses in pumping water for irrigation, mechanization, agricultural processing and post-harvest storage. Developing a domestic energy industry has multiple benefits, because of jobs created in system maintenance and repairs, billing and administration, and power plant operation and distribution, in addition to backward linkages and new domestic markets (UNCTAD, 2017). Positive feedback effects are created as energy provision supports transportation and information and communication technologies (ICTs), which in turn assist in energy generation and distribution.

Like energy, transportation infrastructure (roads, railways, airports, seaports, bridges, waterways and tramways) calls for large-scale investment projects and long gestation periods, although smaller, localized projects with shorter execution periods are also possible. The design of transportation systems shapes social transformations, and how populations and businesses settle and interact (NCE, 2014; Atack et al., 2010). The choice of transport systems, their scale and their spread, matters considerably for structural transformation as well as other economic and social impacts. This is already evident in most developing countries, many of which are still dealing with the legacy of colonial choices in developing transport systems, since these typically emphasized connecting the locations of cash-crop production or extraction of natural resources with towns and ports for export. More widely diffused transport connectivity, by contrast, can assist in more broad-based growth. For example, in road construction, investing in secondary roads in rural areas has been found to have wide-ranging positive impacts and higher benefit-to-cost ratios than investments in highways (United Nations, 2016). Rural roads that increase connectivity for rural areas obviously increase access to markets and related knowledge; they also have benefits for household income, poverty reduction and access to health care and education (Schweikert and Chinowsky, 2012). Efficient transport systems can also reduce production costs, alleviating the need to store large quantities of material and allowing large and small producers to work with just-in-time systems (Nordås and Piermartini, 2004).

The infrastructure services dealing with water provision are recognized to be crucial not just for human welfare but also for economic development. Such services and related physical infrastructure occur at multiple scales and serve urban, industrial, agricultural and rural users, as well as involving ecological considerations (Global Water Partnership, 2009). They include dams and hydropower; water supply; wastewater, sanitation and water quality; storm water systems; irrigation and drainage; river and coastal works; pipelines and canals; and natural water infrastructure (Grigg, 2017). The particular nature of water as a basic human need, in combination with its amenability to being controlled and monopolized in different circumstances, makes public involvement in its provision both necessary and fraught. While everyone needs "access to safe water in adequate quantities for drinking, cooking and personal hygiene, and sanitation facilities that do not compromise health or dignity" (UN-Water, 2015: 37), not everyone gets it. Agriculture depends on irrigation

that raises crop output and is associated with lower inequality (United Nations, 2016) and water infrastructure can reduce vulnerabilities related to food and energy security. Similarly, water is an essential input for manufacturing processes. But distributional conflicts – across locations, sectors, income categories and social groups – loom especially large in the case of water, and the manner of its provision can raise environmental concerns. Longer-term concerns about water overuse and inadequate renewal of fresh water supplies, as well as water pollution, along with the (often unintended) consequences of major water infrastructure projects (such as displacement because of dams, waterlogging and salinity through canal networks, inequality of access and so on) mean that public involvement in its provision and regulation is inevitable even when much of the infrastructure is privately provided.

An example of the strong network externalities associated with infrastructure comes from telecommunications infrastructure, which includes fixed and mobile telephony, radio and Internet systems, along with the machinery that enables information transmission, transmission lines and cables.[3] This is an area that has been dominated by private players, including network and platform operators and technology and content providers, especially as rapid technological change has enabled favourable financial returns (Czarnecki and Dietze, 2017; ADB, 2017; Henckel and McKibbin, 2010; Serebrisky et al., 2015). In addition to facilitating communications in general, such infrastructure is increasingly required by a wide range of activities in banking, trade and production, and has enabled new forms of economic activity to emerge. This impact tends to be higher where levels of penetration are near universal (Estache, 2010: 16), but even where penetration is low there can be many positive effects. For example, Hjort and Poulsen (2017) report that new submarine telecom cables in different parts of Africa brought the arrival of fast Internet, leading to the emergence of technology start-ups and a manufacturing sector that produces Internet-capable devices to serve the region, an improvement of supply chain coordination enhancing productivity in manufacturing and agribusiness, and the creation of jobs in the ICT sector and elsewhere. As the industry moves from traditional fixed networks to software-based network technologies, the scale of investment has been changing rapidly from being predominantly large to including smaller-scale projects (Deloitte, 2017). However, regulatory requirements in this area are complex, involving not just the specification of standards and usage limits, but also the prevention of monopolistic behaviour, which places often serious demands on policymakers in developing countries.

2. Infrastructure and the virtuous circle of growth

Much of the development policy challenge amounts to finding ways to trigger and sustain virtuous circles of increased resource mobilization, faster capital formation, rising productivity, better jobs, higher incomes and expanding markets, both at home and abroad, enabling more resource mobilization. As discussed in *TDR 2016*, industrial development and diversification have been key to most sustained growth and development experiences. As industry – particularly manufacturing – expands, primary activity tends to become more efficient, as a result of both increased demand and the provision of capital and intermediate goods, in turn feeding industrial dynamism. The service sector also expands to complement manufacturing activities and, at higher levels of income, comes to dominate the economy.

Industrial development was central to Hirschman's idea that developing countries should pursue "unbalanced growth" with productive resources targeted at a few sectors. This was based on the belief that the resulting disruption would not only stimulate further private investment in the favoured sectors but would help promote various organizational and other capabilities whose shortage might otherwise curtail the growth process. The unbalanced growth model is based around exploiting scale economies and complementarities in favoured sectors that can induce more investment and productivity growth. Those sectors, in Hirschman's framework, have more backward and forward linkages; the former referring to provision of inputs from other activities and sectors, the latter to demand for new activities. The development policy challenge is, accordingly, about identifying lead sectors, addressing missing linkages and strengthening inter-industry and intersectoral interdependencies to boost productivity growth.

Hirschman believed that this framework would provide the best guide for the efficient sequencing of infrastructure spending, as the shortages revealed to the planning authorities would ensure that public investments in social overhead capital would complement those already under way in the private sector,

thereby further boosting productivity growth. In this sequence, infrastructure would follow rather than lead the growth process. It is largely around this sequencing issue that differences between balanced and unbalanced growth strategies emerged in early development policy debates (see box 4.2). Despite these differences, there was general agreement that in most developing countries, investment in general, and in infrastructure, in particular, involves a series of non-marginal adjustments that are poorly coordinated by markets and for which planning techniques of various kinds are desirable.

There are additional ways in which infrastructure spending can drive productivity and growth. Like other government spending, infrastructure investment boosts aggregate demand, potentially sparking broader-based output growth through scale economies which feed into productivity increases. This typically leads to greater private sector investment, and by extension, also raises private demand for physical capital over a longer time-horizon (Dissou and Didic, 2013). These complementary effects on private capital formation tend to be cumulative, as infrastructure provision affords greater certainty for private industry, and the consequent increased rates of capital formation help to crowd in investments in other sectors of the economy.[4] In turn, increased productivity and rising incomes lead to higher demand for various infrastructure services. In this way infrastructure investment becomes part of the process of cumulative causation, whereby industrial expansion creates employment, incomes and demand, and leads to increased productivity (Myrdal, 1957).

Infrastructure investment can simultaneously address supply-side constraints and thereby raise the productivity of other activities (Straub, 2008; Estache and Fay, 2009). Insofar as this reduces costs and improves the durability of private capital investment, it also enables the private sector to spend less on maintaining its own capital, releasing resources for other productive investment. Infrastructure provision that promotes social inclusion – such as better housing and improvements in health, education, sanitation and nutrition – enhances labour productivity in addition to promoting social welfare (Serebrisky, 2014). At low levels of existing infrastructure, the growth-enhancing and social-inclusion effects of new infrastructure investment tend to be even greater (Straub, 2008).[5]

Conversely, low or insufficient infrastructure can handicap enterprises by increasing production costs

---

BOX 4.2   Balanced versus unbalanced growth

The central issue in the early debates on development policy was how to shift from a resource-dependent to an industrializing economy with a diversified production structure. Industrialization was understood to be an inherently dynamic process, thanks to the presence of increasing returns (both at the firm and sectoral levels), complementarities (on both the supply and demand side), learning economies and various other externalities that if successfully exploited could drive productivity growth and support job creation.

The problem, recognized by most economists, was that in developing countries these features also introduced a large wedge between the private and social returns from investments, making the market an inefficient mechanism for mobilizing and allocating the required resources. Accordingly, the state would have to be involved in connecting the investment and industrialization processes in developing countries. The question was how and where it should make that connection.

For balanced growth theorists such as Paul Rosenstein-Rodan, Ragnar Nurkse and Tibor Scitovsky the major constraint on productive investment was on the demand side. Small markets in most developing countries produced uncertainty about the expected returns on investment and made it difficult to achieve scale economies, thereby choking off the accumulation process and closing down an industrial growth path before it could really get started.

The solution outlined by Rosenstein-Rodan (1943) was a coordinated investment programme (which Nurkse called "a big push") across several industries, to guarantee a sufficient level of aggregate demand to make those investments viable. In particular, expansion of light industries providing consumer goods seemed the most promising option as these could provide local demand for each other's output; and a large-scale and integrated infrastructure programme was seen as the ideal way to break the constraint on self-sustaining growth because it would both stimulate local demand and lead to lower production costs (Nurkse, 1953). Moreover, complementarities across the investments in electricity generation, transport, communications, etc. implied that these too should be organized as an indivisible block if their full benefits were to be realized. The resulting development strategy combined centralized infrastructure planning with infant industry protection and, in the process, introduced a whole range of new planning techniques (shadow pricing, linear programming, etc.) to help manage the subsequent growth trajectory.

Early criticisms of the balanced growth model raised concerns that, given an inelastic supply of factors in many developing countries, it might be prone to inflationary pressures. Also, its emphasis on consumer goods industries seemed to ignore the opportunities for economies of scale in the production of capital and intermediate goods and the potential of tapping into export markets (Fleming, 1955; Sheahan, 1958). Still,

---

(related to transport, logistics and storage), render products that would otherwise be competitive as uncompetitive, limit access to markets and make rural production unprofitable (Escribano and Guasch, 2005, 2008; Donaldson, 2010; Escribano et al., 2010). Indeed, countries that have experienced stalled industrialization or premature deindustrialization (see *TDR 2016*) have tended to have inconsistent trajectories of infrastructure investments, that have been inadequate overall and sometimes pulled the economy in other directions. In India, for example, several studies have noted that underinvestment in infrastructure required for manufacturing sector (Ghosh, 2012; Simon and Natarajan, 2017) has constrained private investment. By contrast, the rise of information technology services and digital products was possible in India because the conditions for the expansion of telecommunications and broadband networks were relatively less costly for the government to deliver

on a wide scale (Douhan and Nordberg, 2007). In several natural resource-rich developing countries, infrastructure investments have pulled the economy in the direction of resource extraction, at the expense of other productive activity.

The resulting infrastructure gaps then become constraints on supply. For example, Mesquita Moreira et al. (2013) found that high transportation costs were associated with falling exports in Chile and Peru, while Escribano et al. (2010: 8) showed that poor infrastructure in Africa increased transport and energy costs for local firms, with severe consequences for manufacturing productivity and competitiveness. Allcott et al. (2016) found that power shortages reduced Indian manufacturing revenues and producer surpluses by almost 10 per cent. When countries have adequate electricity provision with few or no power outages, producers do not need to have costly with the focus firmly on economies of scale, these disagreements were mainly empirical matters relating to the scope for coordinated expansion.

Picking up on both the inelasticity of supply and the importance of capital goods industries, Hirschman (1958) presented a starker contrast between a balanced and unbalanced growth model. Like the balanced growth theorists, he recognized that externalities could disrupt any desired investment sequence. However, for Hirschman growth was always, everywhere and necessarily, an intrinsically uncertain and uneven process – marked by rapid advances in some sectors followed by catching up in others. This made the principal challenge for policymakers the search for complementarities across industries rather than scale economies.

Comparing development to "an endlessly spinning cobweb", he contrasted a big push with a sequential progression of promoting and then reducing "tensions, disproportions and disequilibria", using profits and losses as the metric for identifying disequilibria and the means to induce subsequent investments (Hirschman, 1958: 66). "[A]t each step, an industry takes advantage of external economies created by previous expansions, and at the same time creates new external economies to be exploited by other operators" (Hirschman, 1958: 67). The role of the state planner is to assess whether productive private investment or infrastructure investment will induce the most progress in other industries, through creating excess capacity or shortages. Hirschman introduced the concept of (backward and forward) linkages as the mechanism for simultaneous and progressive expansion in both domestic demand and supply and to better identify the sectors to focus on. This made input–output tables, rather than aggregate demand, Hirschman's policy framework of choice. Since he was unconvinced that most developing countries had the capabilities to undertake big centralized investment programmes, he offered a more pragmatic approach to infrastructure planning that would help break the "interlocking vicious circles" of underdevelopment (Hirschman, 1958: 5). This would occur by allowing infrastructure ("social overhead capital") to lag behind in an investment sequence beginning with productive private investment primarily in the capital goods and intermediate goods sectors (see Hirschman, 1958: 83).

Arguably, the contrast between the two approaches was oversold at the time, as Streeten (1959) recognized and Hirschman (1961, 1987) later accepted. Both approaches were concerned with investment planning and both (albeit to different degrees) recognized that expanding output ahead of demand would give rise to further complementary investments and innovations. This was particularly true of infrastructure investments, given the significant indivisibilities those involved. Indeed, the two theories began with the challenge of a divergence between social and private returns, employed much the same conceptual framework – indivisibilities, externalities, increasing returns, complementarities in supply and demand – and acknowledged a central role for the state. This turns the discussion of investment planning, including with respect to infrastructure, into a matter of empirical detail about where scale economies are located and the political economy question of whether or not the developmental state has the requisite institutional capacities to pursue larger- or smaller-scale projects.

backup generators. Power outages are a particularly acute problem in South Asia and sub-Saharan Africa, as indicated in figure 4.2 by the average number of outages suffered by firms in a month. It has been estimated for sub-Saharan Africa alone that continuous energy supply would accelerate growth by two percentage points per year.[6]

In what follows, we consider whether unbalanced growth through infrastructure investments can really help countries to move to a strong growth trajectory. The historical experiences considered below suggest that they were certainly significant in many success stories. However, even within a framework of unbalanced growth, there are at least two additional issues to keep in mind (Myrdal, 1970). First, some of the supply-side limitations that are common in many developing countries, such as scarcity of skills or the absence of the institutions required to mobilize and

FIGURE 4.2 Number of electrical outages in a typical month

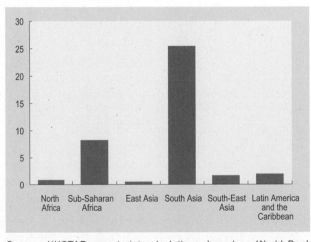

Source: UNCTAD secretariat calculations, based on *World Bank Enterprise Surveys: What Businesses Experience* database. Available at: http://www.enterprisesurveys.org/data/exploretopics/infrastructure (accessed 7 March 2018).

coordinate resources, have to be addressed directly through industrial policies of one kind or another. Second, in addition to expanding the "right" investments, it may also be necessary to restrict certain kinds of private investments and production that pull the economy into unforeseen and undesired directions. In the absence of such disciplining mechanisms, it is also likely that public investments, including in infrastructure, will be captured by certain private interests, with their potential development impact reduced or lost altogether.

3. Historical experiences

While infrastructure can boost productivity growth through a variety of channels, its contribution to sustaining a virtuous development circle does not occur in an institutional or policy vacuum. The gains that infrastructure brought during the industrial revolution, first in England and then in continental European countries, were not only the result of long-standing investments spanning decades or even centuries; they were often built on clear policy visions that placed infrastructure at the centre of nation-building efforts. Indeed, the later industrialization began, the more conscious those efforts appear to have become, given the larger investment push that was usually required to achieve catch-up (*TDR 2003, 2016*).

As Haldane (2018) has noted, the series of successful transformation episodes that have sustained an unprecedented ratcheting up in living standards over the past 250 years have all tended to involve the interlinking of infrastructure, innovation and institutions in ways that have not only supported higher rates of capital formation but also responded to the economic and social disturbances that accompany such episodes. For example, structural change in Britain between 1760 and 1860 was not simply the fortuitous product of technological breakthroughs and entrepreneurial endeavour, but rather the intertwining of a series of industrial, agricultural and demographic changes. The private capital behind these changes was often on a relatively small scale but more significant investments were needed in physical and social infrastructure to ensure the required linkages across the newly emerging activities and to support businesses, workers and society buffeted by these changes. This was particularly true for the turnpikes, canals and railways that accompanied Britain's rise as a global economic superpower. Britain gained an advantage from the early streamlining of legislative

procedures for infrastructure projects and the fact that these projects could be effectively implemented and managed at a regional level, reflecting its pattern of spatially unbalanced industrial development, through ad hoc initiatives among interested private actors. National initiatives only emerged later to better coordinate existing projects in line with the demands of a more sophisticated and integrated national economy.

In Europe, the French architect Michel Chevalier was one of the first to envision a scheme for a multi-country infrastructure network at the heart of efforts to end poverty and conflict in Europe. Conceived in 1830, Chevalier's impressive plan[7] was for a grand European transport system to connect the entire continent with rails, roads and shipping routes, whereby railway lines spanning over 60,000 km would traverse from the Mediterranean, the Black Sea and the Caspian Sea (through northbound lines), linking them to eastbound destinations of Flanders at the North Sea via Warsaw, Vilnius, Riga and St Petersburg to the Russian Pacific (Högselius et al., 2015; Drolet, 2015). He believed that enhanced connectivity between regions would encourage trade, commerce and industrialization in Europe and the Ottoman Empire, and that this was the only way to foster political harmony. This vision tied "public works" (as infrastructure was then known) intimately with the economic, political and industrial progress of Europe at the time. The essential features of this plan were indeed adopted by France as well as a number of European countries that became independent between 1830 and 1871, including Belgium, the German Empire, Greece, Italy, Serbia and Romania; and it even led to cross-country multilateral initiatives for infrastructure expansion (Ambrosius and Henrich-Franke, 2016). Many of these countries saw railways as a means for industrial transformation, with the result that the European railway network expanded from 1,865 miles to over 215,000 miles between 1840 and 1913 (Ambrosius and Henrich-Franke, 2016: 44).

In the United States, the development of transport (notably railway) stimulated several industries such as iron, steel and timber; encouraged financial enterprise by promoting private investments into these sectors and railway construction; and contributed directly to the generation of national income through the provision and expansion of interregional and local transportation services (Jenks, 1944, 1951; Pereira et al., 2014; Shaw, 2014). Rohatyn (2009) provides examples of bold public moves on infrastructure in the United States over two centuries that transformed the country and its economic potential:

- the construction of the Erie Canal, which opened a water route to the west;

- Lincoln's support for the transcontinental railroad, which transformed the country and enabled vast new cities to emerge;

- Land Grant colleges that started in the mid-nineteenth century, which dramatically expanded access to higher education;

- the Homestead Act of 1852, which enabled the westward expansion of population and settlement;

- the construction of the Panama Canal in the early twentieth century, which enabled ships to pass between Atlantic and Pacific oceans and effectively sealed the hegemony of the United States in the region for the next century;

- the Rural Electrification Administration of the Franklin D. Roosevelt government, which brought electricity to the rural United States with all its attendant benefits;

- the GI Bill (Serviceman's Readjustment Act of 1944), which provided free college education and low-interest home and business loans to all veterans with more than 90 days in uniform, thereby creating a secure domestic market;

- the interstate highway system created by Eisenhower's Federal Aid Highway Act, which revitalized the economy and modernized the United States.

As Rohatyn notes, the benefits extended far beyond the purely economic: "Canals, roads, highways, schools, electrical power grids – it was this extensive and innovative infrastructure that made life in the United States more comfortable, more egalitarian and more secure" (2009: 221).

An important feature of the evolution of infrastructure development in these countries was the gradual but increasing significance of public control. While early systems in nineteenth- and twentieth-century Europe and the United States were often entirely private or a mix of public and private (with some significant public investment exceptions), from the late nineteenth century onwards there was a gradual public takeover of responsibility, supported by broader national visions of "municipal socialism" in Europe and "progressivism" in the United States (Marshall, 2013).

The experience with railway expansion in the United States during the second half of the nineteenth century is particularly instructive. In the first phase, extensive state involvement was essentially through subsidies, regulations, legal privileges, military protection, etc. as part of an early public–private partnership model. This enabled the rapid development of a transcontinental network, but also gave rise to financial speculation, market concentration and inefficiencies, business failures and political corruption. The public control that followed, particularly during the time of the New Deal, made it possible for governments to integrate spatial planning at the national, regional and local levels; and enabled an integrated approach to development, whereby infrastructure investments and maintenance were closely coordinated with national economic goals and requirements.

As it became evident with time that infrastructure provision calls for coordination, institutional frameworks to govern infrastructure emerged at the national level, which sought to centralize control with national authorities so as to plan and develop infrastructure integrating spatial, economic and temporal perspectives. Governments began to use bilateral and plurilateral agreements to achieve some level of standardization. As the coexistence of state-run and private rail lines in much of continental Europe, the United States and Britain led to clashes between private and public infrastructure systems (Cootner, 1963; Shaw, 2014), combinations of competitive and cooperative development structures were developed across road transport, telecommunications and postal services (Ambrosius and Henrich-Franke, 2016; Nerlove, 1966).

While the links between development and infrastructure spending appear to have grown closer in the late industrializing economy of the nineteenth century, triggering a virtuous circle augmented by increased international trade, those links were a good deal more tenuous for many developing countries. Indeed, the new communication technologies of that era, railways, steamships and telegraphs, created a global infrastructure network that led to growing income gaps as many developing countries were locked into a vicious circle of increased trade, weak diversification and low productivity growth (*TDR 1997*; Pascali, 2017). In many of the colonized countries, this same infrastructure shaped a highly uneven internal economic landscape: many developing countries inherited city planning or transport and port networks that were built for other purposes,

TABLE 4.1   The role of infrastructure in industrialization of the Republic of Korea

Industrial policy phase	Key infrastructure investments
1960–1970: First five-year development plan, along with policy to promote exporters across sectors such as iron, silk and fishing.	Development of the Seoul–Busan Highway and the Busan Port for exports; construction of power plants to support iron and steel and other core sectors; investment in primary education.
1970–1980: Accelerated industrialization with focus on promoting large exporting sectors, including textiles, plywood, iron ore and electronics.	National land development plan; investments in the Seoul Metro, Honam Highway, Yeongdong Highway and industrial complexes, nuclear power plants to support energy needs for industry.
1980–1990: Rationalization and restructuring, with focus on upgrading products and processes, especially in textiles, electronics, iron and steel products, footwear and ships.	A slowdown in aggregate infrastructure investment; targeted investments to build the regional energy supply system; strengthening of secondary and tertiary education and expansion of national R&D programme to support expansion of high technology sectors.
1990–2000: Transition to a knowledge-based economy, with focus on semiconductors, automobiles, computers and ships.	Expansion of transportation facilities, such as the Incheon Airport and high-speed railway system; information highway and e-government projects; further increase in public investment in higher education.

Source: Bang, 2003.

like natural resource exports, rather than developing a vibrant domestic market, and are still having to address the resultant inadequacies and imbalances (Rodney, 1973; Cooper, 1993). The globalization experience in the nineteenth century serves as an important reminder that simply expecting a combination of new technology, infrastructure spending and trade to deliver sustainable and inclusive growth is not borne out by the historical record.

Only after the Second World War were some developing countries able to establish their own virtuous circle linking infrastructure, industrialization, trade and economic growth. In the Republic of Korea – a prime example of manufacturing-led industrialization after the Second World War – the confluence of technological advance, export promotion, investment and capital accumulation was linked not only to favourable external conditions but also to multi-annual plans from 1962 to 1992 that set out targets and allocated resources for investments in social overhead capital. Infrastructure investment was a key element of these plans (see table 4.1), to the extent that between 1960 and 2002, it amounted to 14 per cent of GDP on average (Bang, 2003).[8]

Similarly, in China over the past three decades, the emphasis on infrastructure had the purpose of creating and enabling high-linkage sectors that were critical for generating growth (Holz, 2011). After the Asian crisis of 1997–1998, the Chinese government increased public infrastructure investment rapidly to stimulate domestic demand and promote economic growth, and these were the underlying reasons for the increase in public infrastructure investment after the 2008 crisis as well. Public infrastructure investment grew in real terms at an average annual rate of 25 per cent over 1997–2010 (Zhang et al., 2013: 91).[9] This was instrumental in creating two distinct types of external economies. First, consistent infrastructure investment resulted in reduction in costs for private sector activity and enlargement of the market, as dispersed and fragmented pockets of small demand were converted into larger markets of effective demand. The expansion of public infrastructure and profitability of private activities raised wages and promoted consumption, while backward linkages led to private investment in new sectors. Second, public investment in strategic sectors created vertical economies in the intermediate stages of production, leading to possibilities of forward linkages between such activities and other lagging sectors to promote growth through "returning" economies (Sutcliffe, 1964).

In both the Republic of Korea and China, infrastructure investments were sequenced according to the needs of the industrial sectors. This is similar to the successful cases of industrializers in the nineteenth century, such as Europe and the United States, where targeting infrastructure investments according to sectoral needs was planned and coordinated so as to avoid bottlenecks that slow down national and regional growth. This also meant that, despite increasing participation of the private sector, the reins of infrastructure planning and coordination were firmly with the government, to ensure the appropriate balance between national economic, social, urban and environmental goals.[10] This strategy implicitly recognized the strong intertemporal dimension, since building infrastructure that promotes structural transformation requires long-term coordination, spanning several decades (Shi et al., 2017).

C. Infrastructure in developing countries

1. Needs and gaps

In the past several years, multilateral financial institutions, private consultancy firms and international experts have provided estimates of infrastructure investment needs, for both developed and developing countries, based on current and medium-term requirements. Table 4.2 summarizes some recent estimates for (mainly) economic infrastructure investment at the global level and by sector, which suggest annual needs ranging from $4.6 trillion to $7.9 trillion.[11] This range includes estimates using both baseline and low-carbon scenarios. The baseline scenario assumes that current growth will continue into the future, while the investment needs for addressing climate change hinge heavily on the concept of sustainable infrastructure.[12]

The large variation (over $3 trillion) across estimates, is because of differences in methodologies, data sources and the types of expenditures considered.[13] All of these calculations involve a wide array of assumptions about future infrastructure demand, prices and technological change. For obvious reasons, all such estimates of future needs for infrastructure investment have problems related to coverage, assumptions and methodologies. There is lack of clarity about the definition of infrastructure and types of investment considered, as well as lack of comprehensive data on current infrastructure investment. The assessment of needs based on quality indicators and the use of expected GDP growth and elasticity of infrastructure investment to growth are problematic.

Few estimates use any calculation of minimum required infrastructure stocks, which are considered more pertinent for low-income countries in need of rapid catching up. The emphasis on a "top-down" approach based on the use of global models is to the detriment of a "bottom-up" assessment of needs based on country-specific circumstances and specific long-term development strategies. The lack of a network perspective fails to take full account of the interdependencies between sectors and types of infrastructure. In addition, rapidly changing technologies make the task of producing accurate estimates

---

TABLE 4.2   Infrastructure investment needs at the global level, annual 2015/16–2030
(Trillions of 2015 dollars)

| | Annual total needs for "core" infrastructure[a] | Annual total needs (baseline scenario) | Annual total needs (low-carbon scenario)[b] | Selected sectors (baseline scenario) | | |
				Power and electricity T&D	Transport	Telecoms
OECD (2017a)	4.9	6.3	6.9	0.7	2.7	0.6
Bhattacharya et al. (2016)	5.4	7.9	.	1.5	2.0	1.0
Woetzel et al. (2016)	3.3	4.6–6.0	.	1.0	1.2	0.6
NCE (2014)	3.8	6.4	7.0	0.7	1.0	0.5

Source: OECD, 2017a: tables 3, A and 4.

   a   "Core" infrastructure investment includes power and electricity transmission and distribution (T&D), transport (roads, rail, airports and ports), water and sanitation, and telecommunications. Total infrastructure includes, in addition to "core" infrastructure, primary energy supply (coal, oil and gas) and energy efficiency.

   b   Under the low-carbon scenario, investment in low-emission, climate-resilient infrastructure is taken into account in order to limit the rise in global temperature to 2°C by the end of the century.

FIGURE 4.3 Current infrastructure investment, selected subregions and economies
(Percentage of GDP)

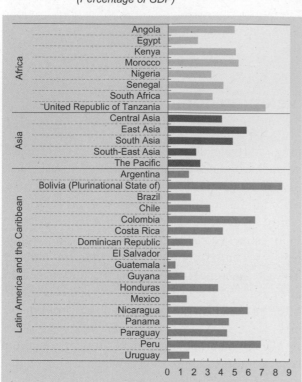

Source: UNCTAD secretariat calculations, based on ECLAC (2017), AfDB (2018: 80), ADB (2017) and Heathcote (2017).

Note: *Asia*: Current infrastructure includes the following Asian subregions and economies: Central Asia (Armenia and Georgia), East Asia (China, Mongolia, the Republic of Korea and Hong Kong, China), South Asia (Bangladesh, Bhutan, India, Maldives, Nepal, Pakistan and Sri Lanka), South-East Asia (Indonesia, Malaysia, the Philippines, Singapore, Thailand and Viet Nam) and The Pacific (Fiji, Kiribati and Papua New Guinea), all for the year 2011. *Africa*: Current infrastructure investment expenditure in the year 2015. Countries included are: Angola, Egypt, Kenya, Morocco, Nigeria, Senegal, South Africa and United Republic of Tanzania. *Latin America and the Caribbean*: Figures are based on InfraLatam database. Current infrastructure investment is from year 2015. Countries included in the figure are: Argentina, Bolivia (Plurinational State of), Brazil, Chile (2014 expenditure), Colombia, Costa Rica, the Dominican Republic, El Salvador, Guatemala, Guyana, Honduras, Mexico, Nicaragua, Panama, Paraguay, Peru and Uruguay (2013 expenditure).

particularly hard, since they would inevitably change future costs and needs (Woetzel et al., 2016: 13).[14] Insufficient inclusion of infrastructure needs for climate change adaptation and mitigation results in more modest estimates (Estache, 2010; Bhattacharya et al., 2016; Schmidt-Traub, 2015; OECD, 2017a, 2017b).

These shortcomings raise doubts about both accuracy and comparability across different estimates. Despite all this, international institutions and experts have reached the conclusion that investment needs are very large, especially when compared with current

investment levels (OECD, 2017b). For developing countries, UNCTAD estimates investment needs of $1.6 trillion–$2.5 trillion per year between 2015 and 2030, against current actual investment of $870 billion.[15] An earlier study by Bhattacharya et al. (2012) projected needs in developing countries to be between 6 per cent and 8 per cent of GDP by 2020, against an actual investment level of 3 per cent in 2012.[16] In Latin America and the Caribbean (LAC), ECLAC (2017) estimated infrastructure investment needs at 6.2 per cent against an actual spending of 3.2 per cent of the region's GDP in 2015.[17] In Africa, projected needs are said to be in the order of 5.9 per cent of the region's GDP over the 2016–2040 period, against current trends at around 4.3 per cent (AfDB, 2018: figure 3.7; and Heathcote, 2017: 28).[18] In Asia, both current and projected investment needs over the years 2016–2030 have been estimated at around 5 per cent of GDP (ADB, 2017). These regional evaluations are not perfectly comparable, since they are produced by different organizations drawing on their own methodologies and data sources.

There are large regional and intraregional variations in current infrastructure investment, as indicated in figure 4.3. In Africa, Ethiopia and United Republic of Tanzania spend well above 5 per cent of GDP on infrastructure, while Nigeria and South Africa (the region's two largest economies) have expenditures of just above 3 per cent and Egypt just over 2 per cent. In Latin America, the regional average is, to a large extent, influenced by low infrastructure expenditure in the region's larger economies, with Argentina, Brazil and Mexico spending less than 2 per cent of GDP in 2015. A few small economies such as Guyana, Trinidad and Tobago, and Uruguay also spend less than 2 per cent of GDP on infrastructure. In contrast, Andean countries such as the Plurinational State of Bolivia, Colombia and Peru spend above 6 per cent, followed closely by smaller economies such as Nicaragua, with expenditure of nearly 6 per cent in 2015. In Asia, at one extreme, East Asia spent 5.8 per cent of its GDP on infrastructure in 2011, but this subregional average was dominated by China, which showed infrastructure expenditure of 6.8 per cent of GDP over 2010–2014. At the other extreme, South-East Asia spent just 2.1 per cent, as the economies hit by the East Asian financial crisis of 1997 (such as Indonesia, Malaysia, the Philippines and Thailand) experienced significant declines in public spending as a proportion of GDP that have not fully recovered thereafter (ADB, 2017: 28–30). Therefore, while on the whole Asia invests more and Africa and

Latin America invest less in infrastructure development, no clear patterns emerge within regions, even in terms of country size or per capita income.

In sectoral terms, Heathcote (2017) indicates that in Latin America there will be a strong concentration of transportation needs in the coming decades (between the years 2016 and 2040), as these have been relatively neglected, while the energy sector seems to be scoring better (Fay et al., 2017: 9–10). In Africa, the biggest infrastructure deficit is thought to be in the energy sector (AfDB, 2013: 3, 2018), although even here, transport stands out as the sector with the largest financing needs over the coming decades (see figure 4.3). In Asia, the largest financing needs are estimated to be in the energy sector, followed by transport.

Another way of estimating infrastructure needs is to look at absolute gaps in existing stock of infrastructure according to various indicators. Road density per square kilometre is a very rough indicator of the development of transport infrastructure, and it must obviously be seen also in the context of terrain, population density and other ecological considerations. Nevertheless, figure 4.4 points to truly shocking differences between Europe and the developing regions, while within Asia (which shows slightly better levels) there are large differences between East Asia and most of the rest of the continent. This confirms the overall logistical problems that are very much a reflection of the overall state of infrastructure as expressed in figure 4.5, whereby most developing regions are still on average able to

FIGURE 4.5 Logistics performance index, 2016

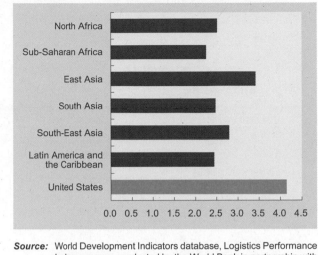

Source: World Development Indicators database, Logistics Performance Index surveys, conducted by the World Bank in partnership with public and private institutions engaged in international logistics.

Note: Respondents evaluated the quality of infrastructure related to trade and transport (e.g. ports, railroads, roads, information technology), assigning values from 1 (very low) to 5 (very high).

meet just above half of the performance standards in the United States.

Figure 4.6 indicates the still-huge gaps in access to energy, in terms of the proportion of the population with access to electricity and clean cooking fuel. Clearly, massive investments will be required in sub-Saharan Africa and Asia to approach anything like the coverage already achieved in advanced economies; and the challenge is made even greater by the large absolute populations in both regions.

FIGURE 4.4 Paved road density
(Km of paved road per 100 km² of land area)

FIGURE 4.6 Energy access, 2016
(Percentage of total population)

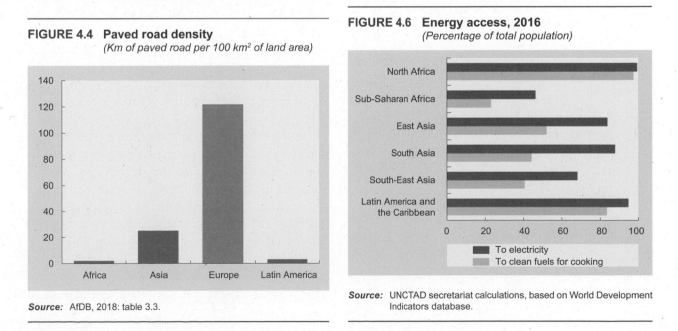

Source: AfDB, 2018: table 3.3.

Source: UNCTAD secretariat calculations, based on World Development Indicators database.

FIGURE 4.7   Telephone access and use, 2016
(Subscriptions per 100 people)

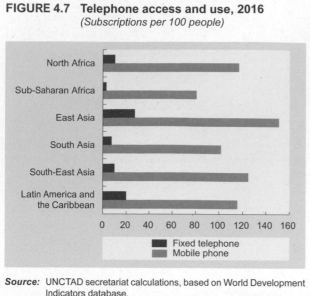

Source: UNCTAD secretariat calculations, based on World Development Indicators database.

FIGURE 4.9   Sanitation facilities access, 2015
(Percentage of total population)

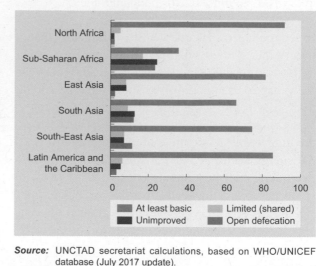

Source: UNCTAD secretariat calculations, based on WHO/UNICEF database (July 2017 update).

Telephone connectivity (whether through landline or mobile telephony) was seen in the previous chapter to be essential for taking advantage of new digital technologies. However, figure 4.7 indicates that, despite the significant recent expansion in such connections, there are still gaps in most developing regions. Meanwhile, access to infrastructure that is seen as essential for social and human development indicates even larger gaps in most developing regions. Figure 4.8 shows how the majority of the population of sub-Saharan Africa and large swathes

of South and South-East Asia in particular do not have access to piped water, especially within homes. Gaps are also huge with respect to basic sanitation facilities, as evident from figure 4.9.

2. The financing gap narrative

Both the historical discussion and the challenges outlined in section B point to the need for countries to have a comprehensive long-term vision that recognizes the need to coordinate across sectors, regions and timelines, along with a more targeted medium-term planned approach towards infrastructure creation. This contrasts, quite sharply, with the current approach to infrastructure investment that looks at individual projects on a case-by-case basis to ensure that they are "bankable" (assuring repayment of loans taken for such investment) and requires that all investors in such projects get adequate returns.

The current approach can be traced back to two important changes that upended the policy discussion from the late 1970s. First, the sharp ascendency of a market-friendly perspective on infrastructure that gained wide currency by the 1980s prompted the emergence of a narrower view related to measuring, understanding and improving conditions for providing infrastructure at the micro level (see e.g. Andrés et al., 2013). This approach, along with intense scrutiny of the entire public investment-driven infrastructure model, led to a widespread privatization of public

FIGURE 4.8   Safely managed water supply access, 2015
(Percentage of total population)

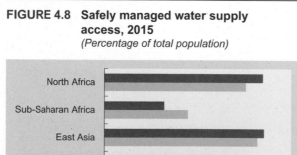
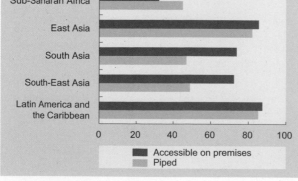

Source: UNCTAD secretariat calculations, based on WHO/UNICEF database (July 2017 update).

infrastructure services in the 1980s, assisted by measures to downsize state spending, reduce regulatory oversight and liberalize financial markets. In the case of the United Kingdom, the resulting reorganization was not just a transfer of state-owned business into private hands; it entailed commercialization of infrastructure sectors in an "attempt to re-engineer public institutions on a model of market exchange" (Meek, 2014: 57). This view was promoted in developing countries, in particular, through the World Bank's *Doing Business Report*.[19] Second, the process of hyperglobalization that picked up steam during the 1990s (see *TDR 2017*) further cemented these processes by promoting a global shift towards privatized infrastructure services and the financialization of infrastructure provision. Priemus and van Wee (2013) note that infrastructure no longer is just a public good, but has now become a widely popular, globally traded, asset class. The long-term, steady nature of infrastructure investments has been instrumental in endearing it to markets, making them the chosen class for institutional financial investors such as insurance companies, pension funds sovereign wealth funds and other foundations (Weber et al., 2016).

The financing gap narrative with respect to infrastructure is built around a few key points. First, estimated infrastructure investment gaps in each country (discussed above) are taken to imply a financing gap of a similar order of magnitude. Second, it is taken for granted that national public sectors in most countries are financially constrained with limited budgetary resources, face governance problems and run the risk of running into debt sustainability issues if they undertake infrastructure investments on the scale needed in the coming years. Third, given this public resource constraint, private capital, which is typically invested in short-term financial assets, should be unlocked for infrastructure projects. Fourth, for this to occur, a pipeline of "bankable" projects needs to be developed.

"Bankable" projects are defined as those "that provide investors with appropriate risk-adjusted returns" (Woetzel et al., 2016: 17). The standard diagnosis is that projects that fit that profile are currently scarce and the risk-adjusted returns of existing projects are too low to attract private investors. Numerous factors are pinpointed as restricting the delivery of "bankable" projects. These include low preparation capacity, high transaction costs, lack of liquid financial instruments, weak regulatory frameworks and legal opposition, along with various types of risks

at the different phases of the life cycle of a project, such as: macroeconomic, political, technical and environmental risks at the phase of preparation; construction risks (overrun, cost escalation) during construction phase; and demand, operating and revenue risks (e.g. price and exchange risks; unrealized projected demand) at the operation phase (Serebrisky et al., 2015; Bhattacharya et al., 2012; Woetzel et al., 2016; G20, 2011).

In order to expand the supply of "bankable" projects, the proponents argue that new paths should be explored to enhance prospective returns and minimize risks that often arise during the life cycle of a project. To enhance returns, projects should be able to generate sufficient revenues over their life cycle, through adoption of user charges, public sector support (typically in the form of "viability gap finance") and additional funding. Proposed measures to reduce risks and uncertainties include: clear identification of actual returns and possible risks (including of default); development of governance structures to ensure approval of stakeholders, including through compensation schemes; provision of de-risking instruments such as sovereign and credit guarantees; and government mapping of long-term investment paths to reduce investors' uncertainty about the future (Woetzel et al., 2016; G20, 2011).

Other proposed measures to increase project "bankability" and thus attract private finance include the development of more liquid security exchanges, with governments acting as market makers (for instance, through issuing of equity and debt on their own infrastructure projects); and adoption of more favourable international investment frameworks, with limits on expropriation, effective compensation and binding dispute-resolution mechanisms. In addition, standardization of contractual terms is identified as important to attract funds to smaller projects, as is project pooling to reduce transaction costs and attract larger investors. Finally, supply-side constraints to additional private financing include strict pension investment rules and regulatory restrictions such as Basel III and Solvency II, which require more capital allocation for infrastructure (Woetzel et al., 2016: 23–26).

The list is long, but an important conclusion is that project "bankability" extends beyond the intrinsic characteristics of the project itself. It depends in large measure on the wider institutional and regulatory conditions in which private finance might (or

FIGURE 4.10 Trends in public investment, 1980–2015
(Percentage of GDP)

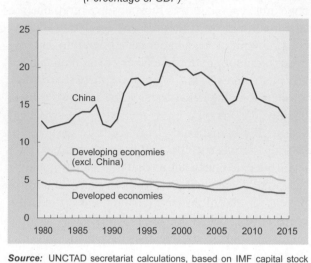

Source: UNCTAD secretariat calculations, based on IMF capital stock data set.
Note: Public investment here is General Government Investment (gross fixed capital formation).

to GDP of 15 per cent to 20 per cent and associated high rates of output growth for several decades. The decline in public investment in developing countries in the 1980s and 1990s can be linked to adoption of fiscal adjustment policies in response to the debt crises and as part of structural adjustment programmes. The world as a whole is, therefore, underinvesting, and consequently creating a cumulative infrastructure gap, even though uncertainty remains as to its exact order of magnitude.

Nevertheless, the financing gap narrative has serious limitations. The first concern is with respect to the expected scale and role of private sector engagement in infrastructure development. As noted in section B, through history, domestic public financing for infrastructure development has been dominant; and experience suggests that such public sector dominance will continue even if private finance grows in the years ahead. Even today, where private finance exists, it comes in together with public funding. In Africa, domestic public finance accounts for 66 per cent of total infrastructure finance (G20, 2011: 7). In Latin America, instances in which private participation in infrastructure (PPI) occur have public finance accounting for a third of total project funding (Fay et al., 2017: 8).[20] In low-income countries, this proportion is nearly 75 per cent (G20, 2011: 10). In Asia, private investment dominates in the telecommunications sector and also has a significant presence in the energy sector, but its participation is very small in transport and virtually non-existent in water and sanitation (ADB, 2017). Thus, while private sector involvement in infrastructure investment may increase with greater supply of "bankable" projects, any rapid recovery of overall infrastructure investment in the future will critically depend on governments' capacities to carry out their leadership roles in planning and executing new infrastructure projects.

not) be made available, such as better developed capital markets and an investor-friendly regulatory framework. In this scheme, planning is identified as necessary to create such "bankable" projects and, as the G20 puts it, "[m]ore resources are needed for project preparation… [as it] encompasses a wide range of activities that have to take place before a project can be of interest to potential financiers" (G20, 2011: 11). In line with this diagnosis, multilateral development banks are stepping in, by establishing joint investment platforms in which they provide technical expertise, capacity-building and financing instruments to increase the supply of "bankable" projects (G20, 2011; UNCTAD, 2018).

The financing gap narrative raises an important concern that is shared by the wider development community: the recognition that infrastructure development is indispensable for sustainable and inclusive growth. In many parts of the world, infrastructure investment has declined since the global crisis (Woetzel et al., 2016: 10). Public investment, which can be used as a proxy for infrastructure investment, in developed countries was at a historic low at 3.4 per cent of GDP in 2015, against 4.7 in 1980 and about 6 per cent in the 1960s. In emerging economies, it fell from above 8 per cent of GDP in the early 1980s to 4.3 per cent in 2000, recovering to 5.7 per cent in 2008 and declining again thereafter (figure 4.10). It is worth noting that the outlier in this respect was China, with impressive rates of public investment

The reasons for public sector dominance in infrastructure have to do with the intrinsic characteristics of infrastructure projects. These include their long gestation periods, capital intensity, difference between private and social returns, complexity of planning and execution, the feedback loops with growth and economic development, the specificities of the countries executing infrastructure projects and the non-linear impacts of infrastructure investments (see section D). In addition, there are macro, institutional and environmental risks and uncertainties, factors that have a strong bearing on the viability and profitability of such projects. "Bankable" projects can mitigate some of these problems when well planned and executed, but they do not eliminate them entirely. More broadly, infrastructure sectors are closely interdependent, and therefore it is critical that infrastructure development is approached systemically by the state, which is the only actor with the required political power and coordination capacity. Leaving the leadership role vacant and expecting the private sector to fill the gaps is likely to lead to an outcome in which a fragmented infrastructure landscape emerges, characterized by underinvestment, sectoral concentration of resources and persistently large infrastructure gaps.

This means that the overall development strategy should determine infrastructure planning (e.g. what scale to target, and which sectors and technologies to prioritize), and to indicate the resources required to achieve these goals. This implies a reversal of the sequencing suggested by the financing gap approach. Instead of starting with the identification of gaps between actual and needed investment for infrastructure, followed by rigid assumptions of government expenditure capacity, estimating private financing required and ending with project design strategies to attract private capital to fill in the gap, the start should be with a national development strategy. This would then be followed by a consideration of the infrastructure development needed to support this strategy, how government planning can support this process, how fiscal space may be expanded and what public–private investment mix could achieve these goals.

A second limiting aspect of the financing gap narrative is that a project is understood as "bankable" in ways that are not necessarily desirable, since the features that might make a project "bankable" may not conform to the sort of development a national government may want to pursue. For instance, to what extent will a "favourable" international investment framework, understood as a condition to make a project "bankable", rob a national government of precious space to pursue its policy goals? Or, to what extent may "bankable" projects entail trade-offs between productive and social infrastructures? Also, "bankable" projects imply de-risking by the public sector through provision of subsidies, which may erode governments' financial capacity to execute other elements of the national development plan. All this suggests that, within a clearly established national development strategy, the terms of project "bankability" should be set not by private actors but – if at all – by national governments to ensure consistency between means and ends. That is, the state should decide both what general (macro, institutional, regulatory) and specific conditions it may want to provide and what projects should be prioritized and (in case it decides in favour of private sector involvement) on what terms this should happen to ensure that private engagement is in line with national objectives.

A third problematic aspect of the financing narrative is the notion that the public sector is always and everywhere financially constrained because of restricted fiscal space and persistent or potential debt burdens, and therefore incentivizing the private sector to invest in infrastructure is the only option. To begin with, these incentives to private actors may turn out to have larger and more prolonged fiscal costs than anticipated, which would adversely affect public finances in any case. But more importantly, in reality, fiscal space and borrowing limits are not fixed, as revenues can be increased through various means and credit from the Central Bank can also play a role. This is important because public investment has the power to crowd in private investment, raising productivity, incomes and taxes. The successful historical experiences described in section B followed just such a trajectory.

Matters of legitimacy, credibility and trust are, undoubtedly, complex institutional issues when it comes to raising public revenue, but it can be argued that effective planning is just as big an issue facing many countries when it comes to the infrastructure challenge. This is considered in the next section.

D. A framework for considering the role of infrastructure in development

A strategy of unbalanced growth, as noted earlier, assumes that there are some sectors that generate more forward and backward linkages than others and that government policy should target those sectors in terms of its efforts to mobilize, channel and manage resources and capabilities in ways that support a more virtuous growth circle. As discussed in *TDR 2016*, this implies the use of active industrial policies, mixing both general and selective measures, to support efforts to diversify and upgrade the economy. The *Report* acknowledged that this would require substantial state capacity, including the capacity to discipline recipients of support as well as to stimulate a learning economy at all levels. In both respects, it also argued that to get the most out of active policies, the developmental state should establish a meaningful dialogue with the business sector and other stakeholders but in doing so should also avoid capture of the policy and regulatory framework by specific interest groups.

This chapter has argued that infrastructure programmes should also be seen as a complementary part of such a development strategy. However, infrastructure programmes do require government to take more of a planning perspective than is the case with industrial policy. The difference is a subtle but important one, particularly as the polarized debate between balanced versus unbalanced growth has tended to pitch industrial policy and planning as being opposed.

1. Some basic considerations

It is evident from the discussion so far that the specific features of infrastructure require moving beyond a purely project-led approach based on the financing gap narrative. Far from simply focusing on "small" mechanisms that identify and remove roadblocks for economic activities, "large" mechanisms that give strategic importance to certain industries play a critical role in promoting linkages through unbalanced growth thus inducing industrialization (Hausmann et al., 2008; Holz 2011: 221). In fact, both theory and experience suggest that infrastructure's role as an inducement mechanism to industrialization is dependent on how infrastructure investments are structured and whether key feedback loops between

infrastructure, growth and economic development are factored into the infrastructure planning process. Some critical considerations that have direct relevance for organizing infrastructure investments in developing countries are as follows.

a. The impact of infrastructure depends on the kind of investment

Some types of infrastructure (such as roads and telecommunications) have a greater impact on productivity than others (e.g. air transport or sewage). Thus, for the development of linkages, it matters which infrastructure investments are prioritized. This in turn will depend upon how the stock of infrastructure has evolved historically relative to income, the pattern and pace of urbanization, the economic and institutional structures of countries (Fay et al., 2017) as well as how the investments are likely to induce linkages with local private sector activity.

b. The impact of infrastructure is context- and sector-specific

The impact of infrastructure on growth is influenced by initial conditions, which explains why infrastructure development has immediate and relatively large impacts on poorer countries, as opposed to advanced countries where there is already a relatively good network of infrastructure in place (Calderón and Servén, 2014). However, even at low levels of infrastructural development, there is no guarantee that new infrastructure of the same kind will result in similar outcomes across countries or sectors. For example, although there is a link between power outages and productivity of firms, these impacts will vary between countries and sectors, depending on how acute the problem of power provision in the country is, and how dependent a sector is on continuous power provision for its production (Moyo, 2013). Similarly, even in a context of overall paucity of roads, efforts to increase connectivity through road infrastructure are likely to have the most impact when targeted to those regions where industrial activity is more easily facilitated.

c. The impact of infrastructure is non-linear

Greater infrastructure investment does not always lead immediately to faster growth. Since infrastructure investment typically has significant economies of scale, it begins to have an impact on private sector productivity only after a threshold level of infrastructure investment has been reached. The relationship between infrastructure and growth can therefore take the shape of an inverted "U" curve, where at initial stages, low or no infrastructure has no impact on growth, until after a threshold where additional infrastructure will contribute to sharp rises in marginal growth, until economies reach a level of infrastructure provision that is almost complete. From that point on, additional infrastructure investments have once again low or no impact on economic growth. As an example, constructing roads will have limited effects on growth until and unless some road networks are developed. At such a point, additional roads will prompt a sharp rise in output, until a large network has been established, after which point, any more roads or maintenance expenditure can be expected to have low or no output effects (Calderón and Servén, 2014).[21]

d. *The impact of infrastructure depends on network effects within and between different kinds of investments*

All forms of modern infrastructure – transport, electricity, telecommunications and broadband – exhibit their own network effects. For instance, in the case of the Internet, the greater the number of Internet users, the greater the possibility of providing various online services. But different infrastructure investments also exhibit network effects between themselves, because achieving economies of scale in infrastructure provision is often not just a case of providing for one kind of infrastructure but also entails complementarities between several other kinds of infrastructure investments (Agénor, 2010; Jiwattanakulpaisarn et al., 2012). For example, energy to promote production in rural areas would not necessarily lead to an increase in the rate of return to enterprises in the absence of other investments, such as roads or telecommunications. Thus, the recent large-scale electricity roll-out in Rwanda did not seem to have a large impact on micro-enterprises because of additional obstacles, such as inadequate transport links, that limit their expansion (Lenz et al., 2017).

In addition to these considerations, other policy choices and macro processes also play a role in determining how infrastructure interacts with growth and productivity. This includes the pace and nature of capital accumulation, technological advancement, institutions that determine the sequencing of infrastructure investment and its interaction with production capacities, linkages that emerge between sectors over time, and eventually, trade relations and international competitiveness (see Gomory and Baumol, 2000). This reiterates the need for planning, which is elaborated upon in the following subsection.

2. *The role of planning in infrastructure development*

Rapid economic transformation is unlikely to occur spontaneously, and throughout the twentieth century successful countries have relied on planning by the state to "initiate, spur, and steer economic development" (Myrdal, 1970: 175), whether in centrally planned regimes, mixed economies or largely market-based private investment dominated economies. However, from the late twentieth century, planning went into decline as a state tool for economic transformation, except in East Asian economies. Recently it has staged something of a comeback, as more developing countries are discovering the long-term costs of unplanned growth.

Planning involves a wide range of choices, from what sectors to prioritize and technologies to adopt, to the degree of macro coordination of investment decisions, to the amount of resources required and how to mobilize them (Chandrasekhar, 2016). Infrastructure planning is likely to assume different forms in different contexts, so plans need to be based on economic, social and geographical realities and aspirations, rather than any pre-established blueprint to guarantee a successful outcome. The design and execution of an infrastructure plan should take into account a country's stage of development, existing infrastructure, industrial capabilities and expansion plans, urban versus rural divides, levels of policy ambition, existing infrastructure institutions and their coordination, availability of new financial, technical or other resources and the existence of political and managerial capacity for effective implementation.

Therefore, infrastructure planning that fits broadly into a national economic development strategy would include the following elements:

- a vision for the infrastructure sector in the long term in the context of the broader national industrial development strategy;

- a consistent time frame to allow for coordination of infrastructure planning with other goals of development planning;

- a life-cycle analysis that allows for feedbacks and improvements and that takes into consideration broader economic and social benefits (market access, poverty alleviation);

- flexibility to respond to possible technological forecasts and potential disruptions or to path-changing contingencies such as the need to promote green technologies as a result of climate change;

- a systemic approach that addresses sectoral inter-dependencies; and

- coordination between different government levels and departments.

Some models of infrastructure planning guidelines have been developed in recent years with the purpose of providing a road map to national governments.[22] These guidelines present additional aspects to those just outlined, such as:

- setting up an adequately staffed central infra-structure unit, under the supervision of the prime minister or president to ensure projects are prepared and executed;

- understanding of the current infrastructure situation and preparation of a list of gaps and deficiencies that need to be addressed;

- looking for solutions with the largest economic and social benefits while minimizing negative social and environmental outcomes;

- laying out the framework and modalities for private sector participation; and

- moving from planning to action by publishing the plan, ensuring the necessary policy changes for the selected projects and finalizing detailed project preparation.

The Infrastructure Consortium for Africa (ICA) defines project preparation as "a process which comprises the entire set of activities undertaken to take a project from conceptualization to actual implementation" (ICA, 2014: 2). But various obstacles to (and shortcomings of) infrastructure project preparation have been identified in recent years, including lack of coordination; lack of funding to cover the project preparation costs, which could be between 3 per cent and 12 per cent of total project costs; lack of

institutional and human capacity for planning, project appraisal and preparation; overly rigid and myopic budgeting, which can limit multi-year costing and thus inclusion of large and long-term projects; a disconnect between decentralized project planning and overall fiscal targets and plans; and lack of a robust public investment management process to deal with the complex interplay between politics and planning (Fay et al., 2017; AfDB, 2018).

Focusing on planning more broadly, Alberti (2015) identifies further shortcomings from country case studies in Latin America, including: lack of inter-sectoral planning; narrow cost–benefit analysis that does not take account of project linkages or externalities and the requirements of regional or sectoral development; failures to anticipate social reactions; no penalties if a national development plan is not followed through; inadequate time for planning activities in public entities crowded out by portfolio administration time; lack of specialists to assist the public sector and poaching of human resources from the public sector during growth phases, when project preparation is needed most due to growing demand for infrastructure services. Looking at both developed and developing-country experiences with large infrastructure projects, Flyvbjerg (2009, 2007) makes the additional point that such projects tend to be characterized by cost overruns, benefit shortfalls and underestimation of risks. In his assessment, much of this has to do with perverse incentives whereby planners deliberately miscalculate costs and benefits to have their projects approved. However, this assessment is project-based and therefore appears not to include the linkages and externalities.

In the early stages of planning, some critical features for success include: clear political support from the top; better coordination between governmental agencies and departments; the recognition of sectoral interdependencies; the generation of political consensus of a kind that incorporates demands from weaker stakeholders; better staffed planning units for effective design of projects; and feasibility studies that take into account broader development benefits. In the later planning stages, a multi-year budgetary approach is necessary to reduce disruption. Procurement practices could be used as a tool to strengthen industry linkages, in addition to serving the purpose of cost reductions. Studart and Ramos (forthcoming 2019) highlight the positive role played by national development banks through their planning capacity, financial clout and available instruments, including taking projects off the ground and contributing to the build-up of an infrastructure financing architecture with cross-party support.

It is likely that de-emphasizing the "bankability" of projects would reduce much of the complexity and costs in infrastructure planning, since the financial arrangements needed to bring the private sector on-board are unduly complicated. The costs involved are not just those of fees for banks or consultants on financial engineering, or upfront financial incentives but, equally important, the contingent liabilities that build up in the course of a project (*TDR 2016*). The latter are hard to anticipate fully, often impacting on future fiscal capacity to maintain support for infrastructure development.

3. Experiences with national development plans: Country evidence

Since the early 2000s, many developing countries have started to prepare and publish national development plans. These initiatives do not necessarily imply that countries rigorously stick to each of their provisions, but rather indicate a vision which countries may want to pursue in terms of their national trajectories. Many countries initially produced these as a follow-up to national (or poverty-reduction) strategies under IMF–World Bank funded programmes, with uncertain government commitment or resources for effective implementation. At the same time, under the broader frameworks of the Millennium Development Goals and now the Sustainable Development Goals, these plans have evolved and in many cases appear to be taking the form of incipient, broad-based national efforts to build a coherent development strategy. Their underlying motivations seem based on the growing understanding that only through development planning will developing countries be able to accelerate growth, develop their productive capacities and achieve greater economic diversification.

This subsection looks at national plans of 40 developing countries, elaborated from the beginning of this millennium, to assess how they fare in terms of including infrastructure plans and the extent to which they address questions of structural change, linkages and productivity growth.

Ninety per cent of all the 40 national development plans considered here contain some sort of

FIGURE 4.11 Infrastructure planning: Country evidence
(Percentage of total)

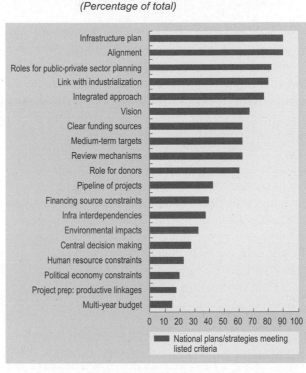

Source: UNCTAD secretariat calculations, based on national development plans (or strategies) of 40 countries.
Note: These countries are: *Africa*: Botswana, Burkina Faso, Chad, Ethiopia, the Gambia, Guinea, Kenya, Lesotho, Malawi, Mozambique, Namibia, Somalia, South Africa, Uganda, United Republic of Tanzania and Zambia. *Asia*: Afghanistan, Bangladesh, Bhutan, Cambodia, Fiji, Malaysia, Papua New Guinea, the Philippines, Solomon Islands, Tajikistan, Thailand, Turkey, Vanuatu, Viet Nam and Timor-Leste. *Latin America and the Caribbean*: Bolivia (Plurinational State of), Colombia, Ecuador, Guatemala, Jamaica, Nicaragua, Peru, Trinidad and Tobago, and Costa Rica.

infrastructure plan. The infrastructure plans are then assessed with respect to their vision of the country's infrastructure into the next 20–30 years, whether the plans are comprehensive or focused, which sectors are covered, and if the links to other policy objectives such as industrialization and economic diversification are clearly stated. Other aspects covered include these questions: Is there a clearly designated centralized decision-making unit or agency? Do countries identify clear funding sources and adopt a multi-year budget approach? Is the role for the private sector, international donors or agencies specified, and to what extent? Are review mechanisms present? Do the plans address specific constraints, such as in the areas of skills, resources, capacity, legislation, environmental impacts and financing sources? Is a detailed pipeline of projects provided, and life-cycle analysis of project preparation? Do projects take into account productive linkages and externalities, going beyond traditional cost–benefit analysis?

The results of the assessment are summarized in figure 4.11. While these cannot provide evidence on implementation within countries, they nevertheless provide an indication of how extensive such national plans are, in terms of their levels of coverage and depth. Overall, plans score well in terms of vision, alignment with the broader country's strategy and links with policy goals such as industrialization or productive diversification. Most plans also identify clear funding sources and a role for the private sector in infrastructure development. However, these plans score considerably less well beyond these broad features. Less than 40 per cent of such plans address the important issue of infrastructure interdependencies, just above 20 per cent make clear references to central decision-making and only about 15 per cent include multi-year budgets. In addition, less than 40 per cent of such plans, and in some cases less than 20 per cent, address different sorts of constraints such as in the areas of skills, environmental impacts or sources of finance.

Even where assessment is more positive, such as in the areas of vision, alignment and links with industrialization/diversification goals, a more detailed reading of the plans suggests that: visions are not fully developed or really long term or do not anticipate possible challenges (of technological nature, other) or obstacles; alignment does not specify the channels through which infrastructure development may support a broader development strategy; and links with industrialization/diversification do not clearly articulate how development of certain types of infrastructure might lead to the latter, lacking description of specific linkage identification or which tools might be needed to establish such linkages.

Experiences with infrastructure development in the recent past might have been richer on the ground than the infrastructure plans surveyed convey. However, if these plans do capture the level of governments' commitment to infrastructure planning and development, then considerably more work is needed, for both more robust national infrastructure and development strategies, to ensure infrastructure development does play the fundamental role it can have in transforming developing economies.

E. Conclusion

Managing structural transformation is a big challenge at all levels of development. In part, that is because the mixture of creative and destructive forces accompanying such a transformation do not automatically translate into a virtuous growth circle while the rents that are inevitably created in the process can be captured by a privileged group in ways that clog the economic arteries and increase the dangers of a political stroke. There are already signs of this happening with the digital revolution. However, this is not inevitable and if history is any guide, public policy, including industrial policy, can help to manage more inclusive and sustainable outcomes. The chapter III set out some elements of that agenda.

This chapter has argued that structural transformation will also need to be accompanied by infrastructure planning. However, even as the funding for infrastructure has begun to recover after decades of decline, serious discussion of what is needed to effectively embed infrastructure programmes in a development strategy has not followed. Indeed, even when infrastructure has been included in national plans, there does not appear to be any clear framework for moving from ambition to implementation. This disconnect is in part the result of a singular ideological drive to limit the infrastructure challenge to a matter of project bankability, leaving it solely in the hands of finance ministries. But it also reflects a reluctance on the part of governments in developing countries to think about the challenge in a more comprehensive and integrated manner and to invest in the techniques, skills and institutional capacities required to ensure that infrastructure will not just build bridges but ensure those bridges deliver on the ambitions of the 2030 Agenda. In that respect, the chapter has suggested that the old debate between balanced and unbalanced growth provides a rich discussion for thinking about those techniques, skills and institutional requirements. The bottom line when it comes to infrastructure spending is that it is too important a development matter to be left to the sole responsibility of finance ministries. ■

Notes

1 A good is non-excludable if people cannot be excluded from consuming it because of non-payment or other criteria and it is non-rivalrous if its consumption by one person does not prevent others from consuming it.

2 According to Markard, 2011: table 3, capital intensity is judged as very high in electricity and water supply, sanitation and road transport; regulation intensity as stronger in water and sanitation; systemic importance is highest in electricity supply, railway transport and telecommunications, and public-sector dominance is found in water supply and sanitation, and railway and road transport.

3 Telecommunications infrastructure is often intertwined with digital infrastructure, but as chapter III indicated, digital infrastructure contains several additional components.

4 This is contrary to the argument made in some recent literature, that infrastructure investment can crowd out private investment (see Agénor and Moreno-Dodson, 2006, for example).

5 For instance, Africa has a power infrastructure investment backlog of over US$40 billion and the world's lowest electrification rate with around 30.5 per cent (Odey and Falola, 2017; Nyambati, 2017). So any additional infrastructure investment in electricity in Africa can be expected to have significant effects on growth, private economic activity and conditions of life.

6 *The Economist*, 2017, based on World Bank calculations.

7 Laid out in Chevalier's book *Système de la Méditerranée*, 1836.

8 The Republic of Korea's first five-year development plan (1962–1966) identified infrastructure as key to support the development of light industries, focusing on the construction of 275 km of railway and many highway projects (Ro, 2002). In the third five-year plan (1972–1976), there were comprehensive programmes to develop airports, seaports, highways, railways and telecommunications (Ro, 2002). Such coordinated infrastructure expansion continued through the subsequent decades, particularly in the 1990s to deal with the emerging extreme infrastructure congestion.

9 This can be contrasted with sluggish public infrastructure investment in India, which has held back the private sector, while in China it has lent a much-needed boost to stimulate demand (Shi et al., 2017).

10 For example, when the Republic of Korea faced additional infrastructure pressures, the Private Capital Inducement Act of the Republic of Korea was formally launched in 1994. This set out the framework conditions for private sector investment in infrastructure provision (World Bank, 2009). The Act identified two categories of investments – strategic infrastructures (roads, railways, subways, ports, airports, water supply and telecommunications) and other infrastructure projects, including gas supply, bus terminals, tourism promotion areas and sport complexes (World Bank, 2009) but the state retained its overseer role in both.

11 These figures are adjusted for sector coverage, are for the period 2016–2030 and are expressed in 2015 United States dollars. The sources are: OECD, 2017a; Bhattacharya et al., 2016; Woetzel et al., 2016; NCE, 2014. As a proportion of global GDP, these figures are in the range 4.8 per cent to 8.3 per cent, assuming global GDP grows in real terms over the years 2016–2023 according to projected rates of IMF WEO Database April 2018 and then at 3 per cent over 2024–2030. These proportions might be compared against investment estimates presented by Woetzel et al. (2016) at 3.5 per cent of global GDP in the past two decades.

12 According to the Global Commission on the Economy and Climate, sustainable infrastructure means, first, that infrastructure is socially sustainable, by: being inclusive and contributing to people's livelihoods and social well-being; and supporting the needs of the poor and reducing their vulnerability to climate shocks. Second, that it is economically sustainable, whereby it creates jobs and boosts growth but does not create unsustainable debt burdens for the government or high costs for users. And, third, that it should be environmentally sustainable by limiting pollution, supporting conservation and the sustainable use of natural resources, contributing to a low-carbon and resource-efficient economy and withstanding climate change impacts (NCE, 2016: 22).

13 Some estimates comprise only capital investment while others include expenditure on operations and maintenance as well. Some methodologies are based on sectoral analysis with consideration of use of more efficient technologies (e.g. OECD, NCE) plus a country-by-country assessment (e.g. Woetzel et al., 2016). In the case of Bhattacharya et al. (2016: 26–28), a macro-simulation is used in which current investment spending is calculated for the base year and then projections for investment requirements are obtained using assumptions on expected growth and investment rates, based on assessments of investment plans from major economies and regions.

14 According to Woetzel et al., 2016, disruptive technologies involve new technologies such as additive manufacturing, advanced automation and modular construction, and new products and services such as autonomous vehicles, drone deliveries and e-commerce, which have the potential to drastically shift the demand between different sources of energy (e.g. from fossil fuel to renewables), reduce the demand

for specific types of infrastructure (e.g. transport – roads, ports) and change how infrastructure is built, with the ultimate effect of radically reshaping the infrastructure sector.

15   These estimates of investment needs are at constant prices and comprise power, transport, telecommunications, water and sanitation; and exclude investment required for climate change. Actual investment is based on latest available year (UNCTAD, 2014: 142). Bhattacharya provides an alternative estimate for developing countries, of $3.5 trillion–$4 trillion (at 2015 dollars) per year over the period 2016–2030, against actual infrastructure investment at $2.2 trillion in 2014, with China alone accounting for $1.3 trillion (Bhattacharya et al., 2016: 21–28).

16   These figures exclude expenditures on operation and maintenance and include additional investment needed to make investments sustainable. See Bhattacharya et al., 2012.

17   Other estimates of infrastructure investment needs for the LAC region fall in the range 3 per cent to 8 per cent of GDP, against actual spending at 2.8 per cent (Fay et al., 2017: table ES1 and box table 1). Serebrisky et al., 2015, and Serebrisky, 2014, drawing on a range of studies, suggest needs of 5 per cent of GDP.

18   In United States dollar terms, the AfDB, 2018: 64, puts the infrastructure needs for Africa at between $130 billion and $170 billion a year, and a financing gap of $68 billion to $108 billion. Previous estimates, produced by the Africa Infrastructure Country Diagnostic, indicated needs of $93 billion a year in 2008, with a financing gap at $31 billion (AfDB, 2018: 64, 2013: 7).

19   That Report attempts to provide "objective" measures of business regulations and their enforcement across 190 economies and selected cities. Higher values on the index are taken to indicate "better" (usually simpler and more liberal) regulations for businesses and stronger protection of property rights, and these results have been used to influence policymakers to move towards liberalizing rules, often without appropriate recognition of the context or broader development considerations. There has been much criticism of both the choice of indicators and the manner of measurement (typically based on interviews conducted in one city of the country concerned) not just from civil society but from the Independent Panel appointed by the President of the World Bank and headed by Trevor Manuel, former Finance Minister of South Africa (World Bank, 2013).

20   This portion of public finance comes from development banks, export credit agencies and other public authorities and companies (Fay et al., 2017: 20).

21   As an example, a recent study on understanding the regional growth determinants in the European Union between 1995 and 2010 concluded that transport and telecommunications investments have a non-linear relationship with growth in the European Union countries (Sanso-Navarro and Vera-Cabello, 2015).

22   Some of these are elaborated in Bhattacharya et al., 2016; Schweikert and Chinowsky, 2012; WEF and PWC, 2012; Alberti, 2015.

References

ADB (2017). Meeting Asia's infrastructure needs. Asian Development Bank. Available at: https://www.adb.org/publications/asia-infrastructure-needs.

AfDB (2013). *An Integrated Approach to Infrastructure Provision in Africa*. Statistics Department, Africa Infrastructure Knowledge Program. April. African Development Bank. Abidjan.

AfDB (2018). *African Economic Outlook 2018*. African Development Bank. Abidjan.

Agénor PR (2010). A theory of infrastructure-led development? *Journal of Economic Dynamics and Control*. 34(5): 932–950.

Agénor P-R and Moreno-Dodson B (2006). Public infrastructure and growth: New channels and policy implications. Policy Research Working Paper Series No. 4064. World Bank.

Alberti J (2015). *Pre-Investment in Infrastructure in Latin America and the Caribbean: Case Studies from Chile, Mexico, Peru, and Uruguay*. Inter-American Development Bank. Washington, D.C.

Allcott H, Collard-Wexler A and O'Connell, SD (2016). How do electricity shortages affect industry? Evidence from India. *American Economic Review*. 106(3): 587–624.

Ambrosius G and Henrich-Franke C (2016). *Integration of Infrastructures in Europe in Historical Comparison*. Springer International Publishing. Cham.

Andrés LA, Schwartz J and Guasch JL (2013). *Uncovering the Drivers of Utility Performance: Lessons from Latin America and the Caribbean on the Role of the Private Sector, Regulation, and Governance in the Power, Water, and Telecommunication Sectors*. World Bank. Washington, D.C.

Arndt HW (1987). *Economic Development: The History of an Idea*. University of Chicago Press. Chicago, IL.

Aschauer DA (1989). Is public expenditure productive? *Journal of Monetary Economics*. 23(2): 177–200.

Aschauer DA (1990). Why is infrastructure important? In: Munnell AH, ed. *Is There a Shortfall in Public Capital Investment?* Federal Reserve Bank of Boston. Boston, MA: 21–50.

Atack J, Bateman F, Haines M and Margo RA (2010). Did railroads induce or follow economic growth? Urbanization and population growth in the American Midwest, 1850–1860. *Social Science History*. 34(2): 171–197.

Bang M-K (2003). Fiscal policy in Korea for building infrastructure and its knowledge based economy. Presentation made at the World Bank-Vietnam-Korea Conference on Public Expenditure. 9 October. Available at: https://slideplayer.com/slide/6321423/.

Bhattacharya A, Meltzer JP, Oppenheim J, Qureshi Z and Stern N (2016). *Delivering on Sustainable Infrastructure for Better Development and Better Climate.* December. Global Economy and Development. Brookings Institute. Washington, D.C.

Bhattacharya A, Romani M and Stern N (2012). Infrastructure for development: Meeting the challenge. Centre for Climate Change Economics and Policy. Policy Paper. Grantham Research Institute on Climate Change and the Environment in collaboration with G-24 Inter-Governmental Group of Twenty Four.

Bom PRD and Ligthart JE (2014). What have we learned from three decades of research on the productivity of public capital? *Journal of Economic Surveys.* 28(5): 889–916.

Bröcker J and Rietveld P (2009). Infrastructure and regional development. In: Capello R and Nijkamp P, eds. *Handbook of Regional Growth and Development Theories.* Edward Elgar. Cheltenham: 152–181.

Calderón C and Servén L (2010). Infrastructure and economic development in sub-Saharan Africa. *Journal of African Economies.* 19(S1): i13–i87.

Calderón C and Servén L (2014). Infrastructure, growth and inequality: An overview. Policy Research Working Paper No. 7034. World Bank.

Calderón C, Moral-Benito E and Servén L (2011). Is infrastructure capital productive? A dynamic heterogeneous approach. Documentos de Trabajo No. 1103. Banco de España.

Cassis Y, De Luca G and Florio M (2016). The history of infrastructure finance: An analytical framework. In: Cassis Y, De Luca G and Florio M, eds. *Infrastructure Finance in Europe: Insights into the History of Water, Transport and Telecommunications.* Oxford University Press. Oxford: 1–38.

Chandrasekhar CP (2016). Development planning. In: Reinert ES, Ghosh J and Kattel R, eds. *Handbook of Alternative Theories of Economic Development.* Edward Elgar. Cheltenham: 519–532.

Chevalier M (1836). *Lettres sur L'Amérique de Nord.* Volume 1. Charles Gosselin. Paris.

Cooper F (1993). Africa and the world economy. In: Cooper F, Mallon FE, Stern SJ Isaacman AF and Roseberry W, eds. *Confronting Historical Paradigms: Peasants, Labor and the Capitalist World System in Africa and Latin America.* University of Wisconsin Press. Madison.

Cootner, PH (1963). The role of the railroads in United States economic growth. *The Journal of Economic History.* 23(4): 477–521.

Czarnecki C and Dietze C (2017). *Reference Architecture for the Telecommunications Industry: Transformation of Strategy, Organization, Processes, Data, and Applications.* Springer International Publishing. Cham.

Deloitte (2017). 2017 Telecommunications Industry Outlook. Deloitte Development LLC.

Deng T (2013). Impacts of transport infrastructure on productivity and economic growth: Recent advances and research challenges. *Transport Reviews: A Transnational Transdisciplinary Journal.* 33(6): 686–699.

Dissou Y and Didic S (2013). Infrastructure and growth. In: Cockburn J, Dissou Y, Duclos J-Y and Tiberti L. *Infrastructure and Economic Growth in Asia.* Springer International Publishing. Cham: 5–46.

Donaldson D (2010). Railroads of the Raj: Estimating the impact of transportation infrastructure. Working Paper Series. No. 16487. National Bureau of Economic Research.

Douhan R and Nordberg A (2007). Is the elephant stepping on its trunk? The problem of India's unbalanced growth. Working Paper Series No. 2007:16. Department of Economics, Uppsala University. Available at: https://ideas.repec.org/p/hhs/uunewp/2007_016.html.

Drolet M (2015). A nineteenth-century Mediterranean union: Michael Chevalier's *Système de la Méditerranée. Mediterranean Historical Review.* 30(2): 147–168.

ECLAC (2017). Infrastructure investment in Latin American and Caribbean countries remain below the needs of the region. ECLAC Press Release. 15 May. Available at: https://www.cepal.org/en/noticias/inversion-infraestructura-paises-america-latina-caribe-se-mantiene-debajo-necesidades-la.

Elburz Z, Nijkamp P and Pels E (2017). Public infrastructure and regional growth: Lessons from meta-analysis. *Journal of Transport Geography.* 58: 1–8.

Escribano A and Guasch JL (2005). Assessing the impact of investment climate on productivity using firm-level data: Methodology and the cases of Guatemala, Honduras, and Nicaragua. Policy Research Working Paper No. 3621. World Bank.

Escribano A and Guasch JL (2008). Robust methodology for investment climate assessment on productivity: Application to investment climate surveys from Central America. Working Paper No. 08–19. Economic Series (11). Universidad Carlos III de Madrid.

Escribano A, Guasch JL and Pena J (2010). Assessing the impact of infrastructure quality on firm productivity in Africa: Cross-country comparisons based on investment climate surveys from 1999 to 2005.

Policy Research Working Paper No. 5191. World Bank.

Estache A (2006). Infrastructure: A survey of recent and upcoming issues. The World Bank Infrastructure Vice-Presidency, and Poverty Reduction and Economic Management Vice-Presidency. World Bank. Available at: http://siteresources.worldbank.org/INTDECABCTOK2006/Resources/Antonio_Estache_Infrastructure_for_Growth.pdf.

Estache A (2010). Infrastructure finance in developing countries: An overview. EIB Papers No. 8/2010. European Investment Bank.

Estache A and Fay M (2009). Current debates on infrastructure policy. Policy Research Working Paper No. 4410. World Bank.

Estache A and Garsous G (2012). The impact of infrastructure on growth in developing countries. Economic Notes. Note 1. International Finance Corporation.

Fay M, Andres LA, Fox C, Narloch U, Straub S and Slawson M (2017). *Rethinking Infrastructure in Latin America and the Caribbean: Spending Better to Achieve More*. World Bank. Washington, D.C.

Fleming M (1955). External economies and the doctrine of balanced growth. *The Economic Journal*. 65(258): 241–256.

Flyvbjerg B (2007). Policy and planning for large-infrastructure projects: Problems, causes, cures. *Environment and Planning B: Planning and Design*. 34(4): 578–597.

Flyvbjerg B (2009). Survival of the unfittest: Why the worst infrastructure gets built – and what we can do about it. *Oxford Review of Economic Policy*. 25(3): 344–367.

G20 (2011). Supporting Infrastructure in Developing Countries. Submission to the G20 by the MDB Working Group on Infrastructure. June. Available at: http://documents.worldbank.org/curated/en/297061468343728311/pdf/655610BR0v20Se0Official0Use0Only090.pdf.

Ghosh M (2012). Regional economic growth and inequality in India during the pre- and post-reform periods. *Oxford Development Studies*. 40(2): 190–212.

Global Water Partnership (2009). Investing in infrastructure: The value of an IWRM approach. Policy Brief No. 7. Technical Committee. Global Water Partnership.

Gomory RE and Baumol WJ (2000). *Global Trade and Conflicting National Interests*. MIT Press. Cambridge MA.

Gramlich EM (1994). Infrastructure investment: A review essay. *Journal of Economic Literature*. 32(3): 1176–1196.

Grigg NS (2017). Global water infrastructure: State of the art review. *International Journal of Water Resources Development*. Available at: https://doi.org/10.1080/07900627.2017.1401919.

Haldane AG (2018). Ideas and institutions: A growth story. Bank of England. Speech given at the University of Oxford. 23 May. Available at: https://www.bankofengland.co.uk/-/media/boe/files/speech/2018/ideas-and-institutions-a-growth-story-speech-by-andy-haldane.pdf?la=en&hash=BDF87B794BCE9110D264BF955E43C1D7A533E593.

Hausmann R, Rodrik D and Sabel CF (2008). Reconfiguring industrial policy: A framework with an application to South Africa. Working Paper No. 168. Center for International Development. Harvard University.

Heathcote, C (2017). Forecasting infrastructure investment needs for 50 countries, 7 sectors through 2040. 19 September. Global Infrastructure Outlook and Oxford Economics. Available at: https://www.gihub.org/blog/forecasting-infrastructure-investment-needs-for-50-countries-7-sectors-through-2040/.

Henckel T and McKibbin WJ (2010). The economics of infrastructure in a globalized world: Issues, lessons and future challenges. 4 June. Brookings Institute. Washington, D.C. Available at: https://www.brookings.edu/research/the-economics-of-infrastructure-in-a-globalized-world-issues-lessons-and-future-challenges/.

Hirschman AO (1958). *The Strategy of Economic Development*. Yale University Press. New Haven, CT.

Hirschman AO (1961). *Latin American Issues: Essays and Comments*. Twentieth Century Fund. New York, NY.

Hirschman AO (1987). The political economy of Latin American development: Seven exercises in retrospection. *Latin American Research Review*. 22(3): 7–36.

Hjort J and Poulsen J (2017). The arrival of fast Internet and employment in Africa. Working Paper No. 23582. National Bureau of Economic Research.

Högselius P, Kaijser A and van der Vleuten E (2015). *Europe's Infrastructure Transition: Economy, War, Nature*. Palgrave Macmillan. Basingstoke.

Holtz-Eakin D (1994). Public-sector capital and the productivity puzzle. *Review of Economics and Statistics*. 76(1): 12–21.

Holz CA (2011). The unbalanced growth hypothesis and the role of the state: The case of China's state-owned enterprises. *Journal of Development Economics*. 96(2): 220–238.

ICA (2014). Effective project preparation for Africa's infrastructure development. Concept Paper. Infrastructure Consortium for Africa Annual Meeting. Cape Town. November.

Ingram GK and Fay M (2008). Physical infrastructure. In: Dutt AK and Ros J, eds. *International Handbook of Development Economics*. Volume 1. Edward Elgar. Cheltenham: 301–315.

Jenks LH (1944). Railroads as an economic force in American development. *The Journal of Economic History*. 4(1): 1–20.

Jenks LH (1951). Capital movement and transportation: Britain and American railway development. *The Journal of Economic History*. 11(4): 375–388.

Jiwattanakulpaisarn P, Noland RB and Graham DJ (2012). Marginal productivity of expanding highway capacity. *Journal of Transport Economics and Policy*. 46(3): 333–347.

Kasper E (2015). A definition for infrastructure: Characteristics and their impact on firms active in infrastructure. PhD dissertation. Technische Universität München. February.

Lakshmanan TR (2011). The broader economic consequences of transport infrastructure investments. *Journal of Transport Geography*. 19(1): 1–12.

Lenz L, Munyehirwe A, Peters J and Sievert M (2017). Does large-scale infrastructure investment alleviate poverty? Impact of Rwanda's electricity access roll-out program. *World Development*. 89: 88–110.

Markard J (2011). Infrastructure sector characteristics and implications for innovation and sectoral change. *Journal of Infrastructure Systems*. 17(3): 107–117.

Marshall T (2013). *Planning Major Infrastructure: A Critical Analysis*. Routledge. Abingdon.

Meek J (2014). *Private Island: Why Britain Now Belongs To Someone Else*. Verso. London.

Melo PC, Graham DJ and Brage-Ardao R (2013). The productivity of transport infrastructure investment: A meta-analysis of empirical evidence. *Regional Science and Urban Economics*. 43(5): 695–706.

Mesquita Moreira M, Blyde JS, Volpe Martincus C and Molina D (2013). Too far to export: Domestic transport costs and regional export disparities in Latin America and the Caribbean. Special Report on Integration and Trade. Inter-American Development Bank. Available at: https://publications.iadb.org/handle/11319/3664.

Moyo B (2013). Power infrastructure quality and manufacturing productivity in Africa: A firm level analysis. *Energy Policy*. 61: 1063–1070.

Myrdal G (1957). *Economic Theory and Under-developed Regions*. G. Duckworth. London.

Myrdal G (1970). *An Approach to the Asian Drama: Methodological and Theoretical*. Vintage Books Edition. New York, NY

NCE (2014). *Better Growth, Better Climate: The New Climate Economy Report*. New Climate Economy. Global Commission on the Economy and Climate. Washington, D.C.

NCE (2016). *The Sustainable Infrastructure Imperative: Financing for Better Growth and Development – The 2016 New Climate Economy Report*. New Climate Economy. Global Commission on the Economy and Climate. Washington, D.C.

Nerlove M (1966). Railroads and American economic growth. *The Journal of Economic History*. 26(1): 107–115.

Nordås HK and Piermartini R (2004). Infrastructure and trade. Staff Working Paper No. ERSD-2004-04. World Trade Organization.

Nurkse R (1953). *Problems of Capital Formation in Underdeveloped Countries*. Blackwell. Oxford.

Nyambati AR (2017). Scaling up power infrastructure in sub-Saharan Africa for poverty alleviation. In: Falola T and Odey MO, eds. *Poverty Reduction Strategies for Africa*. Routledge. Abingdon: 53–64.

Odey MO and Falola T (2017). Introduction. In: Falola T and Odey MO, eds. *Poverty Reduction Strategies for Africa*. Routledge. Abingdon: 1–18.

OECD (2017a). Technical note on estimates of infrastructure investment needs: Background note to the report *Investing in Climate, Investing in Growth*. July. Organisation for Economic Co-operation and Development. Paris. Available at: https://www.oecd.org/env/cc/g20-climate/Technical-note-estimates-of-infrastructure-investment-needs.pdf.

OECD (2017b). *Investing in Climate, Investing in Growth*. Organisation for Economic Co-operation and Development. Paris.

Pascali L (2017). The wind of change: Maritime technology, trade and economic development. *American Economic Review*. 107(9): 2821–2854.

Pereira RM, Hausman WJ and Pereira AM (2014). Railroads and economic growth in the antebellum United States. Working Paper No. 153. College of William and Mary. Williamsburg, VA.

Priemus H and van Wee B (2013). Mega-projects: High ambitions, complex decision- making, different actors, multiple impacts. In: Priemus H and van Wee B, eds. *International Handbook on Mega-Projects*. Edward Elgar. Cheltenham: 1–8.

Ro J (2002). Infrastructure development in Korea. Paper prepared for the PEO Structure Specialists Meeting. Infrastructure Development in the Pacific Region. Osaka. 23–24 September. Available at: http://unpan1.un.org/intradoc/groups/public/documents/APCITY/UNPAN008650.pdf.

Rodney W (1973). *How Europe Underdeveloped Africa*. Bogle-L'Ouverture Publications. London.

Rohatyn F (2009). *Bold Endeavors: How Our Government Built America, and Why It Must Rebuild Now*. Simon and Schuster. New York, NY.

Rosenstein-Rodan PN (1943). Problems of industrialisation of Eastern and South-Eastern Europe. *Economic Journal*. 53(210/211): 202–211.

Sanso-Navarro M and Vera-Cabello M (2015). Non-linearities in regional growth: A non-parametric approach. *Papers in Regional Science*. 94(S1): S19–S38.

Schmidt-Traub G (2015). Investment needs to achieve the Sustainable Development Goals: Understanding the billions and trillions. Working Paper, Version 2. Sustainable Development Solutions Network. A Global Initiative for the United Nations. Available at: unsdsn.org/wp-content/uploads/2015/09/151112-SDG-Financing-Needs.pdf.

Schweikert A and Chinowsky P (2012). National infrastructure planning: A holistic approach to policy development in developing countries. Engineering Project Organizations Conference. Rheden. 10–12 July. Available at: https://www.academia.edu/2755320/National_Infrastructure_Planning_A_Holistic_Approach_to_Policy_Development_in_Developing_Countries.

Serebrisky T (2014). *Sustainable Infrastructure for Competitiveness and Inclusive Growth.* Inter-American Development Bank. Washington, D.C.

Serebrisky T, Suárez-Alemán A, Margot D and Ramirez MC (2015). *Financing Infrastructure in Latin America and the Caribbean: How, How Much and By Whom?* Inter-American Development Bank. Washington, D.C.

Shaw RE (2014). *Canals For a Nation: The Canal Era in the United States, 1790–1860.* The University Press of Kentucky. Lexington, KY.

Sheahan J (1958). International specialization and the concept of balanced growth. *The Quarterly Journal of Economics.* 72(2): 183–197.

Shi Y, Guo S and Sun P (2017). The role of infrastructure in China's regional economic growth. *Journal of Asian Economics.* 49: 26–41.

Simon NS and Natarajan P (2017). Non-linearity between infrastructure inequality and growth: Evidence from India. *Review of Market Integration.* 9(1/2): 66–82.

Straub S (2008). Infrastructure and development: A critical appraisal of the macro level literature. Policy Research Working Paper No. 4590. World Bank.

Streeten P (1959). Unbalanced growth. *Oxford Economic Papers.* 11(2): 167–190.

Studart R and Ramos L (2019, forthcoming). The new development banks and the financing of transformation in Latin America and the Caribbean. In: Barrowclough D, Gallagher KP and Kozul-Wright R, eds. *Southern Led Development Finance: Solutions from the Global South to Boost Resilience and Growth.* Routledge. Abingdon.

Summers LH (2016). The age of secular stagnation: What it is and what to do about it. *Foreign Affairs.* 15 February. Available at: https://www.foreignaffairs.com/articles/united-states/2016-02-15/age-secular-stagnation.

Sutcliffe RB (1964). Balanced and unbalanced growth. *The Quarterly Journal of Economics.* 78(4): 621–640.

The Economist (2017). The leapfrog model. Special Report: What technology can do for Africa. 9 November. Available at: http://media.economist.com/news/special-report/21731038-technology-africa-making-huge-advances-says-jonathan-rosenthal-its-full.

Torrisi G (2009). Public infrastructure: Definition, classification and measurement issues. *Economics, Management, and Financial Markets.* 4(3): 100–124. Available at: https://mpra.ub.uni-muenchen.de/25850/.

UNCTAD (2014). *World Investment Report 2014: Investing in the SDGs: An Action Plan* (United Nations publication. Sales No. E.14.II.D.1. New York and Geneva).

UNCTAD (2017). *The Least Developed Countries Report 2017: Transformational Energy Access* (United Nations publication. Sales No. E.17.II.D.6. New York and Geneva).

UNCTAD (2018). *Scaling Up Finance for the Sustainable Development Goals: Experimenting with Models of Multilateral Development Banking.* UNCTAD/GDS/ECIDC/2017/4. New York and Geneva.

UNCTAD (*TDR 1997*). *Trade and Development Report, 1997: Globalization, Distribution and Growth* (United Nations publication. Sales No. E.97.II.D.8. New York and Geneva).

UNCTAD (*TDR 2003*). *Trade and Development Report, 2003: Capital Accumulation, Growth and Structural Change* (United Nations publication. Sales No. E.03.II.D.7. New York and Geneva).

UNCTAD (*TDR 2016*). *Trade and Development Report, 2016: Structural Transformation for Inclusive and Sustained Growth* (United Nations publication. Sales No. E.16.II.D.5. New York and Geneva).

UNCTAD (*TDR 2017*). *Trade and Development Report, 2017: Beyond Austerity – Towards a Global New Deal* (United Nations publication. Sales No. E.17.II.D.5. New York and Geneva).

United Nations (2016). The infrastructure – inequality – resilience nexus. In: *Global Sustainable Development Report.* Chapter 2. United Nations. New York: 21–40.

UN-Water (2015). *The United Nations World Water Development Report 2015: Water for a Sustainable World.* UNESCO. Paris.

Weber B, Staub-Bisang M, Alfen HW (2016). *Infrastructure as an Asset Class: Investment Strategy, Sustainability, Project Finance and PPPs.* 2nd edn. Wiley Publishing. Chichester.

WEF and PWC (2012). *Strategic Infrastructure: Steps to Prioritize and Deliver Infrastructure Effectively and Efficiently.* World Economic Forum and PricewaterhouseCoopers. Geneva.

Woetzel J, Garemo N, Mischke J, Kamra P, Palter R (2016). Bridging infrastructure gaps. McKinsey Global Institute. McKinsey & Company. June.

Woetzel J, Garemo N, Mischke J, Kamra P, Palter R (2017). Bridging infrastructure gaps: Has the world made progress? Discussion Paper. McKinsey Global Institute. October.

World Bank (2009). Country case study: Korea. In: *Toolkit for Public–Private Partnerships in Roads and Highways.* Public Private Infrastructure Advisory Facility. World Bank. Washington D.C.: 81–90.

World Bank (2013). Independent panel review of the *Doing Business Report.* June. Available at: http://pubdocs.worldbank.org/en/237121516384849082/doing-business-review-panel-report-June-2013.pdf.

Zhang Y, Wang X and Chen K (2013). Growth and distributive effects of public infrastructure investments in China. In: Cockburn J, Dissou Y, Duclos J-Y and Tiberti L. *Infrastructure and Economic Growth in Asia.* Springer International Publishing. Cham: 87–116.

TRADE AND DEVELOPMENT REPORT
Past issues